T0229588

Leadership Principles for Project Success

PROJECT MANAGEMENT TITLES
FROM AUERBACH PUBLICATIONS AND CRC PRESS

Managing Web Projects
Edward B. Farkas
ISBN: 978-1-4398-0495-7

**The Complete Project Management
Methodology and Toolkit**
Gerard M. Hill
ISBN: 978-1-4398-0154-3

**Implementing Program Management:
Templates and Forms Aligned with the
Standard for Program Management —
Second Edition (2008)**
Ginger Levin and Allen M. Green
ISBN: 978-1-4398-1605-9

Project Management Recipes for Success
Guy L. De Furia
ISBN: 978-1-4200-7824-4

**Project Management of Complex and
Embedded Systems: Ensuring Product
Integrity and Program Quality**
Kim H. Pries and Jon Quigley
ISBN: 978-1-4200-7205-1

**Leading IT Projects: The IT
Manager's Guide**
Jessica Keyes
ISBN: 978-1-4200-7082-8

**Building a Project Work Breakdown
Structure: Visualizing Objectives,
Deliverables, Activities, and Schedules**
Dennis P. Miller
ISBN: 978-1-4200-6969-3

**A Standard for Enterprise
Project Management**
Michael S. Zambruski
ISBN: 978-1-4200-7245-7

Global Engineering Project Management
M. Kemal Atesmen
ISBN: 978-1-4200-7393-5

**Effective Communications for
Project Management**
Ralph L. Kliem
ISBN: 978-1-4200-6246-5

Managing Global Development Risk
James M. Hussey and Steven E. Hall
ISBN: 978-1-4200-5520-7

**The Strategic Project Leader: Mastering
Service-Based Project Leadership**
Jack Ferraro
ISBN: 978-0-8493-8794-4

Determining Project Requirements
Hans Jonasson
ISBN: 978-1-4200-4502-4

Practical Guide to Project Planning
Ricardo Viana Vargas
ISBN: 978-1-4200-4504-8

**The Complete Project Management
Office Handbook, Second Edition**
Gerard M. Hill
ISBN: 978-1-4200-4680-9

**Staffing the Project Office for
Competitive Advantage**
J. Kent Crawford
ISBN: 978-0-8247-5477-8

**Project Management Maturity Model,
Second Edition**
J. Kent Crawford
ISBN: 978-0-8493-7945-1

**Optimizing Human Capital with
a Strategic Project Office: Select,
Train, Measure, and Reward People
for Organization Success**
J. Kent Crawford and
Jeannette Cabanis-Brewin
ISBN: 978-0-8493-5410-6

Leadership Principles for Project Success

Thomas Juli

CRC Press
Taylor & Francis Group
Boca Raton   London   New York

CRC Press is an imprint of the
Taylor & Francis Group, an **informa** business

AN AUERBACH BOOK

CRC Press
Taylor & Francis Group
6000 Broken Sound Parkway NW, Suite 300
Boca Raton, FL 33487-2742

© 2011 by Thomas Juli
CRC Press is an imprint of Taylor & Francis Group, an Informa business

No claim to original U.S. Government works

Printed in the United States of America on acid-free paper
10 9 8 7 6 5 4 3 2 1

International Standard Book Number: 978-1-4398-3461-9 (Hardback)

This book contains information obtained from authentic and highly regarded sources. Reasonable efforts have been made to publish reliable data and information, but the author and publisher cannot assume responsibility for the validity of all materials or the consequences of their use. The authors and publishers have attempted to trace the copyright holders of all material reproduced in this publication and apologize to copyright holders if permission to publish in this form has not been obtained. If any copyright material has not been acknowledged please write and let us know so we may rectify in any future reprint.

Except as permitted under U.S. Copyright Law, no part of this book may be reprinted, reproduced, transmitted, or utilized in any form by any electronic, mechanical, or other means, now known or hereafter invented, including photocopying, microfilming, and recording, or in any information storage or retrieval system, without written permission from the publishers.

For permission to photocopy or use material electronically from this work, please access www.copyright. com (http://www.copyright.com/) or contact the Copyright Clearance Center, Inc. (CCC), 222 Rosewood Drive, Danvers, MA 01923, 978-750-8400. CCC is a not-for-profit organization that provides licenses and registration for a variety of users. For organizations that have been granted a photocopy license by the CCC, a separate system of payment has been arranged.

Trademark Notice: Product or corporate names may be trademarks or registered trademarks, and are used only for identification and explanation without intent to infringe.

Library of Congress Cataloging-in-Publication Data

Juli, Thomas.
    Leadership principles for project success / Thomas Juli.
       p. cm.
    Includes bibliographical references and index.
    ISBN 978-1-4398-3461-9 (hardcover : alk. paper)
    1. Project management. 2. Leadership. 3. Executive ability. I. Title.

    HD69.P75J85 2011
    658.4'092--dc22
                                               2010025459

Visit the Taylor & Francis Web site at
http://www.taylorandfrancis.com

and the CRC Press Web site at
http://www.crcpress.com

To my wife, Tina, and
my daughters, Rhea and Aiyana

Contents

PART IV   APPENDICES

PART V   BIBLIOGRAPHY

PART VI   INDEX

Preface

This book is about project success. It reveals a secret for project success: effective project leadership. It shows where pure project *management* falls short and why project *leadership* is the decisive factor for project success. It outlines five simple yet powerful leadership principles which, if applied systematically, can help you pave the path to project success. This book explains these principles and illustrates how you can use them to set up, manage, and align your projects for success. Last but not least, it shows you how to become an effective project leader.

In a nutshell, the five principles state that effective project leaders

1. Build vision
2. Nurture collaboration
3. Promote performance
4. Cultivate learning
5. Ensure results

They thus help secure project success.

These five principles are not based on a particular theory or management concept. A vast amount of literature exists on project management, leadership, project success, and related topics. This literature is important and valuable. Yet, I did not want to write a literature review of the various books on project leadership. Although that also may be a valuable exercise, it was not my intention. Instead, I wanted to write a practical book based on my own personal experience in project management. I wanted to share my insights about project success and my philosophy of project leadership and how it contributes to project success. I was not interested in building complex theoretical models of project leadership. My aim was to develop a guideline for project leadership that can be applied in any kind of project. Thus, the project examples I cite come from all kinds of environments, professional and nonprofessional. They show that the principles are universal and independent of the nature of a project. One third of the book is reserved for practical samples showing the leadership principles in action. In addition, the appendices contain practical and easy-to-use templates and guidelines you can immediately apply in your projects.

I am not in the position to claim that I have worked, managed, or reviewed only successful projects. I have seen and experienced great projects in which everything seemed to work. And I have been exposed to death march projects: doomed for failure from the beginning, or things just did not go well, or the work atmosphere was lousy, or there was no team and instead people were fighting rather than working together. This is not to say that this is normal. Indeed, I claim that most projects can be successful if set up and run correctly. This book will show you how.

It starts with good, solid project management. This is the toolset of a project. As such, it can serve as an excellent vehicle, leveling the way to project success. It is not, however, sufficient. I have witnessed projects in which the project manager was highly skilled in his or her discipline and all tools and templates were based on best practices. And yet the project failed or at least did not go as well as expected. Final project deliveries were good but the road to this delivery was filled with the debris of long hours, low team morale, and dissatisfied customers.

For some time I, too, had thought that project management is *the* critical success factor of a project. Fortunately, I learned that there is much more to it. At the beginning of a project I managed earlier in my consulting career I gathered the complete project team. We discussed how to ensure project success from the very beginning. Then we talked about the hard facts, which in this case was the successful integration of a call center software. And we went beyond these hard factors. We talked about how we could delight the customer, how we could ensure high quality throughout the project, how we could learn from our mistakes during the project, how we could work smart and not hard, and how we could have fun as a team. We set out on the project journey on a high note; we wanted to set a new standard for project success.

Succeed we did. The project was delivered on time and in budget. From this perspective many people would call the project a success no matter what. Analyzing the success, we found that it was actually the "softer" objectives that helped us deliver the project successfully. Project success was more than the sum of deliverables. The path to the final delivery mattered a great deal. And it was about us as the team. We worked together, shared our expertise and experience, grew together, and had fun together. Alas, we were human and consequently we made mistakes along the way. What was different in this project was what we made out of our mistakes. We took them as learning opportunities. We wanted to deliver results and thus accepted mistakes as learning steps toward the ultimate delivery of the final product. It was a very rewarding experience. And it was insightful, for it revealed the five principles I am laying out in this book. We started out the project with a common vision, we nurtured collaboration, we performed as individual experts and as a team helping each other, we cultivated learning, embracing mistakes as learning and growth opportunities, and finally we delivered results. Project management was an important and valuable element in project success. However, it was the vision, collaboration, performance, learning, and results that made the key difference. They were and they are the principles for project success. Our project success was not a one-time phenomenon or happening at the end of the project. It was ongoing; it was a growth process for the duration of the complete project and culminated in the final delivery: on time, in budget, at a very high quality, and, last but not least, delighting the customer.

Project success is like a journey to a final destination. We can compare it with an expedition or tour. Take the image here of a mountain guide showing the path to the summit of the mountain. You can see the path in front of the guide. The planned route is marked on a map and maybe you can see it in the distance. To get to the summit you need to be in a good physical shape and carry the right tools with you. Depending on how experienced you are, you may need the help of others to reach the summit or you may offer your assistance to other members of the expedition. If you have ever hiked a mountain you know that arriving at the summit is certainly the climax of your trip. But it is not the only thing that matters. The ascent to and descent from the summit are just as important. And just as joyful. Reaching the summit may be the driver of the mountain tour. If, however, this is the only thing you focus on, chances are that you will fail along the way and never reach the summit. Hiking through nature, you are exposed to the natural elements and must react to changing environments. You may have a plan that has proven to be reliable in the past. However, at times you may have to change your track. You may need to take a detour or decide to turn back to the base camp and try to reach the summit at a later time or maybe not at all. Good, experienced tour guides know this. They take on the responsibility for their whole group. They want the group to safely reach the summit and return to the base. It is not about the performance of individuals, who may be highly skilled and experienced mountaineers. The mission is to reach the top together and return home safely. This is why the picture I chose for the book cover includes a group of people rather than a single individual reaching the summit of a mountain. A mountain tour is, just like a project, a team effort.

It is misleading to define project success in static terms, focusing only on the final delivery. In the mountain tour example, reaching the summit would represent that final delivery. Project success is dynamic and covers the complete path from initiation to the final deliverable and project closure. Effective project leaders take this into account, just like the experienced mountain guide who plans the tour, takes a group of people to the summit, returns them home safely, and is committed to making the tour a joyful and safe experience.

Project leadership and the principles of effective leadership are not limited to the role of the project manager or project leader. Indeed, you can apply the five principles of effective leadership in any role you fill on a project, whether as the official project sponsor, project manager, team member, external consultant, project auditor, or any other project role. Applying the leadership principles outlined in this book contributes to project success. Alas, by themselves they do not guarantee project success. It takes more than a single individual to secure project success. It takes a team. The question is how you can increase the chances that your project is moving in the right direction. The five leadership principles serve as a guideline to project success. It is up to you to apply them in your role and thus make a difference. It is a question of leadership. I am claiming that you, too, can apply the leadership principles, practice leadership in your role, and thus contribute to project success. It may be difficult at times. But it is possible. Every journey, regardless of how long it may be, starts with the first step. Take this step and move forward. May this book serve as a companion on your journey to project success. I wish you a happy and prosperous journey.

Acknowledgements

Writing this book has been a most rewarding and inspiring journey. It all started with some informal meetings with my colleague and coach, Christian Schmidkonz at SAP in the summer of 2007. Back then we were talking about our understanding of effective project management and leadership. One of the assignments Christian gave me was to list the ten most important principles of leadership. A week later we met again. I explained that I didn't list ten but only came up with three principles: building vision, nurturing collaboration, and cultivating learning. The first principle of building vision has been my own mantra for quite some time. Back in spring of 2007, my wife and I had just passed on the leadership of a local preschool we founded in 2004. We wanted to build a reliable preschool for local children, ages one to three. Building and following this vision were more than a mantra. It helped us start and run the preschool for three consecutive years. It motivated all helping hands and it was still the motto of the preschool long after we passed on organizational responsibility to our successors.

Having come up with three leadership principles, I shared them with other peers. It was a beginning of a very interesting and insightful discussion that is still ongoing. I owe Christian Schmidkonz a great "Thank you!" for asking me what I thought was important in and for leadership. It was the beginning of my book project.

It wasn't until a year later that I first considered writing a book on my experience in project management. About two months before the PMI Global Congress 2008 in Denver, Colorado, John Wyzalek, Senior Acquisitions Editor at Auerbach Publications, sent me an email. He had read the paper I planned to present in Denver, "Realigning Project Objectives and Stakeholders' Expectations in a Project Behind Schedule" (Juli, 2008). Then he asked me if I had ever thought of turning this topic into a book. Indeed I had done so, but had never come to a point of actually pursuing this idea further. I thank John for this simple yet far-reaching question.

The PMI Global Congress in Denver was another important milestone in my book project for other reasons. There were two sessions that inspired me a great deal. They were Tom John's presentation on "The Art of Project Management®

and Complexity" (Johns, 2008) and Michael O'Brochta's session, "How to Get Executives to Act for Project Success" (O'Brochta, 2008). Tom explained the value of complexity theory in project management. He also re-vitalized my knowledge of chunk and systems theory that I worked with during my academic research at the University of Miami in 1997. Michael's remarks on project success were remarkable. It reminded me how important it is to practice common sense in dealing with stakeholders. One year later, at the PMI Global Congress EMEA in Amsterdam, Michael talked about "Great Project Managers" (O'Brochta, 2009). This session, too, encouraged me to delve deeper into the topic of project leadership.

While in Denver I also wanted to share my insights of the three leadership principles with others. For this purpose I organized an informal get together with Alex S. Brown, Joseph and Janice Lukas, Michael Trumper, Lev Virine, and Camper Bull. We shared our experiences and insights on effective project management and leadership. It was very insightful indeed. Outside the PMI Congress I met with Robert Urwiler, CIO of Vail Resorts. He liked the idea of the three leadership principles, but missed a decisive one: ensuring results. How true! From then on I was thinking of four leadership principles. The missing fifth principle of promoting performance "came" to me while outlining the book one year later. Until then I considered performance as being a part of collaboration. While this was and is true, I wanted to emphasize the significance and value of individual and team performance for project success. Hence, the development of five leadership principles.

Writing the book was a project. As such, it was a team effort. It would not have been possible to start, write, and finish the book without the help of others. It is impossible to individually thank the huge number of people who have contributed to the creation of this book. Next to the individuals already mentioned, I am indebted to the many people who shared their experiences and ideas on project leadership with me and challenged mine. They include Christian Baetzner, Elizabeth and James Bowman, Stephen Denning, Giancarlo Duranti, Jesse Fewell, Aslam Handy, John Ikeda, Ginger Levin, Robert Misch, Jim de Piante, Frank Teti, John Watson, Neal Whitten, Eddy Wong, and Stanislas Yanakiev. Thank you for challenging me and making me rethink and clarify quite a few points in my book.

Most of my professional training in project management I acquired working for two consulting companies that have been known for project management excellence: Cambridge Technology Partners and Sapient. The work environments, particularly at Cambridge, were magical and promoted performance on many levels. It was a great and inspiring time as well as a learning experience.

At SAP I had the wonderful opportunity to successfully apply my project management skills in one of the biggest software development projects, SAP CRM 2007. It was also during my time at SAP that I was privileged to attend the best project management workshop ever, conducted by Neal Whitten. I am honored to call Neal Whitten a mentor and role model.

I was fortunate to being part of an online review group of Stephen Denning's new book *The Leader's Guide to Radical Management: Re-inventing the Workplace for the 21st Century* (Denning, 2010). I learned a great deal from him and the many comments in his review group. I liked the idea of an online review group so much that I started my own. This way I could share preliminary chapters of my book and receive valuable feedback. Members of this group were Christian Baetzner, Stephen Denning, Stefan Dieffenbacher, Traci Duez, Sally Elatta, Jesse Fewell, Bala Gopalan, Klaus Helling, Maria E. Kaufmann, Robert Misch, Patrik Olsson, Frank Schabel, Tibor Schiemann, Pedro Serrador, John Watson, Andreas Wirthmüller, Stanislas Yanakiev, and Henning Zeumer.

I would like to acknowledge the help of Michael Huber, an artist and graphic designer, who created the picture of the mountain guide in the Preface. The picture is an excellent illustration of the kind of leadership I am describing in the book.

It has been a wonderful experience working with the team of CRC Press. A special thanks goes to John Wyzalek, who first approached me about the book. Andrea Demby did a fabulous job as the project editor. Not being a native English speaker, I greatly appreciate the art of copyediting the manuscript. Thank you, Christine Morales, for your help.

Personal encouragement, advice, and support came from Annette Ball, Elizabeth and James Bowman, Monika Renn, and, most of all, my own family. Without the help and support of my wife Tina it would not have been possible to start, write, and finish the book. Thank you so much! I dedicate this book to my wife Tina and my two adorable daughters, Rhea and Aiyana.

The book project may be over, but the journey to new insights in project leadership continues. From this perspective the book is only a snapshot of my own experiences, philosophy, and attitude toward leadership and project success at the time of writing the book. Still, I hope the book serves readers as a good guideline and companion for becoming and acting as an effective project leader. I invite readers to participate with me in an ongoing dialogue on project leadership. Share your experiences and let others learn from them. This way it becomes an ongoing journey for all of us.

You can reach me in two main ways:

Email: tj@thomasjuli.com
Web: www.thomasjuli.com and www.TheProjectLeadershipPyramid.net

I am looking forward to hearing from you.

About the Author

Thomas Juli, Ph.D., is an experienced, enthusiastic, and results-driven manager. He provides leading-edge program, interim, and operational management, offering more than 12 years of progressive leadership and management experience in various functions including project and program management, management consulting, business analysis, professional training, and academic teaching. He is a certified Project Management Professional (PMP®) by the Project Management Institute and Certified Scrum Master (CSM®) by the Scrum Alliance.

He is managing director of Thomas Juli Empowerment Partners, a professional service organization for innovative empowerment, consulting, and interim management. Prior to starting his own consulting business, Juli worked for SAP and two leading management and IT consultancies, Sapient and Cambridge Technology Partners. He has consulted for various companies in telecommunications, energy, manufacturing banking and the public sector. He has spoken at conferences on project management and customer relationship management and has written articles on project management for professional journals.

Before entering business, Juli was engaged in research in the fields of economics and U.S. foreign policy. He holds a doctorate with distinction in international studies from the University of Miami, and a masters degree in economics from Washington University in St. Louis.

Chapter 1

The World of Projects

Nothing astonishes men so much as common sense and plain dealing.

Ralph Waldo Emerson (1803–1882),
U.S. philosopher, essayist, and poet, from the essay "Art" (1841)

1.1 The Nature of Projects

So, what is so special about projects in the first place? Actually, nothing really. There have always been projects in our daily life, in both the business world and the nonbusiness world. The difference is that today people speak about projects differently. Maybe it is a modern word and people want to sound important when they say it. But still there is nothing new about projects.

An obvious advantage of projects is that they produce results in a predetermined and agreed-upon time frame. They can be a relatively short duration of only a day or two or long-running projects of several years. The fact is that projects produce results, tangible or not. They produce results.

So, what is the definition of a project? I suggest the following: *A project is a set of activities directed toward commonly agreed-upon objectives to be accomplished in a certain time frame which is not endless. The direction of a project is given by its objectives. It is a unique endeavor.*

In contrast to projects are ongoing activities or routine jobs. For example, assembling a car in a factory is not a project but, at least for the most part, routine work. Tax income form processing by an IRS employee is a routine job, not a project. Taking your kids to school is most likely a routine job.

The Project Management Institute (PMI) offers the following definition of a project: "A project is a temporary endeavor undertaken to create a unique product, service, or result. The temporary nature of projects indicates a definite beginning and end. The end is reached when the project's objectives have been achieved or when the project is terminated because its objectives will not or cannot be met, or when the need for the project no longer exists" (Project Management Institute, 2008, p. 5).

What all common definitions of a project have in common are that a project is a unique endeavor, framed by a given time frame defined by a set start and end date.

Let's talk about some project examples. For most readers, projects in business seem most familiar: development of a new product, integration of new software, building a bridge or a house, and so forth. In politics, the planning of and running an election campaign can be considered a project. It has a set start date and a fixed end date, which happens to be election day, and it yields results. Another example is the founding of a preschool, from the initial planning date until opening day. Planning a summer camp for a youth group is a project. So is the preparation for a party, whether it is a family party or festivities for your organization or company. If you are involved in a club, a fundraising marathon is a project.

One can find endless examples of projects. Tom Peters (2007) goes as far as claiming that all white collar work these days is and actually has to be project work. "And not just any project, no matter how droning, boring, and dull, but rather what … I come to call 'Wow Projects': projects that add value, projects that matter, projects that make a difference, projects that leave a legacy … ."

I was fortunate that most of the projects I worked on or managed, inside and outside of business, met these requirements. It was not the nature of the projects. It was the attitude of the whole team and its desire to create something special. All of my wow projects started with a clear vision; clear enough to become emotional about it. We could see, smell, and feel the expected end results. This was a strong driver in our day-to-day activities. Other attributes of these projects were that collaboration was working: roles and responsibilities were defined, team members' expectations articulated and accounted for, and all were reviewed regularly, adapting them where necessary. We nourished teamwork and the freedom to act for a common goal. Creating and nurturing an innovative learning environment, an atmosphere where feedback was sincere, honest, and constructive, was another success factor. It was about helping and learning from each other. Last but not least, the wow projects were about delivering results, not just the final deliverable. Instead, we set weekly goals to work on and deliver. This meant we always had a good sense of accomplishment. Project success became success for all of us.

Projects are everywhere. They are prevalent. As such, it seems that everyone is, has already been, or will be involved in a project in one way or another. From this perspective, there is nothing special about a project. The distinguishing factor we will shed light on in this book is what *project success* entails. It is easy to talk about a project. It is another matter to lead a project to success.

Before elaborating on project success, let's once more return to the key characteristics of a project. The multitude of characteristics are too numerous to list on this page or even in a single book. Let's review the core ones.

Projects have objectives. They want to achieve something in a given time frame. They need not have a certain duration. Projects can be short-run, such as planning a birthday party, or long-run, such as planning a mission to Mars. The duration does not matter so much to the definition of a project as the fact that every project has an end date. Without an end date, it is most likely not a project and instead an ongoing activity or routine job. Hence, the duration of a typical project is project-specific. No official definition exists for what the duration should be.

A project is usually run by a team of people who serve in different roles. Usually it involves a project manager, whose job is to manage the project to success. In addition to the project team, people outside the project may have an interest in and influence on the project. Let's have a closer look at all the roles, within and outside of the team.

The project team provides for both formal or informal roles. Often there is a distinct role of project manager. The project manager is in charge of the project; he or she is responsible and often accountable for the success of the project. Project players can also be found outside the inner circle of the project. Many people have a keen interest in the success — or failure — of your project, including the customers and the project sponsor who initiated the project. If you work in a corporate setting, your company may have a project management office that coordinates several projects and makes sure they are all in sync with the overall corporate strategy. Other important project players include line managers, who may compete for the same people who are working on your project.

In short, it would be wrong to assume that project players can be found only in the innermost circle of your project. Look outside of your core team and assess your environment. You will find more players than you initially thought possible. Some will play a more significant role than others and may require greater attention.

You may think that having your team in one location is normal. This may be so in some cases but not all. A single project can take place in one or numerous locations. Today's business world is becoming smaller. A couple of years ago it could not be imagined that projects could be run on several continents. It is still the same team but not in the same location. Thanks to technology, it has become possible to communicate with team members no matter where they are located in the world. We call these teams *distributed teams*.

Going a step further, it is now possible to run a project and never meet your own team members. These are called *virtual teams*. This, too, has become normal business to many companies in our global marketplace. The same scenario can happen in your community, in a nonbusiness environment. Say, for example, you are organizing a soccer tournament. You have set up a planning committee, the members of which are distributed across your region. You talk to them on the phone and exchange emails, but may not meet until the day of the tournament. Yet you were part of a team. Thus, distributed and virtual teams are not limited to the business world. They are closer and more normal than you think.

When you set up your project you take people from other groups. In a corporate environment your company is organized in different departments, called line organizations. These departments may follow routine jobs. Your project could be embedded in one department, or it may transcend department boundaries, affecting and involving several departments. In this case, your project adds another level of complexity to the organizational environment. This is called a *matrix organization*. If your project exists in its own environment without breaking or transcending any line organization you may be working in a *project organization*. Which one is best depends on the project. Each has its advantages and disadvantages. Although the matrix organization is the most common in business these days, it is also the most complex. One of its greatest advantages can also be a source of potential conflict. Namely, on the one hand a matrix organization may facilitate cross-functional work across organizational boundaries. On the other hand, some organizational units may oppose this kind of work and withdraw their support of your project. Conflict is predetermined. It takes effective project management to cope with this challenge.

One thing is certain: your project does not exist in a vacuum. In rare cases your project may be totally isolated from others. For example, certain scientific research may fall under this category. Your research project may be isolated to you but not to others. You may not see any dependencies to other projects because your project may be the dominant one. But dependencies may exist if you rely on input from others or vice versa. There may also be interdependencies where other seemingly unrelated projects affect those that have an impact on yours. For example, you have obtained all the required input for your research, but then another project in your organization is given greater priority and a higher budget. That project will thus use money that was originally planned for your research. You may have had no interest in the other project, yet it affected you because now you may be short of money to fund your research.

In a nutshell, projects always exist in a social and organizational environment that can be complex and interdependent. Some projects are totally isolated, as mentioned above. However, for the purpose of this book I assume that every project exists in a social environment that is complex and interdependent. One can also assume that every project, to some extent, exists in a chaotic environment. It is not possible to account for all circumstances in your project plan. This is yet another reason to talk about guidance and leadership. Someone has to tell us which way to go and that there is a light at the end of the tunnel, an answer to this, and project success. This cornerstone to project success is called project management.

1.2 Project Management as a Cornerstone of Project Success

First, let me be quite frank: project management is NOT the only or even single-most-important element to project success. It is a cornerstone, a single stone, not the whole house. It is a very important stone though. It gives the house a frame with which to start. Some people may even consider it to be the first cornerstone. I am not one of them. Project success is not equal to the appropriate application of project management. It entails much more. The end result of your project matters as much as how you get there. We will return to a definition of project success later. For now, let's record that project management can facilitate project success. It is important and necessary for project success, but it is not sufficient. Before I explain why this is so, let's have a closer look at the scope of project management.

Project management is the activity that helps initiate, plan, conduct, monitor, control, and close a project. It encompasses knowledge areas such as scope, time, cost, quality, risk, procurement management, and basic management skills. These management skills are common to other management activities, not project specific. Two examples include communication and team building.

Project management is important. Let there be no doubt. That is, a project cannot be run without project management, be it formal or informal. You need to have something that holds things together. Underlying is the assumption that we need some form of order to organize and run a project. Someone has to do something. In this sense, project management helps set a frame, providing structure and order to potential chaos. Without this structure a project leads to nowhere; it will most likely fail, if it ever takes off.

Project management is not limited to one person. All team members can be engulfed in project management. In other words, project management is not limited to the project manager. Keep in mind that we are talking about the general meaning of project management and not the individual role of a project manager.

So, what are the key elements to project management? There are many, yes. This is not surprising, given that we have just learned something about the complexity of projects. Taking a linear approach to projects and project management, we discover five key activities of project management: project initiation, project planning, project execution, project monitoring and controlling, and, last but not least, project closure. This is more or less the common, most widespread understanding of project management. It is linear in the sense that it makes us believe that a project always goes through these activity phases in this order. Indeed, this may be so in most projects. However, in reality this assumption does not hold true anymore. Projects can fluctuate from one phase to another. Figure 1.1 provides a graph of the first linear approach, where the line depicts the planned, linear project progress. However, after project completion, if you were to graph how things really went, it may look like the graph in Figure 1.2, where the jagged line depicts the actual project progress, which is clearly nonlinear.

Sound too abstract and theoretical? Let's take the example of building a house. Let's say you wanted to build your own home. You even have a picture in your mind of how it will look. You can imagine what it will be like to move in and to live in the home. You foresee the planning phase, talking with construction workers, agencies, your bank, and so forth. You are ready to go. You have sketched a first blueprint and have checked your finances. You think you are ready to start construction when your bank calls to tell you that it needs another form of security from you.

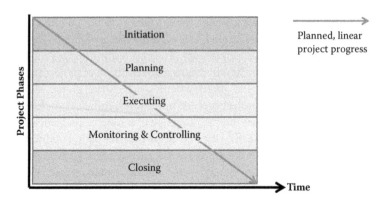

Figure 1.1   Planned, linear project progress.

Or, 2 weeks after construction has started, you find out that the blueprint doesn't include the second bathroom you asked for on the first floor. You must go back to the planning phase — parallel to constructing your house.

There is nothing wrong with the linear approach, taken as a model or framework. It certainly helps structure a project. But it does not naturally explain the key elements to project management. The graph in Figure 1.2 shows very clearly that real life can deviate from the planned line and may go in a different direction. Life is not linear. It is complex and oftentimes chaotic.

So, what are key common elements, even in chaotic projects? I think there are four:

1. *Vision, goals, and objectives.* Every project has a goal. It may not meet formal criteria of measurable results, but still, all projects are meant to achieve something.
2. *People.* Every project involves people, communication, and collaboration. I cannot think of a single project that does not involve people. Projects always exist in a social environment.

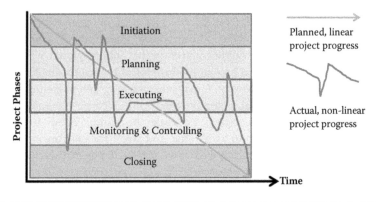

Figure 1.2   Actual, nonlinear project progress.

3. *Results.* Project management is aimed to help produce results. This means that someone or a group of people pick up something (a goal, objective, vision) and want to build toward it. They all want results.
4. *Management skills.* They could be technical or mechanical in nature, such as time, scope, cost, or procurement management, or they could have a social nature, such as communication and team building.

Where does this lead us with respect to a project manager? Who is this project manager? What role does he or she play? Are project managers like superman, running the whole show? Or are they the administrator of some plans? Maybe project managers just facilitate the team to perform and do the work and produce results? The answer is that there is no single answer. It is unlikely that the project manager is always superman, doing all the jobs, saving an ailing project, producing all results alone and taking the glory. There may be projects like this. However, I cannot think of a project I was involved in where this was expected from the project manager. With respect to the other possible roles: coach, administrator, facilitator, leader, and so forth, yes, there are many examples where this holds true. But again, it depends on the situation. Not too helpful, you might think? Take this with you: a project manager may fill many roles. However, one thing is certain: do not expect a project manager to be superman who saves the world — or your project.

1.3 A Common Theme: Projects in Trouble

Let's have a look again at the key elements of project management: project initiation, planning, conducting, monitoring, controlling, closing and vision, objectives, people, communication, and results. All of these elements seem so simple and straight forward. And they are. Project management is a lot about common sense. It is not complicated if you think of these elements as the key to project management. But why then do so many projects fail? Let's have a look at some numbers.

The Standish Group's CHAOS report (The Standish Group, 2009a) contains some of the most quoted statistics of project success rates. Although this report analyzes mostly IT projects, the numbers can be translated to other industries and practices as well. Their press release of April 23, 2009, summarized the main findings of the 2009 report, stating that only 32% of all projects succeeded, in the sense that they delivered the required scope on time and on budget. According to the report, "44% were challenged which are late, over budget, and/or with less than the required features and functions and 24% failed which are cancelled prior to completion or delivered and never used" (The Standish Group, 2009b).

These numbers are frustrating and disturbing. No, they are alarming. Something must be wrong here. Why do so many projects fail? After all, it is all common sense, right? Well, what we can say at this point already is that common sense is not equal to common practice. This is a truism. Granted. And it is true. Actually it may drive people nuts when you ask them why they are not practicing what they think is normal and common sense.

Let's have a look at some common themes of projects in trouble. There can be discrepancies between the goals, scope, budget, time, and quality expectations and requirements. There may be cost overruns. The team atmosphere is lousy. The boss doesn't support you. Politics are involved that make life for your project miserable. Nobody cares about time limits; milestones are regularly missed and not monitored. Let's look at some examples:

- Consider a public project of resurfacing a highway. The project budget and construction schedule had been defined early on. Unfortunately, the project turned out to be over budget and several weeks overdue.
- The goal of an IT project was to replace an existing software application in the marketing department of the company. Development work was finished on time but the marketing department refused to sign off on the new application because it did not meet its requirements.
- The target date for the rollout of a toll billing system for trucks on German major highways was originally scheduled for the middle of August 2003. It was repeatedly delayed. Finally, in January 2005 the system opened, 16 months after the original deadline.

I could go on citing examples of failing projects. But that is not the point. What is important to understand are the underlying reasons for project trouble and failure. The CHAOS report is one example for listing the most common reasons for project failure, and there are other reports available.

My own experience tells me that five key factors lead to project failure:

1. Lack of vision. The objectives are neither clearly defined nor mutually understood by those running and being involved in the project. Consequently, the scope of the project is vague and the timeline leading to the target end date is anything but realistic.
2. Lack of a functioning team. Instead, there is an accumulation of people who may or may not work together. Insular work is common. Communication is held to a minimum. Collaboration is poor.
3. The team as a whole or individuals do not perform as they ought to.
4. No reflection of its own behavior. People do not react to changes, but instead stick to old patterns. Learning does not take place.
5. No regular interim results. People may work together, but they do not produce results. If results are produced, they may be late or of low quality.

Does this apply only to projects in the business world? No. Take the following real example: In my hometown a group of parents was upset about heavy traffic. It was difficult and dangerous for their kids to cross one of the main streets in town.

All the parents agreed that a new traffic light was necessary, allowing the kids to cross the street safely by controlling traffic. They started collecting signatures. In less than 3 weeks they collected 200 signatures. This was an impressive number. They took the signature lists to the local mayor and asked for his support to release the necessary budget money. Unfortunately, the mayor was not convinced of the need for a new traffic light and turned down their request. The parents protested but could not change the mayor's mind. Frustrated, the parents gave up and the project died.

What went wrong? First of all, this project did have a goal: a traffic light. Clearly this was not the cause for project failure. Problems arose because the parents focused solely on support from the mayor. However, the mayor was only one person, and the budget authority lay with the town council. Unfortunately, none of the town council members were informed or involved in the project. Another cause for the project failure was the lack of reflection on the parents' part. Once the mayor signaled his skepticism about the project, the parents did not challenge him, nor did they ask themselves what else they could do to achieve the project objectives. Instead, they gave up.

As much as projects are part of everyday life, so is trouble and project failure, it seems. However, do not generalize this statement that most projects are doomed for failure right from the beginning. When talking about projects in trouble, one should distinguish between those that are merely ailing and those that are indeed doomed to fail. Ailing projects can be realigned to their original or modified objectives if the necessary changes are made. In the case of failing projects, you may sooth the pain, but it is impossible to rescue the project, or at least it is very difficult and unlikely that you will succeed. Project objectives are no longer achievable.

An example of an ailing project was the construction of the Olympic stadium for the Summer Olympic Games 2000 in Athens, Greece. Two years prior to the opening ceremony the construction was way behind schedule. The construction crews managed to catch up and barely finished the stadium before the Olympic Games.

An example of a failing project was the idea to build a high-speed train connection between the Munich Airport and the Munich Central Station in Germany. Whereas public resistance to the project was moderate at the beginning of the planning phase, it strengthened the more it became apparent that the original budgeted project cost would most likely explode and even double. The objectives of building and operating an economical train connection were no longer achievable. The project was canceled before the first construction worker could arrive.

Don't think that if you are faced with or involved in a failing project there is nothing you can do. Regardless of your role, if you want to demonstrate leadership you can always act, and actually you must act. This is even more true in the case of an ailing project, which can still be saved.

You can try realigning the project, by yourself or with others. We will talk about possible approaches for realigning ailing projects later in this book. And even in the case of a failing project there are things you can do. You can run away, hold still, swallow and wait for better times, hope for a miracle, or do nothing. Or, if you are the person in charge of the project, you can cancel the project. Indeed, canceling a project may be the only right thing to do. Don't have the illusion that every project has to finish successfully. First of all, we have learned that a majority of projects do fail for various reasons. Once you realize that your project falls into this category you may seriously consider canceling it. It may save time and resources and, on your part, lots of nerves and energy.

Regardless of whether you have to cancel a project or manage to realign it, you can learn a lot from such project rescue missions. This is true whether you have been actively involved in such a situation or simply read about it. Failing and ailing projects offer valuable lessons. The main thing you want to learn is how to set up a project the correct way right from the beginning. You want to learn how to create and nurture your project right from its initiating stage. There is no law that projects first have to fail in order to succeed. When you start a new project, set it up for success from the beginning. That this is no illusion is shown in the following example.

Let's return to the story of the futile attempt by parents to get a traffic light. One year later, a new group of parents formed. They were aware of the previous failed attempt to get a new traffic light. Although the new group had the same goals, they did not focus only on a safe passage for their own children. They expanded the vision to include senior citizens and everybody else who had a hard time crossing the road. Prior to starting their signature initiative they informed the town council members and secured their support for the project. In addition, they involved local schools and businesses. Last but not least, they talked with the local newspapers, which ran reports on the new project. Initially, the mayor was still skeptical. When he realized the project enjoyed strong public support, he changed his mind and jumped on the bandwagon. Within a few weeks the town council released the necessary budget money for the new traffic light. Six months later the new traffic light was in operation.

This example shows that just because a project failed before doesn't mean it won't work the next time around, provided we identify the root causes of the previous failure and resolve them, or just avoid them right from the beginning. It is therefore wrong to assume that most projects are doomed for failure or that troubled projects inevitably lead to failure.

1.4 Leadership and Project Success

Successful projects are not figments of imagination. They happen. Daily. It is up to you if you want your project to be one of them. Earlier we learned that project management is mostly common sense.

Well, now it is up to you to put this common sense into action. Practice common sense. Follow through. And inspire your team to follow you. Lead the pack and move along as a team.

This does not happen overnight. Some people think that it is sufficient for the team to acknowledge and practice common sense. I am saying that this is not sufficient. Yes, it takes a team to run a project. But it takes at least one person to lead the pack.

The right and appropriate project management skills are crucial. In addition, you must have an understanding of basic leadership principles, and you have to live them. The combination of project management and leadership principles yields project leadership. Corollary, not every project manager is a project leader.

The team is equally important for project success. The collaboration within the team and the performance of each individual team member as well as the performance of the team as one unit are critical factors for project success. Without a performing team it is difficult to secure project success. A performing team does not fall from heaven. It is possible that teams successfully organize themselves into a performing unit. There may even be the absence of formal project management as we know it. But don't be fooled. Every performing team still needs rigid boundaries within it functions.

Performing teams can evolve from within, but you have to ignite this fire of performance and you have to set boundaries within the team for it to function. If you want to generate results out of seemingly chaos you have to build structure that enables creativity, innovation, and results. Helping build and sustain this structure is the leadership we will be talking about in this book. Project management provides excellent tools to build this structure. By themselves the tools are not sufficient for project success. Unless you gear them into the right direction, they remain ineffective. If you want to secure project success you have to understand what it takes to set the right direction. Project management alone will not do the trick. It takes leadership — your leadership. Without project leadership there is no direction in project management. Leadership is the decisive factor for improving the chances for projects to succeed. Consequently, effective project management needs to have a solid foundation based in project leadership. Without leadership, chances are that a project will be "just another project."

It is up to you which project you prefer. If you are interested in successful projects and what leadership principles help you achieve them, continue reading. Leadership principles are not rocket science. Why? Because the five leadership principles I propose in this book are based on common sense. They are not abstract ideas or figments of our imagination. They work because they are based on real-life project experience. Because they are common sense, it is not difficult to understand and apply them and demonstrate true leadership.

This book will tell you what it takes and how to get there. The first part of the book introduces the concept of the *project leadership pyramid*. This pyramid comprises the five leadership principles for project success. The second part of the book will put the project leadership pyramid into practice. It includes practical examples for how you can apply the five leadership principles in your daily project life. The final part of the book (Part III) details how you can become an effective project leader.

1.5 Application Suggestions

Think of two projects of your choice. One should be a project that could serve as an example of a project in trouble, the other one a project that runs or has run smoothly and to your full satisfaction.

1. Answer the following questions about each project:
    a. What are the objectives of this project? Are they mutually understood and even agreed by everyone involved in the project?
    b. Do you have clear roles and responsibilities in the project? How is the atmosphere on the project?
    c. Does everyone speak openly and freely? Or are communication channels obscured and blocked?
    d. Does every person and the team perform as expected? What is done if an individual or maybe even the whole team is not performing as expected and/or required?
    e. Do you stick to your plan? How do you react to changes in the project situation?
    f. How often do you deliver results? Do they meet minimal requirements?
2. Compare your notes and identify the three most important factors that affect or have affected the success of your project.

References

Emerson, R. W. (2000). *The Essential Writings of Ralph Waldo Emerson* (B. Atkinson, Ed.). New York: Modern Library.

Johns, T. (2008). The Art of Project Management® and Complexity. In *2008 PMI Global Congress Proceedings*. Denver, CO: Project Management Institute.

Peters, T. J. (2007). The Wow Project. *FastCompany*. Retrieved from http://www.fastcompany.com/magazine/24/wowproj.html

Project Management Institute. (2008). *A Guide to the Project Management Body of Knowledge* (4th ed.). Newtown Square, PA: Project Management Institute.

The Standish Group. (2009a). *CHAOS Summary 2009*. West Yarmouth, MA.

The Standish Group. (2009b). News release on the new 2009 Chaos report. April 23, 2009. Retrieved from http://www1.standishgroup.com/newsroom/chaos_2009.php

THE PROJECT LEADERSHIP PYRAMID

1

Chapter 2

Introducing the Project Leadership Pyramid

Management is doing things right; leadership is doing the right things.

Peter Drucker (1909–2005),
top management thinker of his time

2.1 The Difference between Management and Leadership

Let's start with the hypothesis I set forth in the last chapter: "Effective project management needs to have a solid foundation based in project leadership." What does this mean for project management and how does it relate to this book? First, we need to distinguish between management and leadership, between managers and leaders, and alas, between project managers and project leaders. There is a difference. A big difference. Leaders define a direction. They take the initiative and take responsibility. At the end of the day they are accountable for the outcome of their projects. Managers, on the other hand, take orders, they do their job to the best of their abilities, and they are assigned to certain roles and responsibilities. Leaders act, managers react.

"Now, wait a minute!" you may exclaim, "I am a project manager and I am taking the initiative. I am not reacting. I am proactive and I am held accountable for the outcome of my project. Why do you still distinguish between a project manager and a project leader?" The answer is simple. As a project manager you can be or become a project leader when you practice the principles of leadership. Combining project management skills with leadership principles constitutes the foundation for effective project management. The difference is that on the one hand you may have a project manager whereas on the other hand you have an *effective* project manager who possesses traits of a leader and lives by leadership principles. This is the difference between an ordinary project manager and an effective project manager and project leader. And yet there are also overlaps. Take, for example, the basic project management skills. The hypothesis claims that project leaders must be knowledgeable and competent in project management skills. Corollary, proclaimed project leaders without project management skills can hardly be good project leaders. As a matter of fact, I would not consider them project leaders in the first place.

2.2 The Power of Simplicity

> It is simplicity that makes the uneducated more effective than the educated when addressing popular audiences.
>
> **Aristotle (384–322 BC),**
> *rhetoric, Greek critic, philosopher, physicist, and zoologist*

Can a project manager become a project leader? Yes, absolutely. Project management is in most cases common sense. Project leadership is no different. It, too, is based on common sense. It is interesting to see that there is a plethora of books and articles about leadership. There are so many things the authors want you to think you have to consider when you want to become a leader. It could very well be so. But does this help you to become one? I doubt it.

Experience shows that we can best work with a few principles at a time. Many factors must be taken into account for effective leadership. Still, you can work best by keeping just a few principles in mind that you actually strive to live. Academically, this is based on chunk theory. Miller (1956) noted that the memory capacity of young adults is around seven elements, called chunks, around seven for digits, six for letters, and five for words. If this holds true for young adults, the rest of us who do not consider ourselves "young" adults anymore likely have a similarly limited capacity. The fact is, it is easier to focus on five principles rather than ten or more.

Some time ago I read an interesting and inspiring book about the management and leadership principles of a very successful company in the entertainment industry (Cockerrell, 2008). It listed ten principles to live by. All of them were convincing and, yes, actually they were common sense. A few days later I told a friend about this book and how much I liked it. My friend then asked me about the first principle. Something unbelievable took place: I could not remember the principles one by one. I understood the overall idea behind them but I could not quote them anymore. Now, you may say that I suffered from temporary memory loss; maybe

I was tired or just had not paid close attention when I read the book. No, none of these were true. There were just too many principles to remember at the moment.

Let me share an example of the opposite case, where a single rule produced amazing results. A couple of years ago I managed a project the objective of which was to integrate a new piece of software in record time. The go-live date of the new application was fixed and so was the budget. In striving for the successful completion of the project right from the beginning, I suggested to the team one outstanding theme to be the main foundation of our daily work: "Work smart, not hard!" I encouraged the team to try to actively live by this theme right from the start. This was reflected in the objective to use a best practice approach to project management and software development wherever possible and to share knowledge, experiences, and methodology. Newly learned lessons were discussed and documented on a weekly basis.[1]

The project turned out to be a huge success. Not only were we able to deliver on time and in budget, but throughout the project life there was a high level of collaboration, performance, and learning on the individual and team levels. We all worked smart — and had a lot of fun along the way. This simple slogan was coined for the project and teamwork from the very first day. In the beginning it was a slogan. Gradually, we internalized it and it became second nature and yielded great results.

This example shows us that you don't need a long list of instructions for how to lead your project to success. I prefer simple rules and principles. In this case, less is more, especially when there are five simple principles we can easily remember, understand, and live by.[2]

2.3 Common Themes of Leadership

So, what are the five leadership principles to which I refer?

There are countless books, articles, and opinions about leadership and what it takes to become and be a leader. Identifying the project leadership principles that I will be describing in this book, I did not limit my search to project management, whether it be project management books, best practices, or my own experience. I expanded my search to our daily world. I asked what distinguishes true leaders from "normal" people and followers. I ended up consolidating the following five common themes.

---

[1] I described the project set-up in a presentation at the PMI Global Congress (Juli, 2003).

[2] By this token, Thomas G. Johns (2008, p. 3) states that "Guidelines for ... a [complex project management] system, as described by Morgan (2006), is to build a good enough 'vision' and replace intricate (complex) strategic plans with a few short, simple statements that describe the general direction that the organization is pursuing and perhaps a few basic boundaries."

All of the great leaders that come to my mind had a vision they talked about and followed. They inspired people. Second, it was not just them speaking and making the magic. They reached a large number of people who were convinced enough to follow them. Then they all worked together to go after the vision. Third, the leaders did not just talk about their vision. They acted and were role models. They knew what they were talking about. Fourth, they were open for feedback, adjusting their strategies to changing environments. Last, they delivered results and not mere words.

There are so many public figures we consider leaders and role models, including Mahatma Gandhi, Martin Luther King, Jr., John F. Kennedy, and many more. Gandhi led an entire nation to independence from the former colonial power of Great Britain. Martin Luther King led the desegregation movement in the United States. John F. Kennedy set out the vision of putting a man on the moon before the end of a decade. All of them had a vision, they inspired people, they walked their own talk, they showed flexibility by adjusting their strategies to changing environments and circumstances, and they made a lasting difference. The question, then, is how we can translate these leadership themes to the needs of the project world. What are the principles of effective project leadership?

2.4 The Five Principles of Effective Project Leadership

The five leadership principles for project success are as follows:

1. *Build vision.* Sharing a common vision and goals and having the same understanding about tracking the progress toward this vision is one of the key factors in the success of a project and team.
2. *Nurture collaboration.* A performing team yields synergy effects; the impossible becomes possible. This is why active team collaboration is crucial.
3. *Promote performance.* Planning is good and important. At the end of the day you and your team have to perform. As a leader it is your responsibility to create an environment that promotes performance, on both the individual and team levels.
4. *Cultivate learning.* As humans we all make mistakes. Effective leaders encourage their teams to explore new avenues and to make mistakes and learn from them. An effective leader builds in sufficient time for the team to learn, create, and innovate.
5. *Ensure results.* Delivering results is both a prerequisite and an outcome of effective project leadership. Project delivery is a team effort, not an individual effort. The effective project leader builds and guides the team to deliver results by incorporating the first four leadership principles.

All five leadership principles combined encompass the core of effective project leadership.

Take again the earlier leadership examples of Mahatma Gandhi, Martin Luther King, Jr., and John F. Kennedy. They had many things in common. They talked about their visions of building something new (vision principle). They inspired and motivated people to make the necessary changes (collaboration principle). They utilized their strength; they did what they preached (performance principle). Their vision was not built in a vacuum; it was based on facts, taking the environment into account (learning principle). And, last but not least, they all ensured long-lasting results (results principle).

2.5 The Metaphor of the Pyramid

Together, the five leadership principles described here build the *project leadership pyramid* (Figure 2.1). The principle at the top of this pyramid is the first principle (build vision), followed by nurture collaboration, promote performance, cultivate learning, and, at the base of the pyramid, ensure results.

The pyramid is a powerful image. I use this image for a simple reason: Although I think building vision is probably the most important principle of effective leadership, the bottom line most people see or want to see is results. Thus vision is at the top and results at the foundation of the pyramid. Collaboration, performance, and learning are necessary building blocks of the pyramid. They are framed by vision and results.

Visually speaking, when you approach a pyramid from a far distance, you first see the top. In our case, vision is at the top of the pyramid. As you get closer, you see more of the pyramid until at last you are standing in front of the first row of the building blocks (results). Looking upward, you may feel overwhelmed by the size of the pyramid. It may not even be possible to see the top of the pyramid (vision). Alas, you know that it exists. It was the first thing that you could see and what caught your attention. It guided you all the way to the base of the pyramid. If you

Figure 2.1 The project leadership pyramid.

now want to understand the secrets of the pyramid, you have to go inside. You have to explore the pyramid. This book explains the structure of the project leadership pyramid and reveals the secrets inside.

2.6 Structure of Part I

In the following chapters we will first elaborate on each of the five principles separately. We then analyze how the five principles interact with each other. You will find that there is not one single principle that is the most important element of effective project leadership. Instead, effective project leadership is made up of the whole project leadership pyramid. Effective project leaders apply all five principles as one unit. Each chapter in Part I will conclude with a discussion of how to apply the specific principle to various roles. What we will see is that regardless of your role on a project, may it be as the project sponsor, project manager, team member, or auditor, the principles hold true. They are project independent. This makes them quite powerful.

2.7 Application Suggestions

Think of five leaders in your environment (personal, business, or public life):

1. What distinguishes them from others?
2. What are the key principles you can distill from analyzing their behavior?
3. How could you transfer these principles into your daily project life?

References

Cockerrell, L. (2008). *Creating Magic: 10 Common Sense Leadership Strategies from a Life at Disney.* London: Vermilion.

Drucker, P. F. (2006). *The Effective Executive: The Definitive Guide to Getting the Right Things Done* (rev. ed.). New York: Harper Paperbacks.

Drucker, P. F. (2008). *The Essential Drucker: The Best of Sixty Years of Peter Drucker's Essential Writings on Management.* New York: Collins Business Essentials.

Johns, T. (2008). The Art of Project Management® and complexity. In *2008 PMI Global Congress Proceedings.* Denver, CO: Project Management Institute.

Juli, T. (2003). Work smart, not hard! An approach to time-sensitive project management. In *2003 PMI Global Congress Proceedings.* The Hague, Netherlands: Project Management Institute. Retrieved from http://www.thomasjuli.com/work_smart_not_hard.pdf.

Miller, G. A. (1956). The magical number seven, plus or minus two. *The Psychological Review, 63,* 81–97. Retrieved from http://www.musanim.com/miller1956/.

Morgan, G. (2006). *Images of Organizations* (updated ed.). London: Sage Publications.

Chapter 3

Principle 1: Build Vision

The reason most people never reach their goals is that they don't define them, or ever seriously consider them as believable or achievable. Winners can tell you where they are going, what they plan to do along the way, and who will be sharing the adventure with them.

Denis E. Waitley (1933–),
American motivational speaker and writer

3.1 Vision

There are several reasons why building vision is the first leadership principle. From an image approach, it is the tip of the pyramid you see from the distance. It guides you; it gives you a direction to walk toward. From a content perspective vision, it gives your project meaning, the reason for its existence. Let's look at an example.

A couple of years ago my wife and I were deeply frustrated that there was no reliable preschool in our town. Our eldest daughter had just finished attending a preschool that, unfortunately, closed shortly after, and there was no other preschool in our community. This is why we were looking for a preschool for our youngest daughter. There were other preschools in the region. However, they were overpriced or had a waiting list of 1 year or longer. This was clearly no solution to our problem. We needed to have a reliable preschool, allowing my wife to return to work for at least a few hours every week. In addition, we were convinced that a preschool was good for our children. One evening we met with other parents who faced a similar situation and were equally frustrated. We talked about what a relief it would be to have a reliable preschool in our town. We visualized the daily routines, the happy kids, you name it. At one time I stopped the discussion and asked why we couldn't found a preschool by ourselves. We had a vision of the preschool — saw its daily operations, the happy and smiling kids. We saw how happy we were. Soon our initial skepticism of founding and running a preschool was replaced by excitement and an entrepreneurial spirit. We had nothing to lose and everything to gain. One week later we met again and founded an organization as the legal prerequisite for the preschool to develop. Only 9 months later we opened a preschool in our town. Six years later, the preschool is still operating and has expanded in size. It has become an institution in our community.

There were a number of reasons why this project turned out to be a huge success. The cornerstone of our success was our vision and our belief in it. The vision of founding and running our own reliable and affordable preschool drove our daily doing, planning. In the beginning we did not have the faintest clue how exactly we could realize our vision. And there were a lot of obstacles ahead of us. People and other organizations told us that it would take at least 2 to 3 years to found a preschool. Well, we proved them wrong. Our vision carried us, helped overcome obstacles. Maybe our vision even caused us to overlook the obvious obstacles and master them without much hassle. We proved our critics wrong and accomplished the seemingly impossible in less than a year.

This story illustrates that having the right vision can carry you a long way. The right vision defines the direction of your project. It constitutes the reason for initiating your project in the first place. It sets the tone of the overall project and what you want to achieve. It helps overcome obstacles because it is a driving force. You may compare it to a 10 hurdle dash. The sprinter has to run over 10 hurdles. He takes each hurdle one by one. What drives him, though, is the need to cross the finish line before his competitors. The vision is to win the race. Crossing the hurdles, which are actually obstacles, does not constitute vision but milestones on the way to the finish line.

A vision need not be described in "hard" words, like a formal project objective statement (to be discussed later). Indeed, you may want to describe your project vision in soft, flowery words. What is most important is that your vision is motivating and inspiring on a personal and emotional level. It needs to be able to create excitement and a drive in those who will help achieve it. It needs to move people to action.

Some time ago I came across a vision story about a construction project (Simmons, 2006, p. 16–17). A visitor wanted to find out what all the people in a town were working on. He approached each worker to ask about his or her tasks. The first worker replied that he was a brick layer. The second worker told him that he was building a wall. Then he asked a third worker. This one explained to him that he and the other people were building a cathedral.

What do you think was the most powerful answer, carrying the whole team toward the goal: the first, second, or third answer the visitor got? The vision of building a cathedral moved hundreds of people over a long time. They could not see it yet but they visualized it. The vision constituted a purpose of individual projects such as building a wall.

I can transfer the story to a project of mine where we integrated new software for a call center of an online bank (Juli, 2002). The vision that drove this IT project was not technical in nature. The vision of the company was to improve overall customer service and make the customer calling technical service happy. The project was technical, but the vision went beyond the technology and was purely business driven, putting the end customer at the center of attention. The project of integrating new call center software was a mere stepping stone toward this vision.

The key to building vision is that people need to be able to relate to the vision in their daily activities. Give them the chance to identify themselves with the vision. Involve them in building this vision and participate in making it real. This helps build rapport and the necessary buy-in from those people to realize the project. Make them fans of the vision. Let it constitute their motivation and passion. Let them rave about it.

The secret of a good project vision is that it portrays a direction of the project in a way that people can relate to it. The right project vision is the foundation of every successful project. It is the cornerstone of success.

3.2 Project Objectives

Building vision does not mean that developing and defining formal project objectives is of little or no importance. The opposite is the case. Actually, defining project objectives is one of the key project success factors, no doubt about it. Take the example of our preschool. The vision we had was to build and run a reliable and affordable preschool. From the start we had very specific ideas in mind. We said that we wanted to open the doors of the preschool within a year, that the preschool should stay affordable (actually, we set explicit maximum target fees), that the building should be safe and big enough, and so forth. We filled the vision with life, not mere words. We broke down the vision until we had very specific objectives on which to focus.

A vision sets the overall picture of your project. Project objectives qualify this vision, make it specific. Project objectives thus constitute the concrete foundation of your specific project, for planning, conducting, monitoring, and closing activities.

Recall the quotation of Denis Waitley at the beginning of this chapter: "Winners can tell you where they are going, what they plan to do along the way, and who will be sharing the adventure with them." Project objectives are not vague about the direction. Just like the vision, it should be described such that you and everybody else on the project team can relate to it in your daily activities. Be specific about what you want to achieve. On the other hand, don't be too detailed; this may limit creativity and inspiration. Furthermore, you want the objectives to be relevant; i.e., in sync with the vision. The project matters to the organization and the people for whom and with whom you are working. It is relevant to the clients of the project as well, whether within or outside your organization, be they customers or co-workers. Know who they are for they are your clients you want to delight.

Project objectives provide a very specific and concrete direction. Stay on the ground though. They still need to be achievable. This may be difficult to state at the very beginning of your project. There is no rule that serves as a guideline. Sometimes you have to rely on other people's estimates; sometimes it may be a good decision to rely on one's gut feeling and firm beliefs.

For example, when we first decided to pursue opening a preschool we were well aware that it took other communities up to 3 years to found a preschool. We didn't have this much time. First of all, in 3 years the preschool would be of no benefit to us because our own children would be too old and attending regular school. We were driven by our immediate needs and desires. We were aware that our plan might not work out as intended. At least we could say that we tried. This was sufficient for all of us to start work.

Your project objectives must have two other characteristics. They have to be measurable and time-boxed. You may want to argue about the characteristic of measurability. It is true there are projects for which it is difficult to think of measurable objectives. In such cases you could ask how you want to evaluate if and to what extent the project results will satisfy the actual requirements of the project. Trying to answer this question causes you to be more specific about your goals. The objectives may turn out to be measurable after all.

Project objectives frame a project; they set the boundaries of the playing field. Without boundaries, the project journey may take you anywhere but the desired destination.

Once more citing the example of our preschool, we set maximum target fees and agreed on opening hours. When you train for a marathon you may set a target time within which you want to run. Set the measurable target in such a way that it helps set a boundary around the project and yet is still motivating enough. Don't raise the bar too high or leave it too low. If you find out that you need to adjust it along the way, you may have a chance to do so.

Let's talk about the last characteristic of good project objectives: being time-boxed. This means you need to have a target end date for your project. This is important. Without a target finish date we are not talking about a project in the first place but about an ongoing activity. A project always has a start and an end date. The dates may change for many reasons. But without an end date you don't have a project. You may not even have incentives to start or finish it any time in the future. Why have the project in the first place if you cannot even say when you want to finish it?

All the characteristics of good project objectives — specific, measurable, achievable, relevant, and time-boxed (abbreviated SMART) — help set boundaries around your project. They help streamline your intended efforts. The aim of all characteristics is to help you focus on the ultimate project goals.

Make no mistake, it is not an academic exercise to ensure a SMART project objective. Describing your project objectives to meet these requirements forces you to think through what you really want to achieve. At the end of the day your project has to yield results. After all, this is why you start your project in the first place. Both a vision and project objectives set the tone of your project, define the direction of your project. But how specific is your goal? If you describe it in words that are too general it will give room for many different interpretations.

For most projects you are working with a team, with other people. You want to make sure everyone has the same understanding of your goal. The vision may be described in fairly general terms (e.g., we want to found and run a preschool). The project objectives have to be much more specific for people to understand the scope of your project. In the case of the preschool, we talked about the future location of the preschool, opening hours, fees, group sizes, and so forth.

Yet another example may be building a house. You take your vision to an architect. The architect will ask you what exactly you have in mind. If you stay on the abstract level you may end up with a house that looks totally different from what you had in mind because you did not express your vision explicitly or appropriately for the architect to understand.

In short, make sure that you have project objectives that are SMART. They need to be crystal clear and understood by everyone actively involved in your project.

3.3 Vision vs. Project Objectives

Both project vision and project objectives have to be worded in a way that your project team can relate to them. They serve as guidelines. As such, everyone on your project team needs to be able to translate them into directives for their daily project work. This is why they need to have the same understanding of the meaning and scope of the vision and the project objectives.

Needless to say, your project objectives need to be in sync with your vision. To a certain extent you can say that project objectives are a subset of the project vision. Project objectives solidify your vision, help produce tangible results. The project objectives describe the means to achieve your vision in a given time frame, the means to make it happen. From this perspective, project objectives concretize the project vision.

When you use the picture of the pyramid project objectives, ensure that there is a link between the vision (the tip of the pyramid) and the foundation of the pyramid (the results). The vision provides the overall direction for your project. The project objectives do the same but are more specific about the desired project results at the lowest level of the pyramid. The closer you get to the pyramid, the better will be your understanding of what exactly the project results will look like. You will get a clearer picture the closer you get to the final destination of your project journey.

At the beginning of this journey you may have a faint idea of the end results. SMART project objectives frame the lowest level of the pyramid. The closer you get to the pyramid, the better picture you will have of what else comprises the base of the pyramid (i.e., project results).

For example, when you train for your first marathon you may set out a target time (e.g., less than 4 hours). The more you train you will get a better idea if the original set target time is feasible or not. Once you have mastered preliminary races as preparation for the marathon, such as a half marathon, you will get an even better idea how fast you can run the whole marathon. Right before the marathon the objectives are clearest. But it is not until after the race that you know if you have achieved the goal you initially set and possibly modified during the weeks of training.

Both project vision and project objectives are crucial for project success. Together they set the direction and tone of your project journey. They complement each other. The vision inspires your journey. It defines the purpose of your project. The project objectives tell you more about the destination. You lose or skip either one of them and your project is unlikely to succeed. A project vision without project objectives may give you an idea of the direction, but you may never get close enough to the destination to produce tangible results at a certain time. On the other hand, project objectives without a vision may describe the desired end result and time frame, but they cannot inspire the necessary enthusiasm in your team to drive the project to success. They do not form an underlying meaning for the work. It makes a difference if you tell workers to put one brick on top of another, to build a wall or to start work on a cathedral. If you prefer project objectives without the corresponding project vision you will end up with lots of brick layers. Their main motivations may be to earn the money. They come in the morning, work, and leave in the evening. The workers who have a vision of building a cathedral may actually conduct the same activities as the first worker, but their work attitude and motivations are likely to be different. They know that they are devoting their time and effort to something big.

The closer you get to the pyramid (i.e., the closer you get to the end of your project), the clearer a picture you will have about project results. In most situations it is virtually impossible to describe the final project results at the beginning of the project journey. However, the vision in its nature changes less frequently. It thus serves as the compass for the project objectives. However, it is *the combination of project vision and objectives* that sets the direction and describes the destination of your journey.

3.4 Building Vision: First Steps

There are endless ways and means to build vision. I can sketch only a few in this book. In Part II of the book I offer concrete examples and templates you may want to apply in your project. They are far from being complete but should give you an idea of what is possible. At this point let me suggest some basic principles of what it takes to build vision in your project.

To begin, you need to acknowledge your utmost motivations for the project. The motivation can be to solve a problem or to create something new. Let's first have a look at the motivation to solve a problem. For this purpose, answering the following three questions will help you pinpoint the core of the problem:

1. What are the top issues or risks?
2. Who is affected by these issues or risks?
3. What are the impacts of the issues or risks?

Going through this exercise makes you analyze your present situation and isolate the actual problem. Who knows, maybe you find out after this exercise that there is actually no problem. Even better. Or you may realize that the problem is different from what you initially thought. This, too, is great. It helps save a lot of energy. Can you imagine if you started a project to solve a problem that does not actually exist?

In addition to the first three questions, you can ask, "*why?*" For example: *Why* are these the top issues or risks? *Why* do these issues or risks affect the identified persons or organizations and not others? *Why* do these issues or risks have such a great impact on them? If the answers do not get down to the true core of the problem, continue to ask "why?" until you have identified the true core of the problem. It is this issue you want to address and which drives your effort to find a solution.

Once you have identified the cause of the problem, go beyond it and outline possible solutions. Answering the next three follow-up questions will help you in doing so:

1. What needs to be done to resolve the situation? Why?
2. What benefits can we expect from the improved situation? Why?
3. What do we need to do to achieve this? Why?

If the motivation to start your project is not problem oriented, but instead you want to create something new, you can modify the questions, as follows:

1. What are the top solutions or opportunities you envision? Why?
2. Who is interested in these solutions or opportunities? Why?
3. What are the effects of the solutions or opportunities? Why?
4. What needs to be done to bring about the new situation caused by the solutions or opportunities? Why?
5. What disadvantages will the solution have or bring with it? Why?
6. What do we need to do to overcome these disadvantages and obstacles? Why?

Input for answering the questions may come from several sources. You may account for company goals, market demand, results of previous projects, responses to competitors, etc.

Once you have answered all questions, summarize your findings in one or two sentences. This is the *motivation statement* of your project. It may be tedious to find the right wording, but it is worth it. This exercise forces you to specify the motivation. Just like you did for the project vision and objectives, you want to phrase it so that everyone on your team can understand and relate to it.

Composing a *vision statement* comes next. In your vision statement, describe the *ultimate* solution to your motivation. Start with the end in mind. The answers to questions 4 through 6 above should provide you enough input. At this point it is less important to describe all details of the desired end state than to get a broad picture of *what* the end result will be and how it will feel to get there and have it.

Next, document your vision statement. This is not a formal or administrative exercise. Documenting your vision statement helps you to phrase it in a way that is understandable to others, because you don't want to keep this vision to yourself. You want to share it with others. Understanding the vision is one thing; ensuring the support of others to achieve it is another thing and actually one key to project success. This is why sharing your vision is so important.

Building vision cannot be done overnight. Plan sufficient time to build the vision, involve others (especially your team), request feedback, and refine and qualify your vision. Note that it may not be possible to have a vision that is shared by everyone actively involved in your project. In this case you may want to start your project with a set of workshops that help clarify the vision and break down its elements into project objectives and requirements. We will return to this point in Chapter 10.

3.5 The Person Who Builds Vision

At this point you may ask if it is always the project leader who develops the project vision. For example, you may be assigned to a project management role where the vision and project objectives have been defined for you. You may have no influence on the project vision statement. True, this can indeed happen. It is probably not so uncommon in the first place. Note, however, that we are not talking about the role of the project manager but the role of project leader. Project leaders make themselves responsible for both project vision and objectives. If there is neither, the project leader is responsible for developing them and ensuring that they are mutually agreed upon by everyone actively involved in the project.

If there is a vision, whether a project vision or corporate vision that has to be taken into account when realizing your project, it could have been defined, authorized, or given out by a project sponsor. Regardless, as a project leader you *must* make sure that both are in place. Corollary, project leaders do not start a project without a project vision and objectives. If you want to be or become a project leader, you either build vision and project objectives or make sure that both are in place, are crystal clear, and are mutually understood by every single person actively involved in the project.

3.6 Characteristics of Vision Builder

This distinguishes a project leader from a project manager. Project managers may accept what is given to them. They swallow whatever they are given to eat. They react, don't ask questions, and manage the project according to the principles and side constraints set out for them. Project leaders ensure that the direction is defined and clear. They go beyond the dutiful administration of a project.

You may want to compare a project leader with the skipper of a ship. Experienced skippers know where they have to go. They have a mission to fulfill. They will not leave the harbor until the mission is clear and all preparations for the journey are complete. It is their job and responsibility to lead the crew in the right direction. Of course, they cannot achieve the mission by themselves. They need to build and have a functioning crew. Every crew member fulfills a distinct role. But it is not the accumulation of individual crew members that make up the functioning crew. All crew members must know what is expected from them. And vice versa, all crew members have to know what they can expect from others. The skipper then has to build a crew that functions as one unit. Only together can the skipper and crew sail the boat and accomplish the mission.

In the end, however, it is the skipper who is responsible for the direction of the journey and who communicates it to the team, ensuring that everyone understands the direction of the journey.

Ask yourself who you are on your project. Are you the project leader who acts as the skipper? Or are you just a crew member, fulfilling your duties as a project manager. When we talk about project leadership we expect the characteristics and responsibilities of a skipper. This means that you are well aware that you need your crew to accomplish the project mission. This is why you want to build a functioning and performing team. At the end of the day you initiate this process. You start with building vision, developing a performing team, and ensuring delivery. In other words, project success starts with you as the project leader.

3.7 It Takes a Project Leader — and a Team

As the skipper, as the project leader, you are responsible and accountable for leading your team. You are accountable for setting up, running, monitoring, delivering, and closing the project. Now, in the real world, project managers are often held responsible but not accountable for the outcome of a project. But even if you are not accountable, that is, your head is not at stake, project leaders *always* act as if they are accountable. This does not mean that a project leader is the most important person on the team. This is as far from the truth as it can be. Project leaders know that they cannot achieve the project objectives alone. It takes a team to do so. You, as the project leader, are part of this team.

It is a misconception that project leaders are the "boss" of their teams, in the sense that they are the autocratic leader of a number of people formed more or less loosely together in a team. Officially, you may lead your project team, supervising the individual team members. But make no mistake; project leaders understand that they rely on their team. As such, they are part of the team, behaving and acting as members and fulfilling their role and responsibilities. Without the team, project leaders cannot achieve anything substantial. Take again the example of a skipper at sea. Skippers may certainly dictate the direction. From this perspective they may be the #1 person on the ship. And they need all others to fulfill the overall mission. A project leader may tyrannize the team, and this could actually help achieve the project objectives. However, it is highly unlikely that things would be done smoothly and this approach will hardly ever produce long-lasting effects.

We will look at the significance of team building and involvement in the next chapter. For the time being, keep this in mind: It takes a project leader to build vision — and a team.

3.8 Timing of Building Vision

Now, let's briefly talk about the seemingly obvious: When is the right timing to build vision? You build a vision of your project *before* project initiation because the project vision sets the overall tone of your project. It defines the direction of the project and puts it into perspective. It frames the project environment and constitutes the purpose of the project existence in the first place.

But why is it then that the most obvious is way too often not too common after all? This is an excellent question. It takes us back to our insight in Chapter 1: Common sense is not equal to common practice. Once I worked on a technical project where there was no vision, where the project objectives were neither clear nor mutually understood. The project was doomed to fail and fail it did. The lack of vision moved the project to a roller coaster, to a maze without a clear end in sight. When the project manager in charge realized, he tried to correct and adjust the course midway, while everything was at full speed (i.e., during the project, while all other project activities were still in full swing). Did it improve the overall situation? Yes, insofar as the project manager could say that he tried to build vision and adjust project objectives to a changing environment. No, because the project did not change its overall direction at all. Actually, there was no overall direction to start with and no direction after the little "vision building" by the project manager. The project continued to slide down the path to project failure. Frustration grew and quality suffered. The interesting thing was that the project did produce results.

However, it did not meet the originally stated requirements. In addition, the project vision was neglected and forgotten. Interestingly, the original vision of this technical project was not technical in nature at all. It was business driven and it was about the end customer. Forgetting about this vision, the team focused solely on the technical features of the solution. Business factors and aspects of user experience were given less importance. This became obvious during the end-user acceptances tests. Simple yet typical end-user scenarios were flawed or did not function at all. In the end, the project failed from both a technical and a business perspective.

What we can conclude from this example is that you want to make sure that you build vision before the actual start of your project. If you want to build vision during the course of a project, this is possible. However, you should be well aware of the fact that you may have to throw away some or everything of what you produced to that point in time. After all, by building or adjusting vision you are changing the course of the project. It may be possible to use some of the past deliverables, but there is no guarantee. What counts is that the new vision sets the right direction for the project.

You may even be tempted to build project vision after the project is over, maybe to justify poor project results. This is possible. But note that this has nothing to do with project leadership and certainly nothing to do with project success. Instead, it is an example of poor judgment and lack of business ethics. If you want to build a solid foundation for project success, build vision *prior* to project start and refine it with the help of project objectives and regular deliverables.

3.9 Value of Building Vision

As time consuming as vision building may be, it yields precious rewards you cannot live without if you are interested in leading your project to success. The motivation statement describes the initial environment. It helps you focus on a specific situation you want to change or create. The vision statement describes the solution you have in mind. You break down the vision into its various specifications and develop a SMART project objective statement. The project objectives help structure your solution requirements.

The motivation, vision, and project objectives statements all form a solid foundation for successful projects. If you miss any one of them, the chances for project success are decreased. This is why you want to make sure you develop all of them at the beginning of your project. Ensure that they are consistent, that they complement each other, and that they form one unit.

Make sure that this unit is commonly understood and supported by everyone involved in your project team. Ideally, you involve your team in developing the motivation, vision, and project objective statements.

Things change during the course of a project. For example, specific requirements may have to be modified and even some of the project objectives may change. The vision should be least likely to change; it stays stable. If it changes, the overall direction of your project changes. In this case it may be best to terminate your initiative and launch a new one.

Start with a unified vision and know where you stand before and during your project. This is your utmost responsibility as project leader. A project leader takes the initiative to build vision. This is the #1 prerequisite for project success. Also, as a project leader you do not work alone. Know your environment, know your potential, and identify your limits and overcome. Build and involve your team and nurture effective collaboration across the board. This brings us to the second leadership principle: nurture collaboration.

3.10 Application Suggestions

1. Analysis of the past:
   a. Think about a past project that succeeded.
   b. What motivated the project in the first place?
   c. What was the overall project vision?
   d. What were the official project objectives?
   e. How did you contribute to the development of the project motivation, vision, or objectives? What could you have done differently?
2. Application of principles in the present:
   a. Think of a present or upcoming project.
   b. Write down a motivation statement for the project.
   c. Develop a vision statement.
   d. Break down the vision into its components and derive project objectives. Make sure that they meet the SMART criteria.
   e. Compare them with official statements of your project. Where and how do they differ?

References

Juli, T. (2002). Closer to the customer: The successful CRM strategy of HVB Direkt. *Banken & Sparkassen, 3*, 40–42.

Simmons, A. (2006). *The Story Factor: Inspiration, Influence, and Persuasion Through the Art of Storytelling*. New York: Perseus Books Group.

Waitley, D. E. (1980). *The Winner's Edge: The Critical Attitude of Success*. New York: Berkley.

Chapter 4

Principle 2: Nurture Collaboration

Players win games, teams win championships.

William C. Taylor,
American businessman

4.1 The Heart and Soul of a Project

We all strive for project success. But what does "project success" mean? What does it entail? And even more important, *how* do we achieve it? We have already learned that project success is more than the accumulation of project deliverables. That is what most people may perceive as project success, but there is more to it. Actually, project results may be the last things we can see in our projects.

Let's take the image of the project leadership pyramid. The first thing we see on our project journey is the tip of the pyramid (i.e., project vision). We have an idea of what the eventual results should look like, the project objectives, but we cannot see them yet. We need to know how to get from vision down to project results (Figure 4.1).

Project results are at the bottom of the pyramid. Before we describe project results in detail, we will be able to see what is between vision and results. We will see what links the top with the base of the pyramid. This is the middle of the pyramid; it is the central part of the pyramid.

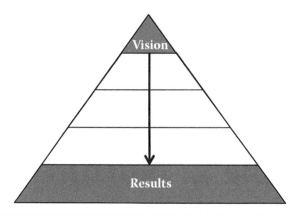

Figure 4.1   From vision to results.

The next three project leadership pyramid principles fill the gap between vision and results. They level the path from vision down to results. Understanding these three principles will provide answers to the question about what it takes to get from project vision down to project results. The next three chapters will elaborate on each of these principles. They are distinct and all equally important. And they all have one aspect in common: They require the active involvement of the project team. You can also say that it is these three principles and the team that connect project vision and results. This is why the team is the heart and soul of a project.

Thus far we have learned that it is the project leader who is responsible for building vision and making sure that the project starts in the right direction and stays on course. This is the top of the project leadership pyramid, yet it is not sufficient to produce results.

To move closer to results we have to have a deep understanding of the heart and soul of every successful project: the team. As important as they are for project success, project leaders are powerless if they do not build and involve a team and do not nurture collaboration.

There are several reasons why the team is the heart and soul of the project. A project leader alone does not have the time to conduct all activities (unless it is a one-man project). In most cases, several people are involved over the course of a project. It is the individuals on the team and the team as a whole executing the various activities. The project manager is one of them, fulfilling his or her role and responsibilities.

Furthermore, project leaders often do not possess all the necessary expertise to deliver the project. Even if they do, they likely do not have the time to conduct all activities by themselves.

It is the team doing the work. And you, whether in the role of project manager, sponsor, expert, or even client, want to play an active part in this team.

4.2 Team Building

The team and teamwork are significant factors for project success. Be aware, though, that teamwork does not just happen. It evolves. As project leader you need to understand that teams go through various development phases. At the beginning of a project you form the team. Roles and responsibilities are defined and distributed. The project moves along. After awhile you find out that things are not working as smoothly as intended. For example, you may find out that a team member does not completely fill the role of IT architect because he lacks certain technical skills. As a consequence, the assigned architect cannot and does not review the source code of the new software being built, the new software is implemented, and now the complete system does not function as required. The team atmosphere is at a nadir. Some team members blame the architect, others the developers, yet others the project manager. This scenario is an example of a *storming phase* of a project team. The situation may differ from project to project. Still, you get the idea that the team is in a so-called storming phase.

A storming phase is by no means necessarily a bad thing. The opposite can be the case. If a storming phase is taken as a chance to make the necessary changes in the project team set-up, it serves a purpose.

You as the project leader have to understand that roles and responsibilities need to be adjusted to cope with the changing environment. This is a prerequisite for team building to take place. Revisiting roles and responsibilities and making necessary adjustments is called the *norming phase*. In the previous example, you may assign the "old" architect to a new role where he feels more comfortable and can prove his strengths. Another person may now take over the responsibilities of the old architect, such as code reviews. You may actually take advantage of the opportunity to review other role assignments and collaboration rules and see if they still meet the present project requirements. As a consequence, collaboration in the team becomes easier, more efficient and effective. The team enters the *performing stage*.

This is the stage where team synergy effects can be viewed. It is the stage where teamwork is more than the sum of individual workloads. Team magic takes place. All of a sudden seemingly impossible tasks become possible. Why? Because you have overcome obstacles to collaboration, the team works efficiently, and synergy effects can unravel. This is where you as the project leader want to take your team. The *Guide to the Project Management Body of Knowledge (PMBOK® Guide)* aptly describes the connection of project leadership and team building resulting in teamwork. It states: "Team building is the process of helping a group of individuals, bound by a common sense of purpose, to work independently with each other, the leader, external stakeholders, and the organization. The results of good leadership and good team building are teamwork" (Project Management Institute, 2008, p. 418). The quote underlines the importance of teamwork. At the same time it reveals once more that the team-building process needs to be initiated. If it doesn't happen by itself, it is your responsibility as the project leader to initiate and facilitate it.

Teamwork is more than the sum of individual contributions on the team. Teamwork is the symbiosis among all individual team members. It can thus take the team as a whole, as one unit, to a higher level of performance. This is why team building is so valuable and has to be on the map of every project leader.

This concept is not limited to the world of business. Take, for example, a championship team in soccer or any other sport. The team may be made up of a few exceptional players, but this by itself is not sufficient for the team to win as a team. It is the dynamic interactions in the team that make the difference. Teamwork can help overcome the weaknesses of individuals by giving them the chance to unleash and play out their strengths.

There is no doubt that teamwork takes time to develop. It takes a lot of training, setbacks, and adjustments in the team structure, order, and collaboration rules. It is worth the effort. As the *PMBOK® Guide* explains, "outcomes of team building include mutual trust, high quality of information exchange, better decision making, and effective project control" (Project Management Institute, 2008, p. 418).

4.3 The Juice of Teamwork

Collaboration is the juice of teamwork; it is what makes teamwork possible in the first place. It encompasses communication, individual and joint execution, as well as the delivery of results on both the individual and team level. Communication is part of collaboration.

It is true that open communication is critical for project success, but it is not an end in itself. Rather, see communication as being an important element of collaboration. That is, open communication is a critical success factor for effective collaboration.

The following example shows that communication alone is not sufficient for teamwork to play out. On a soccer team the players talk with each other. They play and support each other by passing the ball and hopefully scoring a goal. Although a single player scores the goal, the team effort prepares the right environment for that player to overcome the goalkeeper of the other team.

Another example is the Alinghi sailing team. (For an extensive review of this team's success story, see Jenewein & Morhart, 2006.) Exchanging commands by itself does not constitute effective teamwork. The individual team members must execute their respective tasks. The combination of all individual tasks moves the ship across the ocean, fast and efficiently.

4.4 The Project Leader and the Team

When you are the project manager, you may oversee the team. Be aware, though, that first and foremost you are a member of the team. As such, it is your responsibility to support your team.

If you want to nurture collaboration you need to start with yourself. You need to be a role model to others. You share information openly. You give and accept open and constructive feedback. You work with your team. You realize your own weaknesses, because you cannot know and do everything by yourself. You rely on others and acknowledge their strengths. This is why you trust their expertise.

You do not want to micromanage them because this would be counterproductive. Your responsibility is to ensure that they can do their jobs. And let them do their jobs, especially when they are more skilled than you are in their particular activity. When you and your team set up rules of communication, you should be the first person to follow these rules. Realize that it is the whole team as a unit performing the work and not just you or a group of individuals. You want to actively participate in the daily business of your team, being an active team member and team player.

Ernesto Bertarelli, the president of the Alinghi sailing team, knew very well that his title alone did not earn him the respect of the team. He participated in all team-internal trials, the aim of which was to find out who is best for each position on the boat. They applied to him too. He gave his best in the team trials and trainings. This is what earned him the respect of his team — and vice versa. Ernesto Bertarelli was the president of the Alinghi sailing team as well as an active team player.

This is what distinguishes good and effective leadership from a simple, old-fashioned, top-down leadership style. Understand that the project is about the team. From this perspective you may actually call a project leader a *team* leader. Note the first word is not "leader" but "team." This is for a good reason. If you want to be an effective project leader you have to be a good team player as well.

On the other hand, you need your team to support you in your role. Both you and your team need to help each other fulfill their roles and responsibilities. Being a role model to your team is not a one-way street. When you act as a role model to others and are open to constructive feedback you will soon find out the strengths of others on your team who now may serve as role models to you. This is why project leadership calls for being a team player too. One doesn't go without the other. When you call for active and open collaboration on your team, walk the talk, practice it by yourself. Show everyone the power of open collaboration and swim with the flow of your team you helped build. Do not micromanage but facilitate teamwork. This is what nurturing collaboration means. You have to ensure that collaboration takes place and start with yourself. Create an environment where collaboration is practiced on every team level. This is the best guarantee for team synergy effects to develop.

The alternative is that your team degenerates into an accumulation of individuals, each focusing solely on his or her work package, not caring about anybody else. I doubt this is what you are striving for. No doubt, it is possible for this kind of "teamwork" to eventually secure the delivery of project results.

Let me tell you a story about a project where teamwork and collaboration were mere words on a piece of paper hidden away in a drawer. I once worked on a project where the project manager not only did not invest any time building a team at the beginning and throughout the project, he also did not care about team spirit. He did not see (or maybe he did not want to see) the need for and potential of a performing team. In this particular project and company the regular line activities of the team members were given a higher priority than project activities. In addition, the various line organizations or departments in this company functioned as separate units. They interacted with each other where necessary but that was pretty much it. They kept to themselves and everybody seemed to be happy with it. Any project manager would have a hard time building a team across different line organizations in the first place. The project I was working on was no exception. Directions given out by the project manager could easily be overruled by line managers. Team members, for example, did not first ask the project manager for approval of their vacation requests but went directly to their line managers. If the project manager was lucky, he was informed about the vacation a few days prior. In addition, line managers held the overall power to allocate people to other line activities, resulting in limiting team members' availability for the project. As a consequence, planning the project became quite challenging. At least once the project deadline had to be postponed because a line manager withdrew team members from the project for work on another organization in his department. The sad and fatal thing was that the project manager could not do much about it but swallow. It was fatal in the sense that the project initially planned for 6 months was delivered 6 months late with a reduced scope and lower quality than required.

From an outside point of view, everyone in the project and company lost. And yet, the project results were celebrated as if they were delivered on time. Indeed, the whole project was considered a "success."

You could conclude that teamwork and active collaboration is not that important after all as long as the project delivers results. As this story shows, you may be right — if you don't mind additional effort and a high level of frustration for people involved in your project. Alas, not valuing teamwork and active collaboration enough do not have much to do with true project leadership and the understanding of project success propagated in this book.

4.5 Self-Organizing Teams

Agile team environments make use of self-organizing teams (Beedle et al,. 2001). In this scenario there is no single person overseeing or leading the team. Rather, the team as a whole agrees on the distribution of work packages for a given time frame. There are no additional hierarchies. The team organizes itself.

Make no mistake, though; self-organizing teams do not promote a laissez-faire approach toward collaboration. Self-organizing teams require a high level of discipline among individual team members. The motivation in these teams is very high, driven by a common vision and a mutual understanding of the project objectives.

In the absence of these elements, it is unlikely that self-organizing teams can evolve or even exist.

This brings us back to the first principle: building vision. Unless a team already has a common vision, it takes a leader to help build the vision and secure an understanding and support of it by every single team member.

A closer look at self-organizing teams furthermore reveals that there is an institution or role that directs the work of the team. This can be a vision, project objectives, a requirements catalog, a timeline, you name it. In addition, self-organizing teams follow detailed rules of engagement (i.e., communication and escalation rules).

Collaboration does not just happen. It is proclaimed. It is nurtured by the team as a group and by its self-defined and agreed-upon rules of collaboration. This combination promotes collaboration within the team.

Still, even self-organizing teams go through the team development phases of forming, storming, norming, and performing, mentioned previously. A coach facilitates this development process and mediates in cases of disruption.

4.6 The Project Team as the Power Base of the Project Leader

By now we have learned that the project leader relies on his or her team and vice versa. You can say that the project leader and the team form a symbiosis. By this token, the project leader is as strong as the team and vice versa. As you help build vision and nurture collaboration you set the direction and shape the heart and soul of the project. You thus have great influence on the outcome of your own project, even considering that it is the team and not you as the project leader who is doing the work. The actual power to save or kill a project is with the team, of which you are a part. This means that when you build vision as a guiding force for collaboration and nurture active and open collaboration, you strengthen the base of your own power and influence: your own team.

Corollary, the power you have as a project leader is built on your own team. The team is only as strong as its level of collaboration. This again depends on the direction given by the vision that you help build. With a performing team the project leader has the greatest influence and thus power.

This, too, could be abused. As a project leader you could abuse this power for your own personal gains. What does this mean to the project and the chances for project success? They will both deteriorate. By abusing the power given by team synergy the project leader weakens his or her foundation of power. Unless the organizational structure and environment of the project allows or even supports this kind of behavior, the project is doomed to fail. Effective collaboration prevents this from happening.

4.7 Collaboration beyond Team Boundaries

The project core team is the backbone of project success and the foundation of the project leader's power. It does not stop there. The project core team is important for the daily work of the project. Yet, the team members of the core team are not the only project players. The extended project team includes stakeholders and maybe even the clients of your project. Hence, when you promote and nurture collaboration, do not limit your efforts to the core project team. Expand your efforts to the extended project team. This applies to the principle of building vision as well as nurturing collaboration.

This is especially important when members of the extended project team are everything but supportive of your project. Recall the story of the company where line activities had a greater priority than work on a project. This can be extremely frustrating for the project manager and the team. They are constantly sitting between two chairs — their own department on the one hand and the project on the other hand. In a situation like this both parties lose. This need not happen. Actually it is a call for action. Reach out to the extended team. Talk about the project vision and explain how everyone will benefit from the project. Show the skeptics the value of the project and its results. Find out how they want to be involved in your project. Share relevant information that clarifies this value. Market the accomplishment of your project on a regular basis throughout the project life and show how everyone, including the extended project team, contributes to project success.

Collaboration is not limited to your own project team. It goes beyond the boundaries of the project core team. The rewards of building and sharing the project vision and nurturing collaboration are similar to those of your project core team. They significantly increase the chance for project success.

4.8 Nurturing Collaboration — First Steps

There are numerous ways and means to nurture collaboration for every project phase. First of all, start your efforts early. To be specific, plan activities that nurture collaboration right from the beginning of your project until project closure. This is not a one-time but a continuous effort.

My own experience shows that every successful project I either led or was a member of started with a *team norming workshop*. The purpose of this team norming was multifold: (1) to explain to the team the motivation, vision, and objectives, including the scope of the project, its timeline, interdependencies, and other constraints, (2) to discuss and define roles and responsibilities, (3) to agree on communication rules, including meeting structures and escalation mechanisms, (4) to account for personal motivations of team members, and (5) to refer to and use former lessons learned from other projects or team normings. Please have a look at Chapter 10, in which I explain how to plan and conduct a team norming workshop.

If there is one thing you want taken home from a team norming workshop it is that every single team member understands the need and the immense value of active and open collaboration and the resulting teamwork. They need to understand that although you as the project leader may facilitate teamwork, every single team member is expected to participate and contribute to the team. The project leader is no exception, as he or she, too, is a member of the team.

Given the importance of effective teamwork, you cannot make compromises on setting the groundwork for effective collaboration. By this token, if individuals on your team do not share this philosophy, you may want to consider replacing them with individuals who do.

You may not always have the chance to select individuals for your team. When you do have the freedom to choose your team, you should look for certain strengths in potential candidates. In addition to the required skill set, potential team members should also be passionate and have the proper character and mindset to work on a team.

First, you want them to be passionate about the project and the expected work. If they are not, it could be because they truly do not care or they lack the necessary information about the purpose and vision of the project. If they do not care, think twice about whether you want to have them on board. Personally, I advise against it. If they lack passion due to lack of information about the project, you and possibly also the rest of your team should step in and fill this gap.

Second, the candidates need to have the character and mindset to be open to and supportive of active teamwork. Project work is teamwork. Even the best expert in his or her field has to share knowledge and expertise with the team. The willingness to share information, exchange ideas, and actively work with others in the team is a prerequisite of effective collaboration and teamwork.

When you recruit team members during a project you may not have to do it by yourself. Involve your existing team. Ask them to help select the right candidates. Not only can this yield new perspectives from which to assess candidates. It may also help integrate new team members into the group faster because the existing team wants to have them on board.

The team is the base of power of the project leader. Selecting the right team and conducting a team norming are two activities that help build this power base. Team selection and norming are two of the first steps to nurture collaboration. They are a starting point toward the development of a performing team.

Don't stop here. In addition to the team norming, plan for and conduct more formal team-building activities. Chapters 10 and 11 cite a number of examples. Team building takes time. This is why you want to review and improve collaboration rules and their practice on a regular basis. Involve your team in doing so, either as a unit or in one-on-one meetings with your team members. From time to time, seek outside help, asking other experts to review your project and identify areas of improvement.

There are endless ways and means to build a performing team. Note though that at the end of the day by far the most effective assurance for developing a performing team is teamwork itself. This is what nurturing collaboration is all about.

4.9 The Value of Collaboration

Collaboration is necessary for the team to achieve the vision and project objectives. This has become clear by now. By the same token, the project vision must include the concept of collaboration; it needs to be part of the vision as well as the project objectives. Collaboration is a means to achieve the objectives and thus to come closer to achieving the vision. It is a central element of every project. This is why vision and collaboration go hand in hand. You cannot move from the top to the bottom of the project leadership pyramid without collaboration. On the other hand, collaboration without a common cause leads nowhere.

Project success is not about individual accomplishments. The project team delivers the project. As such, the team is the heart and soul of the project. Corollary, project success is, or at least should always be, the success of the team. Effective project leaders understand the value and huge potential of teamwork and team synergy effects. This is why they actively nurture collaboration. They serve as role models and are part of the team. They thus actively participate and contribute to teamwork.

Team success, and therefore project success, is not about the individual. What matters are the leadership principles and the nature of collaboration.

Nurturing collaboration can be hard at times. It takes a lot of effort and can be quite time consuming. The payoffs, however, are worth every minute invested. Having mutually understood and supported rules of engagement, characterized by open communication and effective collaboration, makes project life much easier. Once you have helped create an atmosphere of trust, team spirit, and fun, team synergy effects emerge. Magical things can happen, productivity increases, and the quality of your deliverables is higher. Nurturing collaboration prepares the ground for performance on the individual and team level. As a project leader you want to cultivate this soil of performance. This leads us to the third leadership principle: promoting performance.

4.10 Application Suggestions

1. Review the roles and responsibilities in a past or present project of yours. How have you accounted for the personal motivations of your team members?
2. Are you following the same collaboration rules of your team? If not, why are you deviating from them?
3. Core and extended project team:
   a. Who is in your core project team?

    b. Who is part of your extended project team?

    c. How have you nurtured collaboration beyond the boundaries of your core project team?

4. How can you promote open and active collaboration with and among the extended project team?

5. What obstacles to collaboration with your extended project team exist?

6. How can you overcome these obstacles?

7. Think of a past or present project that had or has a very strong team. How did it feel to be part of the team? How did you sustain ongoing teamwork?

References

Beedle, M., Bennekum, A. V., Cockburn, A., Cunningham, W., Fowler, M., Highsmith, J., et al. (2001). *Manifesto for Agile Software Development*. Retrieved from http://agilemanifesto.org/. (see also http://agilemanifesto.org/principles.html).

Jenewein, W., & Morhart, F. (2006). Sieben Manöver zum Teamerfolg. *Harvard Business Manager, July*, 2–12.

Project Management Institute. (2008). *A Guide to the Project Management Body of Knowledge* (4th ed.). Newtown Square, PA: Project Management Institute.

Taylor, W. C., & Labarre, P. G. (2006). *Mavericks at Work: Why the Most Original Minds in Business Win*. New York: HarperCollins.

Chapter 5

Principle 3: Promote Performance

Don't tell people how to do things. Tell them what to do and let them surprise you with their ingenuity.

George Patton (1885–1945),
U.S. general during World War II

We have spent time building vision and nurturing collaboration. Now it is time to act. You can plan your project in every detail and agree on collaboration rules. Then you have to start work. This is performance. You execute your plan, realizing the project objectives and reaching for the vision. It is also a time when you want to reap the rewards of effective collaboration. Having built a vision and done the necessary things to nurture collaboration are useless if you cannot move your team to the performance stage. In other words, you have to create an environment that helps promote performance. This is what the third principle is about.

5.1 The Performing Project Team

In Chapter 4 we talked about the project development phases: forming, storming, norming, and performing. The last phase is where you want your team to act. This is where synergy effects take place. Both individual and team performance are at a peak. If you have ever experienced this stage in a project you know that magical things can happen. Seemingly unsolvable and insurmountable challenges turn out to be manageable with your team. Productivity is high, quality is great, and your project moves along according to plan and maybe even faster. It may even feel effortless. Everything is running smoothly. People don't talk about plans, they execute them. And everyone knows exactly what to do, when, and how. At the same time, every team member knows what the other team members are doing. The single team member can totally trust the team as a whole and all of the team members. All the little wheels work together. The team forms one unit and performs as such. It is an atmosphere of complete trust. It is not that there are no problems arising. But the team embraces them, taking them as challenges and chances to prove its individual and group competencies. The team is more than the accumulation of individuals. It is performing synergy.

This is no illusion or fairy tale. It is real. And as a project leader you can get there — move your team to this performing stage. Let's have a look at some of the basic rules to comply with and apply.

5.1.1 Rule 1: Be a Role Model

The first rule of successfully promoting performance is that you want to lead by example. As important as a team is, it is you as the project leader who builds and helps norm the team. Corollary, promoting performance has to start with you. Not only are you committed to your role and its responsibilities, but your actions are in sync with the project vision and you follow all collaboration rules. You deliver on time and as expected. In short, you serve as a role model. As such, you encourage your team members to do the same.

Take the example of the president of the Alinghi sailing team, Ernesto Bertarelli. He participated in every team competition. The goal was to find the best team member for each position. He did not exclude himself from the team norms. He was and acted as a team member, like everyone else. He lived the team values and was judged by the same measurements as every other team member. What counted was the purpose of finding the best team. To find the best person for each role, you must not exclude yourself from the quest. You actually start with yourself, participating with the rest of the team. This behavior and these actions help build trust and respect within your team.

As an example, let's look at the captain of a soccer team. He is formally leading his team on the field. He also acts as a role model during training. He actively participates in the team's training. He teaches junior team members, integrating them into the team. He knows that it is not the individual player who can be the decisive factor but the integration of the whole team that wins a championship.

When Lee Iacocca became CEO of the then-ailing Chrysler corporation, he realized that he had to cut salaries. This was only one of the many steps he had to undertake. And he started with himself by cutting his own salary to $1. You could say that this was easy for him because he could afford it. This is true. What counted, however, was the gesture of applying the same rules to himself. This sent the message that, "I am one of you. Let's do it together."

The new CEO of a telecommunications giant realized that customer service was one of the most critical areas of improvement of the company. Managers lacked understanding of the basic needs of end customers. The new CEO wanted to change this and thus ordered that every senior manager spend at least one day each quarter in a company storefront, selling products and services to end customers.

You don't have to be a CEO to be a role model. It can start with small things. For example, actively participate in the discussion when conducting project reviews as team members state what they like or dislike. This shows everyone that you are open and receptive to feedback from others. You take it seriously and act upon it. Or, you could ask a third, neutral person to facilitate project reviews. This may make it easier for team members to provide feedback on your performance.

No matter what project you are working on, be aware that as project leader you are a role model to your own team and others. Act as such. Walk your own talk and be true to your own principles. Demonstrate authentic leadership.

5.1.2 Rule 2: Create the Right Environment

The second rule of successfully promoting performance is that you as project leader want to create an environment in which your team can prosper. In the team norming workshop mentioned in Chapter 4, not only does the team talk about roles and responsibilities, but they also want to find out what work environment is best for the team and for individual team members. This starts with the location, which includes the office space.

In today's world, virtual teams are becoming more and more common. Technology helps link the various team members, who may sit in different offices or even be distributed across the globe. There is email, the telephone, online chats, video conferences, online document sharing, you name it. Still, there is no substitute for bringing the team together. If it is not possible for the team to sit and work together, maybe there is the possibility to set up a permanent room that is reserved for team meetings. If parts of your team are located in a different country, it helps a great deal to visit them at least once so that they get to know you in person.

Find out how flexible working hours can be and when you have common working hours where everyone needs to be present. If at all possible, account for the individual motivations of your team members.

In one of the projects I managed we had a very experienced senior business analyst. He performed on a very high level. The quality of his analysis and documents was impeccable. Alas, I noticed that the work packages he worked on in the late afternoons did not have the usual quality. We talked about this. In the conversation I learned that in the afternoon he was thinking of his little kids, wondering what they were doing at the end of the day. He wished he could be there with them, getting them to bed. We agreed to change his working hours. From that day on, he left our project office at 5 pm, giving him enough time to spend with his kids. In return, he finished any open work packages in the evening or early morning.

Within days, all his work packages yielded the same high quality. He was highly motivated and contributed a great deal to the success of the project.

This little episode taught me how important it can be to account for personal motivations and interests. We are not working machines but human beings. Just as we have to know the underlying motivation of a project, we need to understand the motivations of our own team and every team member. If you are working with a large team, focus on those you are working with the most. You want to know what makes them tick, what motivates them on a daily basis. Maybe it is their love of the work, or maybe it is just the money. Whatever it is, try to find it; not to control them but to understand them better. Take them seriously and value their motivations. Treat your team members as you want them to treat you. For example, if you have to leave early because you have tickets for a concert of your favorite band, it motivates you to start early on this particular day and finish on time. Would you expect other team members to honor this? Would you do the same for them?

The motivations of each individual on your team drive their daily work and their attitude toward it. You do not want to make assumptions about them that turn out to be flawed. This could lead to quite a few misunderstandings, especially when you are working with cross-cultural teams. If you want to promote performance in your team, take the time and find out what motivates the team as a whole and each individual on your team. Discover what your team and the individual team members need to perform. Learn how you can help the team perform.

It may not be possible to fulfill all needs. Try to fulfill the most important ones and see how this impacts team performance. Find out what blocks team members from performing and try to remove these blocks. Cover the team's back so that it can focus on the job. In return you can expect that the team will cover yours.

For example, in a past software development project I limited the time developers had to face the customer, sitting in endless meetings while their code was waiting for them. Whenever there was important information affecting their work, I shared it with them. On the other hand, team members did not let me stand in the rain when I needed a realistic assessment of possible technical problems we had and how they were progressing in their work. It was a win–win situation. I covered their back and vice versa. This, too, is what teamwork and team performance is about: helping each other.

5.1.3 Rule 3: Empower Your Team

Being a role model and creating the right environment for team performance are important ingredients to promote performance. Alas, *team* performance is about your *team*. Acknowledging the strengths of individual team members and the potential synergies from teamwork are one thing. But it does not stop there. You have to enable your team to do its job and perform. This is what the third rule to successfully promoting performance is about: empower your team. This means you have to give your team the power and all the information it needs to do its job and perform.

Give your team and each individual member the opportunity to prove their strengths. Empowerment is the opposite of micromanagement and top-down leadership. Empowerment is about trusting your team. It calls for you to show every team member how to solve problems by themselves. Empowerment means that you teach your team how to become less reliant on you as a project leader and instead to trust and show their own strengths and the power of the team. Embrace the previous rule of creating an optimal environment where the team as a whole and each team member can best fulfill their roles and thus contribute to collaboration, sharing, and the purpose of the project.

In a nutshell, if you want to promote team performance you have to empower your team to perform. Give your team the opportunity to excel and have an active hand in project success. Empower your team through your effective leadership. This goes in two directions. On the one hand, apply all five project leadership pyramid principles and contribute to project success. On the other hand, help your team as a group and team members as individuals become leaders in their own roles and thus contribute to project success. Give your team the freedom to act, and share the information and power necessary to do so. This doesn't mean the end of your leadership. Empowerment does not come for naught. It is directed toward a common goal: the successful delivery of your project. "Empowerment means you have freedom to act; it also means you are accountable for results" (Blanchard et al., 1998, p. 90). Accountability is two sided. If an individual team member is successful, so are the team and leadership; if an individual fails, so do the team and its leader. It is therefore your responsibility as project leader to make sure that your team understands this and supports each other practicing it. This is why empowerment takes effective leadership — your leadership.

5.1.4 Rule 4: Develop a Solution-and-Results Orientation toward Problems and Risks

One of the characteristics of performing teams is that they focus on solutions and results rather than problems. As project leader you want every team member to understand how important it is to identify problems and risks. Furthermore, it is even more important that they not despair and stop thinking and acting when facing a problem. Instead, they should analyze the root of the problem or risk and take appropriate measures to solve or control it. From this perspective a problem or risk is not seen as a potential show-stopper but a chance to learn and prove skills and competencies on the individual and/or group levels. The question is not what a problem is all about but how to solve it for the benefit of the project and move on. This distinguishes a problem orientation from a solution-and-results orientation. The latter one is forward looking toward achieving the project vision. A problem orientation, on the other hand, holds the person accountable for solving the problem in the past and present. As a consequence, performance becomes impossible. This is why the fourth rule of successfully promoting performance is to help your team develop a solution-and-results orientation toward problems and risks.

Practicing a solution-oriented approach to project challenges by itself is no guarantee of performance. It is an ingredient. It helps the team to be or at least become proactive and work toward achieving the project objectives.

As project leader it is not your responsibility to solve every potential problem or risk. What you want to do is empower your team to solve problems by themselves. This improves problem-solving competency and self-confidence on the individual and team level. You don't talk so much about problems, mistakes, and shortcomings. Instead, you elaborate on future chances and perspectives.

The last thing you want to do is seek a scapegoat for a problem. It is counterproductive. All it does is deteriorate team morale. Team members end up withholding problems from the team, information flow ebbs, and collaboration is held to a minimum. This is the end of teamwork and team performance. Instead of trying to find a scapegoat, attack and solve problems as a team.

The chances of a group finding the solution to a problem are much greater than letting the accountable individual try to solve it by him- or herself. Accountability for solving a problem does not imply that the person has to solve the problem alone. It means that that person or group drives the solution. If the accountable individual is not able to do so alone, it is his or her responsibility to ask for help.

In cases where the team cannot solve a problem even with a joint effort, you still have the chance to escalate the issue and ask for help. If you do, outline what you have found out about the root causes of the problem or risk and share what you suggest doing. If you do not have a clue about a possible solution, say so.

If you cannot or do not want to escalate an issue, you may be able to work around it or live with it. Similar to developing a project plan, you cannot account for every possible detail. Nor will you be able to solve every problem or risk. As a matter of fact, oftentimes you will not even want to. In other words, do not attempt to solve or control every single problem or risk. Sometimes problems disappear or dissolve without you doing anything about them. Keep the big picture and overall direction in mind.

5.1.5 Rule 5: Invite Productive Competition

In some project situations you may want to conduct team internal competitions to promote and improve team performance. This is especially the case when the project takes place in a competitive environment such as the world of sports. Corollary, the fifth rule of successfully promoting performance encourages you to invite productive competition in your team.

The team internal trials of the Alinghi sailing team serve as an example. The goal of the trials was to find the best person for each role on the boat, which secured the optimal team performance. The individual performance was seen in light of the overall team performance. In other words, the trials were not about individual performances but to find the best collective performance. The ambition was to improve the team performance and become a better team.

Team internal competitions may also be useful, for example, in software development projects, where two teams follow different approaches for a technical solution. They develop a prototype that illustrates their approaches. The aim is to learn which approach and solution may work best. From this perspective the team internal competition serves the purpose of promoting creativity and innovation.

Both examples show that competitiveness, for example, in the form of team internal competitions, *can* help promote performance. The prerequisite is that the competitiveness aims at improving team performance; it is linked with collaboration and social sharing.

5.1.6 Rule 6: Let It Happen

Suppose you are acting as a role model and you have created a supportive environment in which team performance can prosper. What else can you do to promote performance? Simple: Let it happen. This is the sixth rule of successfully promoting performance. Let the team do its job. By the time a soccer match starts, for example, there is not much the coach can do about the team performance. It is showtime. Now the team has to prove its talents and show what it has learned.

There comes a point when you actually do *not* want to push individuals to perform. If you sense this is still necessary at this stage, you have probably missed something at an earlier stage, say during team norming or in one-on-one meetings with your team members.

Project leadership also deals with trust. You have to trust your team and let the team do its job. Alas, you are part of the team. You do not have time to micromanage your team members. Micromanagement is usually a sign of distrust and poor planning. It is poor leadership. When you have built a common vision and developed collaboration rules jointly with your team, there should be no need to micromanage team members. Promote performance by being a role model, creating the right environment, empowering your team, and then trusting your team. Do not force and micromanage your team members. Project leadership is not about micromanagement. It is about enabling and empowering your team to perform and produce results. It starts with you as the leader and culminates in teamwork, team performance, and team results.

5.1.7 Rule 7: Celebrate Performance

The final rule for successfully promoting performance calls for celebrating performance. There are at least two reasons to celebrate performance.

First, you should celebrate when you see the results of performance. These can be the delivery of a product, the approval of a project phase, or whatever the performance was intended to achieve.

Another reason to celebrate is the performance process itself. This is the behavior of individual team members or the team as a whole. You want to "look for behaviors that reflect the purpose and values, skill development, and team work, and reward, reward, reward those behaviors" (Blanchard et al., 2001, p. 190). The reward can be formal (in the form of a pay increase, a prize, or a promotion), or it can be informal (simply acknowledging the performance, enjoying the act of team performance). Things are running smoothly. Team members get a kick out of solving formerly insurmountable problems. They are happy to be a part of the team. They enjoy work and have a good time. Performance on the group level is high and in return helps improve individual performance. You can observe this, for example, when you watch a sports team on which individual players all of a sudden play exceptionally well, like they have never played before. It is because the team performance is helping unleash individual skills. This, too, is team magic. It is highly rewarding to the team and the individual members of the team. That is, experiencing team magic is a reward by itself.

With every celebration you know there is an end. Make sure that this celebration coincides with the successful project delivery. If you and your team are not there yet, stay focused on the project purpose. Performance is great as long as it is geared in the right direction. You do not want to be overindulged with team performance, lose sight of the changing environments and circumstances, and then have to find out that, although the team performance was great, it did not yield the required results. Celebrating performance is great. But make sure you and your team keep your sights on the project vision and produce results.

5.2 The Extended Project Team

The rules of promoting performance apply to both your core project team and the extended project team. You serve and act as a role model, you create the right environment, and you let performance develop and take place. Period. In the case of the extended team, you also ask what they, the stakeholders, need to perform in their extended project role. For example, what kind of information do they need? How much do they want to be involved in your daily project work? In return, you tell them what you need from them for project success. Note that you do not ask for what you need from them for yourself. This is not about you. It is about project success. This is what counts and this is what should drive you, your core team, and your extended team throughout the life of the project, from initiation to close. When you ask what the stakeholders need from you and tell them what you need from them to secure project success, it becomes evident that you, your core team, and your extended team are interdependent. Any one of you cannot achieve project success without the help and support of the others. Nurture and cultivate this interdependence to the benefit of the project.

This is not a call for trying to please everyone. If individual needs are within the scope of the project and actually help achieve its vision, you have to account for them. Other needs may be important to the specific person but may be out of the scope of the project. Recall that your first and foremost responsibility as project manager and project leader is to manage your project successfully and fulfill its objectives. This directs and bounds all of your activities. Corollary, it gives you an idea which special needs, requirements, and desires of your key stakeholders outside the core project team are consistent with the overall project vision and project objectives and thus may need special attention. At the same time, you will know which are beyond the scope of the project.

5.3 The Right Timing

Applying the performance rules is an ongoing activity. Building a performing team takes time, patience, and endurance. Corollary, the sooner you start promoting performance on the individual and team level, the better. This will help you build a common project vision and nurture collaboration. Remember, though, that you cannot force people to perform if the necessary conditions are not met. Two of the top requirements are a common vision and collaboration. They are the necessary conditions for promoting performance. Do not expect performance if there is no common vision as a driver of daily project life and rules of engagement. They all go hand in hand, linked with each other. Alas, it starts with you as project leader.

5.4 Value of Performance

The most obvious reward of performance is results. The results may be the final project deliverables or smaller milestones on the way to the final project delivery. In either case, results give the person or team a sense of accomplishment. This is important and rewarding. But there is more to performance than results. The process of performance itself is valuable. Top athletes talk of a "flow state" when they are performing. It is as if they lived and acted in a different world where everything seems to be possible. It can actually be this flow state people are after, what motivates them. If you have ever worked on a performing team and experienced synergy effects from teamwork, the results of the team performance could be amazing. But it is the special atmosphere in such a performing team that creates magic and motivates you and everyone else on the team. It takes the team performance to a higher level. No doubt, this is a desirable state you and your team may want to experience. Still, it is not automatically the ultimate state. A caveat regarding flow state created by team performance: you can create a tunnel vision within which you neglect or ignore the outside world, which changes and may affect your project vision and objectives. You are performing, but the end results you deliver may no longer be needed. For example, you may work on a project building a bridge across a major river. The project duration is 18 months. You are really excited that you have built a performing team. Everything seems to work smoothly. After 18 months you finish the bridge on schedule and in budget. Yet, nothing seems to be right because the customer, the government, is not willing to pay your bill. They claim that you did not account for desired and required changes expressed during the project. You did not realize that the project objectives and requirements changed during the course of the project.

This example shows us that although team performance is desirable, as the project leader you also have to ensure that it leads in the right direction. This means you have to be sensible to changing circumstances that may affect the project objectives and requirements. You and your team have to be aware of these changes and plan accordingly. As the project leader, you must ensure that your team is open and flexible enough to adjust to a changing environment. You have to create and nourish a culture of ongoing learning. This brings us to the fourth principle of effective leadership: cultivating learning.

5.5 Application Suggestions

1. Think of a situation in which a role model inspired you to higher performance.
2. Describe the ideal environment you need to be most productive in your present role.
   a. What exactly makes this environment special to you? Why?
   b. What do you need to change in your present situation to create this environment? Why?
   c. What disadvantages would this environment have or bring with it? Why?
   d. What do you need to overcome these disadvantages and obstacles?
3. Now analyze a past or present project environment:
   a. How productive was/is this environment to team performance?
   b. Describe the ideal environment for optimal team performance.
   c. What exactly makes this environment special to your team? Why?
   d. What do you and your team need to change to create this environment? Why?
   e. What disadvantages would this environment have or bring with it? Why?
   f. What do you and your team need to overcome these disadvantages and obstacles?
4. List all criteria that make performance in your present project more likely?
5. Describe what "magic" in general and the phenomenon of "team magic" in particular mean to you.

6. How can you account for individual motivations and interests on a project?
7. Think of a winning championship team. What did it take this team to get there?
8. What does it feel like to be part of a winning team? What were some of the obstacles you experienced on the way and how did you manage to overcome them?

References

Blanchard, K. H., Carlos, J. P., & Randolph, A. (1998). *Empowerment Takes More Than a Minute*. San Francisco: Berret-Koehler Publishers.

Blanchard, K. H., Bowles, S., Carew, D., & Parisi-Carew, E. (2001). *High Five! The Magic of Working Together*. New York: HarperCollins.

Patton, G. S., & Atkinson, R. (1995). *War as I Knew It*. New York: Mariner Books. Retrieved from http://en.wikiquote.org/wiki/George_Patton.

Chapter 6

Principle 4: Cultivate Learning

Take chances, make mistakes. That's how you grow. Pain nourishes
your courage. You have to fail in order to practice being brave.

Mary Tyler Moore (1936–),
U.S. television actress

6.1 Certainty in an Uncertain World: Change and Mistakes

If performance is what we are striving for, lasting performance must be the Holy
Grail. How true is this statement? Well, there is certainly some truth to it. We want
to secure lasting performance in order to achieve our project objectives. Lasting
performance by itself, however, is not sufficient if it does not account for change.
We live in a dynamic, ever-changing world. This is a truism. Also, we know that we
can expect lots of changes in long-lasting projects. This, too, is common sense. The
same applies to the statements that we make mistakes and that knowing everything
is an illusion. But, if we know all this already, why is it then that reflection, learning,
and plan adjustments are not common practice in so many projects? Maybe it is not
common sense after all that learning is important in life and thus in projects.

If we want to secure lasting performance we have to be able to cope with
changes. Changes come in many forms, caused by ourselves and others. Sometimes
we can influence them and sometimes we cannot. The fact is that we can expect

changes to take place. Knowing this, the question becomes how we can best cope with changes. Take the example of a soccer team in a major tournament, say the World Cup, which has won its first matches. The team already plays at a very high level. Experts consider it the favorite to win the tournament. Then, one day, one of the key players on the team gets injured during training. What happens next? Quite a few things can happen. Some people may freak out, lose control, and maybe even give up all hope of winning the next game. A performing team and, even more important, an effective leader stay calm. The leader (the head coach or the coaching team) assesses the alternatives, changes players' roles, and adjusts the strategy to compensate for the missing player. The team's only choice is to react to the changing circumstances. The question is how it handles the new situation. An experienced coach, knowing that players can get injured, can help prevent this from happening. For example, the coach ensures that the players have the necessary physical fitness to play in the first place. The coach may read signs of a player's fatigue in a game and may replace the player with someone "fresh" from the bench. Still, there are and always will be circumstances the coach cannot control. This is no excuse not to be prepared for the unforeseen circumstances. It is a matter of attitude. The coach can freak out, lose control, and despair about losing one of the leading players, or he or she and the team can do something about it. This is when you know whether you are dealing with a truly performing team.

Performing teams are much more likely to cope with changing circumstances. They realize that there may not be enough time to despair. Instead, they embrace the situation and act. They show the necessary flexibility to step in and resolve the situation. This is where you want your team to be. For this to happen, not only do you have to fulfill the first three leadership principles, you have to cultivate an environment of learning, both on the individual and, even more important, on the team level.

This distinguishes effective and proactive leadership from ineffective and reactive management; this is the difference between performance and learning on the one hand and failure and inflexibility on the other. On what side do you want to be?

When you know that changes are likely to occur in your project, you and your team need to be prepared for them. Objectives, requirements, and collaboration rules are subject to change, performance levels may fluctuate, and even the vision may vary. Knowing this is one thing. Doing something about it is another thing. Do not fool yourself. You cannot account for every possible change. Indeed, it would be foolish to try to prepare for every single circumstance. Developing plans for every possible situation does not reduce uncertainty. It may give you some idea of what you could do, but there is no guarantee that it will work. We cannot foresee the future. A plan, therefore, can serve only as a road map, which itself is subject to change.

We can all make mistakes regardless if we have a rough, high-level plan or a very detailed plan accounting for every feasible problem. The question is what we make out of our mistakes. Do we learn from them or do we despair and give up?

We all make mistakes. This is especially so when working in a fast-paced and uncertain environment. It is impossible to plan for every possible scenario. Expect mistakes to be made and build in enough flexibility to adjust your plans accordingly. A prerequisite is that you as the project leader create a culture of learning in which team members are not punished when they make mistakes. Making mistakes is normal. You want to build a team that is capable of learning from mistakes and mastering change. This cannot happen overnight. The key is that from the very first day you establish learning routines in your project. You want learning to be part of your daily project routine. How so? Let's have a look at some examples.

6.2 The Status Report

One of the prerequisites of learning is the accessibility to information. This applies to both your core and extended project teams. The content you provide in project status reports is a sign of the amount and quality of information you are sharing with your team. It is a good snapshot of your project. The requirements of a status report differ from project to project. Usually a status report consists of an executive summary of the overall status of the project. It lists achieved milestones or key activities since the last report, any upcoming milestones or key activities, and the top issues and risks. A status report is both backward and forward looking. Assessing the present status, you list and analyze the achievements of your project teams. The key question is whether or not the project is still on track and if you can achieve the project objectives. The sooner you identify any discrepancies, the easier it is to realign your project. Asking the right questions will help you and your team identify actual or potential discrepancies early on, giving you enough time to learn from your mistakes and move on. Go beyond the usual status report questions and information. The five leadership principles serve as an orientation. In preparing a status report you want to check if your activities are still in sync with the principles. Determining whether you are still following the principles will tell you if your vision, objectives, and requirements have changed or need to be modified. The same applies to the team's collaboration rules, performance routines, and even results. If any one of the five principles have been violated, chances are that your project is no longer on track. Therefore, when you prepare your status report, monitor the milestones, list accomplishments, identify issues and risks, and outline steps to resolve and control them. In addition, check if you and your team are following the five leadership principles for success. This will help you identify root causes and possible problems that could cause harm if they are not detected and resolved early on. Once more, the sooner you identify any discrepancies the easier it is to realign your project.

6.3 Review Sessions

A simple and pragmatic learning routine is to conduct regular feedback sessions with your team. You can conduct them daily, weekly, or monthly, depending on the nature of your project. The key question you and your team want to answer is what everyone has learned since the last feedback session. Personally, I like to start by asking everyone what is going well in our project, what we have to improve to secure project success, and how to do so. See Chapter 11 for sample formats.

There are a few things to keep in mind when you plan, prepare, and conduct review sessions.

6.3.1 Regularity

Make the feedback session a regular event for your project, starting the first day. Let it become an early and regular routine. Do not wait until your project or a project phase is completed. That will not allow you to find out what you could be doing better or differently while you have the chance. Conducting a lessons learned session upon completion of a project may be valuable if you can apply those lessons in a future project. True. However, they are useless for the past project. Thus, feedback sessions need to be a constant part of your current project.

6.3.2 Focused Lessons Learned

Collecting feedback is a first important step. Next, prioritize the lessons learned and discuss the most important ones. Go a step further and ask what actions you can derive from these lessons. Consolidate them into a motto for the whole team to work on till the next feedback session.

In a past project we conducted daily stand-up meetings where every team member talked about their work package and most pressing issue of that day (Juli, 2003). Once a week we expanded this session to include lessons learned. It was interesting to see what the various team members learned each week and what they wanted to work on the next week. In addition to individual goals, we derived team goals to work on each week. Examples were "Work smart, not hard," "Focus on small time savings," or "Let's do it right the first time instead of learning by trial and error." The feedback session quickly became our team round of learning. And it didn't stop there. It resulted in greater and faster sharing of breakthrough experiences. Team members started posting their lessons learned on the whiteboard even before the feedback session for open discussion. Often we did not wait till the next review session and started sharing lessons learned on an ongoing basis. Learning became an early routine on a daily basis.

Prioritizing feedback helps you and your team focus. It is impossible to focus on several activities at the same time. It scatters your resources. It is inefficient and ineffective because it does not yield the desired, tangible results. Instead, focus on one or only a few action items at a time.

6.3.3 Rotate Positions

There is no law that dictates that the project leader must always facilitate the feedback sessions. Indeed, I encourage you to rotate the facilitator role on your team. This has a number of advantages. First, it gives you a chance to participate more actively in the feedback session as a normal team member. Second, it gives every team member the opportunity to develop facilitation skills. You may want to start the session by asking the facilitator to share his or her own observations and lessons learned. Tell the team member beforehand about opening and leading the review session, so he or she has sufficient time to prepare.

6.3.4 Vary Locations

In most cases you will probably run your regular feedback sessions at the site of your project. From time to time, you may also want to consider conducting the sessions at an off-site location, away from your usual place of work. Ask a third person to facilitate this workshop, and actively participate in the workshop, not as a project leader but as a team member.

Off-site meetings offer a number of advantages. The different location may help team members think more clearly, because of the distance from their daily jobs. Maybe you can combine the workshop with a team event and/or team-building exercises to help boost team morale and collaboration. Thus a simple review session can contribute not only to learning but also to improved team morale, better and more effective collaboration and performance, and clear expectations about the road ahead.

6.4 Training

The ideal scenario for a project is that everyone on your team possesses the right skills and competencies to master the challenges ahead. Reality, however, looks different. First, you may not be able find the persons with the right skills. Second, you may think you have all the required skills and competencies covered and then find out that this is not the case. Or, individual team members may fall out or leave the project. The team then has to compensate for the missing skills and competencies. This may work out, but there is no guarantee.

There may be times when you can compensate for missing skills. At other times, you have to fill the gaps because your team is simply missing the required skills altogether. The sooner you can identify these gaps, the better, because it may give you sufficient time to fill them. Formal training may help. However, sending team members to such training during a project may cause them to fall behind schedule on their work packages. Therefore, it is best if you can conduct formal training before the start of your project. If this is not possible, plan for sufficient time during the project.

An alternative to formal training is team internal training, where experienced team members help less experienced members learn the missing skills and competencies. You may organize teaching sessions for this purpose or pair experienced with less experienced team members. This allows team members to share information and expertise across your team.

It is not just the project leader calling the shots. In a functioning team, every team member is responsible for identifying and addressing possible gaps in skills and competencies and finding a solution. This is why it is important that you set up the expectation that all team members be open and receptive to learning and sharing their own knowledge and experience. It cannot be that it is just you sharing information. Everybody has to participate. As project leader, you serve as partner and coach for learning and information sharing. You *facilitate* learning. You are not the sole source of information. Help build a learning environment and invite the complete team to join and support you.

6.5 Timing: It Is Never Too Late to Learn, Unless …

Learning is an ongoing activity. As much as circumstances can change and some changes are beyond our control, you want learning to be a part of your daily project work. Always. In a past project of mine a team member revealed in a team meeting that he would not be able to finish his work package on time and thus we could not deliver on time. This may not be too uncommon a situation. What made this situation a bit more peculiar was the fact that the team member revealed his little secret just 4 hours before the final delivery deadline. This was bad news. The project manager was anything but happy about this delay. The team saved the situation. It analyzed the problem and jointly developed a solution. It did not spend a single moment blaming the team member for not telling the team earlier about his delivery problems. The team focused on finding a resolution and executing it together. This is an excellent example of teamwork and a solution-oriented attitude toward challenges. It shows that it is never too late to learn — as long as the project delivery date has not passed or you could not deliver because you did not learn early enough. This is why you want to create a learning environment from day 1 of your project.

6.6 Banning Learning

To illustrate what can happen if you do not make learning a constant part of your daily project routine, let me tell you a story of another project I was working on. At the beginning of the project, the project office encouraged the project manager to conduct a team feedback session or lessons learned workshop at the completion of each project phase. The project manager agreed. On the day of the lessons learned workshop everybody appeared and stayed throughout, with one exception: the project manager bailed out literally at the last minute for another meeting. When he reviewed the prioritized feedback after the workshop, he was upset. Rather than addressing the results of the lessons learned workshop with the team, he took the concerns raised by the team as a personal assault against him. As a consequence, he forbade the project office to plan and conduct any future single lessons learned sessions with the team. The team on the other side wanted to have regular feedback sessions. It was seeing the value they got out of the first session. This was of no interest to the project manager, however, and he insisted on the ban of future feedback sessions. The decision disappointed the team a great deal. For awhile individual team members continued to share their experiences and lessons learned. However, it didn't capture them in a consistent way and share them across the complete team. Soon, fewer team members expended the energy to share their thoughts and experiences. Openly talking about mistakes was perceived as a sign of weakness. People became afraid of talking about shortcomings, problems, or risks. They focused on their own activities, deliverables, and performance. Individual performance did not suffer, but team performance deteriorated and so did team morale. There was hardly any room to openly share experiences and new ideas, which was critical because the various work packages were dependent on each other. Toward the end of the project the deliverables of the subprojects were integrated. Not too surprising, they did not function together as required. The resulting integration effort took longer than planned and moved the original deadline. At the end of the day, the project was delivered late and was over budget.

This story is not meant to imply that not conducting lessons learned workshops will automatically cause your project to fail. What it does tell us is that blocking the development of a pulsating and active learning environment characterized by open and constructive feedback and team learning sends a wrong, negative message. In the example, banning feedback sessions had a ripple effect. It decreased team morale, questioned the value of open collaboration, caused people to focus on their own performance and deliverables rather than the team's (thus undermining the seamless integration of the different work packages and deliverables), and endangering final project delivery. Clearly, this was far from what the project manager intended, but he was still accountable for the mess he helped create. I admit that there were other reasons for the failure of this particular project. The behavior of the project manager was no excuse for other team members to stop learning altogether. Not all of them did, which probably saved project delivery, even though it was late and over budget.

A small group of team members including myself continued to synchronize, sharing information, experiences, and concerns, and we kept our performance level high. It was frustrating to witness the vanishing team morale. Still, we continued our small team effort, focused on our deliverables, thus contributing to saving delivery (at least partly) and making a difference.

6.7 Invite External Project Reviews

Usually project reviews or audits are perceived as bad. This is understandable. Nobody likes being criticized. As project leader, however, it is a matter of attitude. Project reviews can be a great learning opportunity. They can help the project manager manage the project to success. An outside view offers different perspectives; fresh and unspoiled perspectives. In contrast, the longer we work on a project, the more likely it becomes for us to develop tunnel vision. Understanding the power of learning and innovation, we should avoid this by all means. Project reviews can help achieve this.

Sharing your lessons learned does not stop with your team, core or extended. Invite others to challenge you on your project vision and the progress of your project. One of my former employers conducted project reviews of every project prior to the close of a project phase. The purpose of the review was multifold. For one, it ensured that the respective project manager and project team complied with the quality delivery standards. Second, reviewers wanted to find out if there were areas of improvement and where the reviewers or the organization could help the project team succeed. It was not the goal to find construction areas and blame the project manager and team for issues or risks. Instead, the company goal was that all projects were delivered to the fullest satisfaction of our clients. The project reviews were mandatory for all projects. Everybody expected them, although they did not necessarily like them. The bottom line was that they helped keep delivery quality at a high level. This in return helped the project manager and his team to become a better team. They were able to deliver the project on time and delighted the client, the team, and their own organization.

6.8 Extended Team Learning

When you cultivate learning, expand the learning environment to the extended project team. Although you may not have the chance to meet with the extended team on a regular basis, do not allow this to be an obstacle to soliciting regular feedback. Checking for expectations regularly will tell you if the side constraints you have accounted for in setting up and planning your project are still valid or if they have changed. Remember that stakeholders can have a significant impact on the project vision and objectives. They can affect the way you work in your core team and thus influence team performance. For example, the line organization in which some of your team members usually work may undergo a restructuring. Consequently, the line manager you reported to in your role as project manager changes. The new line manager may not share the views of the predecessor and thus opposes your project. Given the newly gained influence, the line manager threatens to withdraw team members from the project team unless the special desires of the line managers are accounted for in the project. Now you have to react quickly. You must find out what motivates the new line manager and what explains the resistance to your project. Take this input and align the project accordingly so as not to threaten the project vision.

Expanding the learning environment to the extended project team enables you to become sensitive to changes that are outside the inner realm of the project but that can still affect daily project operations and ultimately the successful project delivery.

6.9 Learning and Innovation

We do not live in a world of certainty. Projects are no different. We constantly face uncertainties, have to make decisions, and act on incomplete information. In such a situation, making mistakes is inevitable. They are normal and part of our daily life. If we learn from them, they are not a bad thing at all. They can actually enforce learning effects. From this perspective, punishing mistakes is counterintuitive. If you want to be or even have to be creative in your project, you can expect to make mistakes. The key is to embrace these mistakes as learning opportunities and move on. Innovation comes from learning. And there is no learning without mistakes.

In some situations you may actually want to encourage your team to make mistakes if it satisfies a higher purpose. For example, if you want to find a new approach or develop a new technical routine the only way to approach this may be by trial and error. In this case you cannot learn if you do not make mistakes. It would be fatal if you punished your team members for errors committed. As long as they learn from their mistakes, this is a good process and valuable learning experience.

If you are seriously interested in creating something new, you have to go new ways. Given that every project faces many changes, you must take paths that you did not and could not plan in every detail. You have to take new approaches and, yes, you will make mistakes. The big question is what you will make out of them. The way you react to mistakes makes a big difference. Learning from them and moving on to a higher level is key to innovation and innovative results.

You may have heard of Google's and 3M's learning models. In both companies employees work 4 days on their assigned project. The fifth day is reserved for innovation: 50% of this time should be project related, and the remaining 50% can be the team member's pet project. In both cases the team member is expected to produce a tangible result or at least an insight. It may be a bit far-fetched to claim that this time-sharing model is the most important key to Google's and 3M's innovation power. It certainly is an important factor.

The neat thing is that we can copy it to our project world 1:1. You can argue whether you want to or can reserve a full day each week for innovative exercises. I would say that you should plan a minimum of 10% of your time for innovation that is project related. Create room for your team members to be creative, to try something new, share their ideas, and learn from each other. Note that the 10% is not a time buffer used to compensate for late deliverables. Of course, it can be, but this should be avoided. Personally, I don't believe in time buffers. Instead, spend sufficient time estimating your work packages and accounting for risks. This should do the trick and make additional time buffers unnecessary. However, when you tell your team that you have reserved 10 or 20% of their time for innovation benefiting the project, this sends out a strong and positive signal. You expect your team members to think outside the box, beyond the known path traveled, and to find new avenues to reach the goals of the projects. Since every team member has the luxury of this innovation time, it helps create a team learning culture. It is learning for the purpose of the project. And the team and each individual may benefit from it. This is a win–win situation.

6.10 The Value of Learning

We started the chapter with the preconception that if it is performance we are striving for, lasting performance must be the Holy Grail. By now we know that this not necessarily true. Lasting performance can be achieved. It takes practice, training, endurance, and a results-driven attitude toward project challenges to develop and sustain it.

Look at any sports team. Training (i.e., learning) is one of the key activities of the team. The goal is to become a better team. It culminates in performance on the day of the competition. The competition shows whether the preparation was good enough; it decides if the team's performance is sufficient to ensure and deliver the desired results. Finding out that this is not the case can be valuable if there is another competition in the near future and the team can improve its performance next time around. Once again, save for a very few exceptions, there cannot be performance without training or learning. Performance and project success do not fall from heaven. You have to prepare and work for them, learning from mistakes and failures. Just make sure that it is not project failure you are learning from, because then it is too late to adjust. The show is over. When you or your team make mistakes, learn from them. Correct your shortcomings, improve your performance, and continue to work toward accomplishing the project vision, before it is too late.

Cultivating learning starts with you as the project leader. But it does not stop there. For learning and performance to yield the desired results, you have to involve your team. It is your responsibility as project leader to help create a learning environment and culture in your team. Set the expectation that you want everyone in your team to join and support you. Empower your team to perform, make mistakes, learn, and innovate. This helps reduce uncertainty as information flows more freely, people are not afraid of making mistakes because they see them as learning opportunities, and team members help each other solve problems. Innovation can prosper and lead to new and better products.

In the last chapter we saw that promoting performance is an ongoing exercise. Cultivating learning is no different. Promoting performance and cultivating learning must go hand in hand. Combine the two principles and they become ingredients for lasting performance.

By cultivating learning from the beginning of your project you significantly increase the speed at which your team can move from the forming to the performing stage and then stay in this stage. Once you have created a learning environment, the storming phase of the project team turns into an opportunity to adjust rules and responsibilities and allow for team performance to develop and prosper at an even faster pace.

Note that in the project leadership pyramid, *learning* is embedded between *performance* and *results*. For good reason. When you move from the pyramid level of *performance* to the level of *results* you pass through *learning*. This means if you want performance to yield the desired results you have to cultivate learning. There cannot be lasting performance without learning, and there cannot be results without performance.

6.11 Application Suggestions

1. How are you securing a creative and innovative learning environment in your project?
2. How do you involve your own project team in cultivating learning?
3. What three factors do you value the most in an innovative learning culture?
4. What factors can you think of that impede continuous learning and self-improvement in a team? How can you remove these impediments?
5. How do you expand the learning environment from your core team to the extended project team of stakeholders?
6. How do you identify and cope with changes in the external project environment that may affect your project?

References

Juli, T. (2003). Work smart, not hard! An approach to time-sensitive project management. In *2003 PMI Global Congress Proceedings*. The Hague, Netherlands: Project Management Institute. Retrieved from http://www.thomasjuli.com/work_smart_not_hard.pdf.

Chapter 7

Principle 5: Ensure Results

> However beautiful the strategy, you should occasionally look at the results.

> **Sir Winston Churchill (1874–1965),**
> *British Prime Minister*

7.1 Project Success Is Not Measured Solely by Results

Finally we have reached the base of the pyramid. We can see each stone of the pyramid clearly. Looking up, we may even see the top of the pyramid. We certainly are impressed by the mere size of the pyramid.

So, is this the end of the journey? Is this what the whole journey was about? You may be tempted to say yes. First of all, how do we know if we delivered the right result? Maybe it is just an interim result. For example, a soccer team may have won a qualification match for the World Cup. Is this the end? No. The vision is to win the World Cup. And there are a lot of steps on the path to this vision. Winning a match is an example.

Don't be fooled. Delivering your project is important, very important indeed. It is one of the objectives of every project. It is the most important responsibility of a project manager. The question, though, is *How* did we get there? Project results are important. Oftentimes they are what people care most about. But is project success only about delivering results? Is project leadership only about ensuring results?

Of course, we know the right answer is "no." We have seen in the previous chapter that project success and project leadership are not defined solely by results or their delivery. Vision, collaboration, performance, and learning are just as important. They culminate in results. When you talk about project success, the path

69

to project results matters too. Corollary, an effective project leader always looks beyond the delivery of results.

Consider the opposite position for a moment: results are all that matters in project leadership. If this statement were true, we might see a project manager who forces the team to deliver a project, team morale that is low because the project manager constantly intimidates team members, a project manager who is the only person calling the shots, dictating what to do and when, and team members who are micromanaged and monitored around the clock. If this were the case, yes, the heart of leadership would be about delivering results.

If, on the other hand, and I hope this is the case, you have reservations about this scenario, continue reading.

7.2 Responsibility for Results: Project Leader and Team

Let's agree on the point that project leaders are accountable for project results. However, they are not the sole individuals who are delivering. It is their team. Delivering results is a team effort. The team is the heart and soul of a project. Project leaders are members of the teams they help build. It is their responsibility to take the initiative and ensure that team synergy effects can take place.

Hence, although results are important, they are only one element in project success. And you as the project leader have to ensure results. But you do not deliver them by yourself. Actually, you cannot. Effective project leaders do not forget their base of power: their team. Without their team nothing will be delivered. The project leader and the team have to build one unit. In other words, as far as delivery is concerned the project leader and the team are one unit. Of course this is so, because the project leader is also a member of the team. If there is a bottom line it is that the project leader has to ensure results. This is what he or she stands for. However, results are not delivered by the project leader alone but by the project leader and the team as one unit.

Project results are not about individual performance and delivery. They are about team performance and team delivery. After all, we are talking about a "team" as one unit and not a group of individuals who care only about their own individual goals and work without looking left or right.

As project leader you lead your team to results. The team delivers, not the project leader. This is the difference between a want-to-be project leader who acts like a dictator or tyrant and an effective project leader. Who do you want be?

7.3 Critical Success Factors of Results

Results are about team effort. And a good team starts with leadership. In this sense, a team starts with you. And you start with building vision and following the other principles. If you want to build a team, be part of the team, and lead your team to results, you have to nurture collaboration, you have to promote performance on the individual and most important on the team level, you have to create an environment of learning and reflection and cultivate it, and you have to ensure results. If you neglect the last principle, ensuring results, you act like a skipper without direction who stays on the ocean until all resources have vanished. Without food or water you and your crew will eventually die. This is a guarantee. The same applies to a project. If you do not have any direction and you do not ensure delivery, your project is basically "dead." And who knows, maybe it was not alive in the first place.

This is why the fifth principle of ensuring results complements the first four principles of the project leadership pyramid. It is the combination of all five principles that constitutes the project leadership pyramid. Applying all five principles is what effective project leadership for project success is about. If you miss any one of them, your leadership is flawed and you will most likely not secure project success. The fifth principle of ensuring results reminds us that we have to make sure the results of the other four principles are in sync with the project vision and objectives. They have to serve the project purpose. Whenever any of the project leadership pyramid principles yields results, they have to build up to the final product or service of the project. *Ensuring results* is thus not an activity focusing only on the final project deliverables. It appeals to us that our project activities shall be results oriented, keeping the end deliverables in mind. It is a call for results-driven leadership — with the necessary flexibility outlined in the fourth principle of the project leadership pyramid. And, although the team delivers results, it is not responsible for project failure; that falls to you as the project leader, for not having lived by the five principles of effective leadership. In other words, you are one of the sources of failure or success for your project. Act responsibly.

7.4 Interim Results

I doubt you want to be blamed for a project failure. Actually, I am sure you do not want your project to fail in the first place. Why would you? You want to make sure you set up your project for success right from the start and ensure throughout the project that you stay on the right course. One way to find out if you are, is by feedback from your sponsor, from your team, and from your stakeholders. And you get feedback in the form of results. You do not have to wait until the end of your project to see them. If at all possible — and in most projects this is the case — define milestones with interim results and agree on them with your sponsor and your team. In addition all efforts should be results driven, benefiting the purpose of the project. Delivering results throughout your project is *the* insurance for delivering the final result as required. This is true for a number of reasons.

Interim results reveal if you are on the right track. Say, for example, you are leading a software project but the client is not sure what exactly it wants or needs. If you happen to work in the IT industry, you know this scenario is quite common. In this case, you and your team can build an early prototype and demonstrate it to your client and sponsor. Asking them if this is what they have in mind gives you valuable input. Maybe they do not like it and request some changes. Because it is a prototype you still have enough time to make the necessary adjustments. Another example is a soccer team trying to qualify for the World Cup. A practice match gives the coach an idea if the team structure works or if changes must still be made.

Note that regular deliverables or interim results need not always constitute a tangible product. It could be that you have a formal checkpoint at which you reflect on the project's progress and the overall results thus far and how you plan to proceed.

Another example showing the value of interim results is the Alinghi sailing team. Driven by the vision of winning the America's Cup, the team ran regular trials under real conditions. Team members were not guaranteed a spot on the A or B team. Performance fluctuated throughout the preparation phase. So did the composure of the team. Due to this internal competition, individual and overall performance improved significantly. Everyone knew that eventually it was not about the individual performance. It was about finding the right team, where every single team member helped form one unit with the team. All that mattered was overall team performance. Getting to this point was a long-term effort. It took time. This is why interim challenges in the form of trials were so important. Ensuring these interim results was crucial to finding the right team, to secure team performance at the highest level, which eventually led to victory for the Alinghi sailing *team* in the America's Cup.

These examples show that regardless of how regular deliverables or interim results look, they give you and your team the chance to learn whether you are on track. In this sense, interim results reduce uncertainty. This is extremely helpful in long-term projects, such as finding the best sailing team, constructing a bridge, or building a house. In the latter case, the architect may first build a small model or create a simulation on the computer. This is much better than being surprised by an end result, finding out that you had something completely different in mind when you ordered the house.

Another benefit of interim results is that they can give you and your team a sense of accomplishment early on. This can be a morale booster. Feedback on interim results shows you where you and your team need to make changes, choose a different approach, switch roles within the team, bring somebody else onto the team, or, who knows, maybe kick out nonperforming team members if all fails.

Interim results also give you a reason to celebrate the accomplishment with your team. This, too, can be important for team morale and motivation. Celebrating accomplishments with your team throughout the project life helps boost morale and create a stronger sense of community. It helps improve collaboration and team performance. It is a win–win thing to do. Don't miss it.

7.5 Timing of Results

If you wait too long to deliver and present results, it may be too late. For example, a project I assessed some time ago prepared a prototype of the final product. The reason was multifold. First, the team wanted to showcase the project. Second, the team intended to tell coworkers about the new product the project was developing.

Last but not least, the team was interested in feedback from the client and sponsor, finding out to what extent the prototype met expectations and requirements. There was nothing wrong with this approach. Actually, the intentions were excellent and laudable. There was just one major flaw. The team did not finish the prototype until 2 weeks prior to the delivery and go-live date of the final product. Although the prototype created a lot of interest from coworkers, it was useless in the sense that the team ran out of time to accommodate any feedback from the client in the final product and project delivery. Failing to plan and deliver this interim result on time showed a number of things. Not only did it show a lack of understanding of proper planning, it also sent a signal to the client that the team did not care about their feedback nor did they have a sincere interest in finding out the true needs and desires of the client.

This example tells us that interim results are important. It also illustrates that interim results have to be delivered at a time when they still serve their purpose, be it to solicit feedback, showcase the project, demonstrate a new technology, present new ideas, etc. Plan for and build in interim results in your project plan and deliver them at a time that still gives you and your team sufficient time to react and account for the feedback in the remainder of your project. If delivering an interim result reveals that your project is off track, you have to react immediately and realign your project. And you need to have enough time to do so. If you deliver interim results too late (i.e., at a time where it is impossible to accommodate any feedback and make any adjustments to your project), they are useless. In this case they create more effort than they add value to you, your team, and your client.

The intervals of interim results depend on the nature of your project. There is no strict rule regarding the length of these intervals. For some projects you will want to have regular deliverables every 2 or 3 weeks. In Agile software development the team builds and delivers workable pieces of software in iterations of every 2 to 4 weeks. For other projects you may have only one interim milestone. The important thing to keep in mind is that interim results have to add value. They have to benefit the purpose of the project. It doesn't do any good to produce interim results every 2 weeks just to present something. The various interim results should build up and form a whole that eventually constitutes the final project deliverable. In addition, you and your team as well as your client and sponsor have to understand the value of the interim results. As much as you talk about the final project results and ensure a common understanding of the project vision, the primary project players have to understand why and how interim results add value. The results have to be in sync with the project vision and its objectives.

When you plan for interim results keep the ultimate project goal in mind. For example, the goal could be a prototype that aims to demonstrate the viability of new technology. Or it may be a presentation to your stakeholders in which you list the team's accomplishments and outline the next steps. The objective of the presentation is to involve the stakeholders and win their continuous support, necessary to achieve the project objectives.

Another example may be teaching a new technique in sports, say skiing. You break down the new technique into its various components, teach and train each individual skill, and link them together one by one until finally they form one movement and the technique you originally had in mind.

When you train for a marathon you probably plan races of shorter duration. The shorter races tell you where you stand in your training. They give you feedback about your condition and show you what you still need to practice. The shorter practice races constitute interim results in your project of preparing for and running a marathon.

7.6 The Value of Ensuring Results

What we have seen in this chapter is that, although delivering results may be the bottom line of a project, project success and project leadership are not defined solely by results or their delivery. Vision, collaboration, performance, and learning are just as important. They are the prerequisites for project results. Consequently, when you talk about project success, the path to project results matters too.

Ensuring results is not solely about end results. The fifth principle calls on us to keep the project vision in mind in all our activities and produce results that benefit the purpose of the project. Ensuring ongoing results builds the base of the pyramid until it is complete. Project success is not defined by a single product or service delivered at the completion of a project. It is the accumulation of the many results yielded from each and every principle in the project leadership pyramid.

Project delivery is a team effort, not an individual effort. You have to lead your team to project delivery. You as the project leader have to ensure that you and your team deliver results on an ongoing basis. Prerequisite is that you are forming and building a performing team. As project leader it is your duty to build and prepare your team for performance. Empower your team and let team magic evolve and fulfill its potentials. Give your team enough freedom to unravel its strengths and talents. This does not mean that you give up control of your team and your project. You continue to guide your team toward fulfilling the project vision and objectives. You are responsible for making sure all results are in sync with the project vision and contribute to achieving the project objectives. Ensuring results thus means that as project leader you guide your team in this direction. Be aware that although the team is responsible for delivery, as project leader you remain accountable for project success, which entails results and reflects the quality of collaboration, performance, and learning you helped set up.

Accountability for project success is not limited to the final project delivery. It includes the complete process and ongoing results. A project is a journey to the base of the project leadership pyramid. Hence a project is not just the final destination or delivery. There may be endless ways and means to the final destination. All are part of the journey. As project leader you must ensure that the team stays on the right path to the final destination. The sooner you learn if you and your team have departed from the right path, the sooner you can correct it and return it to the right direction. Interim results and/or interim milestones help you determine whether you are still traveling in the right direction or if you need to realign your project. They serve as orientation points for project progress.

In a sense, interim results are also elements of the fourth principle of cultivating learning. They provide excellent learning opportunities. Also similar to learning, ensuring results is an ongoing activity. Without interim results, learning stays on the abstract level. For example, when you conduct a formal project review and fall short of deriving tangible follow-up action items you deprive yourself from true learning and its benefits. As a matter of fact, you undermine the purpose of the project review. Remember, the goal of a project review is to identify what works and what does not and agree to do something about the areas that need improvement. However, just planning and talking about improvements and not executing them will not do any good and does not add any value. It is a waste of time.

Learning in a project environment without results that contribute to the eventual project success is useless. Learning has to be directed toward the project vision and objectives. For example, why invest in a formal training of new technical skills if you cannot apply the skills in your project? Consequently, if you want to ensure results from learning, they have to serve the purpose of the project. It is not sufficient to cultivate learning. You have to ensure that learning yields results and benefits the project vision. This is why regular results are so important and you want them to be a constant part of your project.

Ongoing project results serve as a reflection of project leadership and how well the five principles of the project leadership pyramid are practiced They reveal the true quality of team collaboration, team performance, and team learning. It is a form of quality assurance of effective project leadership for project success.

No single principle is the most important. It is the combination of all five leadership principles that helps secure project success. Building vision is the principle to start with, but you cannot achieve results if you do not embrace all five principles together as one unit. Furthermore, you need to understand the dynamics of the principles and how they interact with each other. This takes us to the last chapter of Part I of this book, where we take a close look at these dynamics and gain an understanding of the holistic pyramid.

7.7 Application Suggestions

1. Can you think of a project that fell short of delivering results and yet was considered a success? If so, why? What were the factors that made people think or believe that this particular project was a success nevertheless?
2. Can you think of a project that resembled a death march (e.g., team members worked overtime to meet the deadline, team morale was low throughout,

there was an absence of effective collaboration), yet in spite of the death march character, the project produced the required results and the sponsor and clients were happy?

    a. What was the definition of "project success"?

    b. How did the team members define "project success"?

    c. How would the team members define "project success" the next time around?

    d. What could you do differently, applying the five project leadership pyramid principles?

3. When and how did interim results help boost your performance, quality, and collaboration?

4. What are other rewards of ensuring results?

5. How can you ensure results during the initiation phase of your project?

6. How can you utilize teamwork to ensure results?

7. How can you involve the extended project team in your effort of ensuring results? When is the best time to do so?

Chapter 8

The Dynamic Pyramid

Everything should be made as simple as possible, but not one bit simpler.

Albert Einstein (1879–1955),
physicist[1]

8.1 Five Principles, One Project Leadership Pyramid

The pyramid is complete. We have learned about all five leadership principles for project success. Together they constitute the project leadership pyramid. End of story? Not quite. It is important to understand these five principles. However, understanding the individual principles is not sufficient. In the last chapter we saw that the principles affect each other. It is difficult to isolate them from one another. For example, interim results offer excellent learning opportunities, which in turn help boost collaboration, improve performance, give rise to innovation, and thus move us closer to realizing the project vision. This shows that the principles are interrelated and interdependent. They are not isolated principles. Instead, they have to be seen as one unit.

This should not come as a surprise to you. After all, we are talking about one project leadership pyramid, not five. As small as this detail may be, it has a very

[1] Quote attributed to A. Einstein based on Herbert Spencer Lecture, "On the Method of Theoretical Physics," delivered at Oxford (10 June 1933); also published in *Philosophy of Science*, Vol. 1, No. 2 (April 1934), pp. 163–169. The original quote from his lecture was: "It can scarcely be denied that the supreme goal of all theory is to make the irreducible basic elements as simple and as few as possible without having to surrender the adequate representation of a single datum of experience." (Retrieved from http://en.wikiquote.org/wiki/Albert_einstein on January 27, 2010.)

deep and important meaning. Leadership is not merely the sum of applying the five principles. It is understanding and living the dynamics within each principle as well as all five principles as one unit.

8.2 The Resulting 5×5 Pyramid

If you want to gain a deeper understanding of one principle, you need to account for the remaining four principles and how they relate to the one you are looking at. Corollary, we are not talking about one pyramid consisting of five parts. Rather, we have a 5×5 pyramid consisting of five principles, where each principle accounts for itself as well as the other four principles. This is illustrated in Figure 8.1.

Let's look at each principle once more and this focus on the interrelatedness of the principles.

8.2.1 Principle 1: Building Vision

First and foremost, this principle is about the vision of your project and its environment. The vision provides an orientation point for your project. It sets the overall direction. Again, using the picture of the pyramid as you approach it from the distance, the first thing you see is the top of the pyramid. In our case it is the principle of building vision. Vision comes first. This implies that if there is no vision in your

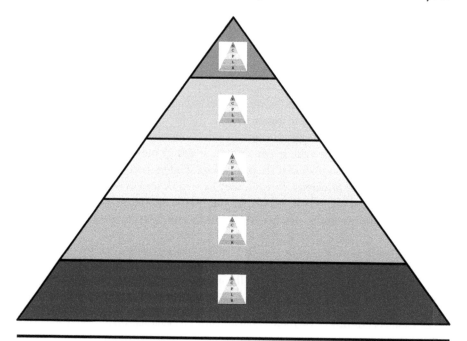

Figure 8.1   The 5×5 pyramid.

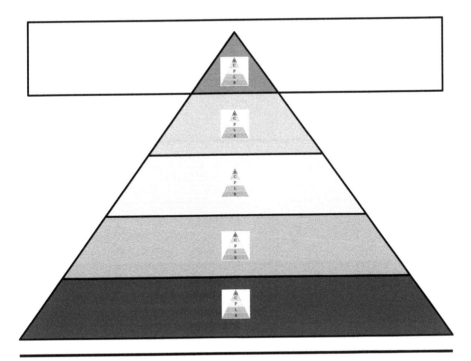

Figure 8.2 The dynamic principle 1: Building Vision.

project, there may not even be a project at all. Consequently, if you have a project without a clear vision, your project is doomed to fail.

The vision describes *what* the journey will be about. It also elucidates *how* you plan to get to the final destination of the journey. It is crucial that everyone involved in the project has the same understanding of the vision. Thus, the vision needs to be worded in a way that everyone can relate to on a day-to-day basis. The vision defines the destination of the project. Plus, it provides practical guidance to the project team about how to get there. It defines the purpose of the project on the abstract and individual levels.

Recall that the first principle does not consist simply of defining a vision of your project. It involves breaking down the vision into project objectives from which you derive requirements. This helps define the scope of your project. Speaking in pictures, it portrays the frame of the results at the bottom of the pyramid. In addition to the project objectives and their related requirements, principle 1 also calls for a strategy for how to achieve the vision (i.e., how to get from the vision to the base of the pyramid). To achieve this, you have to address and account for the heart of the pyramid, made up of the three other principles. These middle principles all have in common that they talk about the necessity and value of empowering your team. Thus the project vision also must address *how* you plan to nurture collaboration, promote performance, cultivate learning, and ensure results. Knowing that

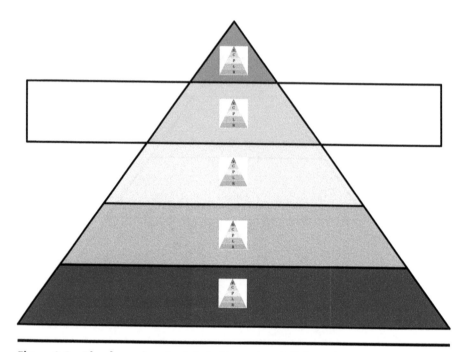

Figure 8.3   The dynamic principle 2: Nurturing Collaboration.

the remaining four principles are critical in securing project success, you include them in your vision building at the start of your project.

8.2.2 *Principle 2: Nurturing Collaboration*

Principle 2 addresses all the areas of collaboration outlined in Chapter 4. The overall direction is given by the vision (principle 1). Next you must link collaboration to this project vision so that collaboration benefits the purpose of the project.

The team norming workshop is a central exercise of principle 2. In addition to defining the rules of engagement, you address how you plan to promote performance on the individual and team levels, how to build a creative and innovative learning environment, and how to ensure ongoing results of all project activities. You also determine how you can make sure all your activities stay in sync with the vision and the project objectives, to meet project requirements.

8.2.3 *Principle 3: Promoting Performance*

Principle 3, promoting performance, refers to individual and team performance. It is in the middle of the pyramid, halfway between the vision and results, embedded between collaboration and learning. Promoting performance begins with finding avenues to secure and constantly improve performance throughout your team. Activities must comply with the rules of engagement set forth using principle 2.

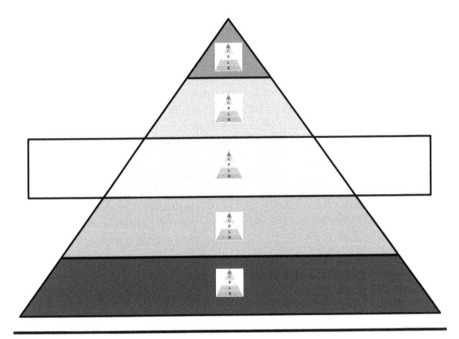

Figure 8.4   The dynamic principle 3: Promoting Performance.

On the other hand, you need to be flexible enough to react to a changing environment regardless of whoever or whatever caused the change to occur (principle 4). Performance without yielding results is useless. Thus, you need to ensure that performance is results oriented (principle 5). Last but not least, the actions of your team must move the team closer to realizing the vision of your project and must be in sync with the direction given by that vision (principle 1).

One of the keys to promoting performance is to empower your team. To empower your team effectively, satisfy the following critical success factors:

1. *Vision.* The team needs to have an understanding of the vision and objectives, purpose and drivers of the project. Use common sense: not everyone on the team needs the same amount of information or even to be actively involved in every single vision-building activity. The idea is to secure a common understanding of the purpose and direction of the project.
2. *Collaboration.* Norm and build your team. Treat every team member with respect. Good project leaders are also good team players. Hence, you want to communicate *with* and not down *to* your team. In addition, account for individual interests and motivations as long as they are compatible with the project vision. Utilize the strengths of each team member for the purpose of the project.
3. *Performance.* Give your team the opportunity to excel. Teamwork is not about hierarchies; it is about team performance. Help identify and remove impediments to team performance.

4. *Learning.* You and your team must be open to new ideas. Encourage your team to try new things, make mistakes, and learn from them. Learning and self-improvement are continuous activities. By this token, review your own performance regularly and adjust where necessary.

5. *Results.* The team sees the need for and value of delivering regular results. Each member takes accountability for the results, understanding that accountability is two-sided: if a team member fails or succeeds, so does the rest of the team. The team does not focus on problems, but instead identifies the root causes of problems and resolves them. Team members are solution and results oriented in their actions toward achieving the project objectives.

This list is far from complete. Every project is unique and thus contains many nuances. Nevertheless, the list shows that empowerment involves all five principles of the project leadership pyramid. It thus underlines once more the dynamic nature of the pyramid.

8.2.4 Principle 4: Cultivating Learning

In Chapter 7, we sketched the interrelatedness of this principle with the other four. Cultivating learning means that you create an environment of open and constructive feedback. In this environment the soil is fruitful for individual and team creativity and innovation to prosper. We learn by looking at the results (principle 5) and comparing them with the requirements (principle 1). Learning gives us the

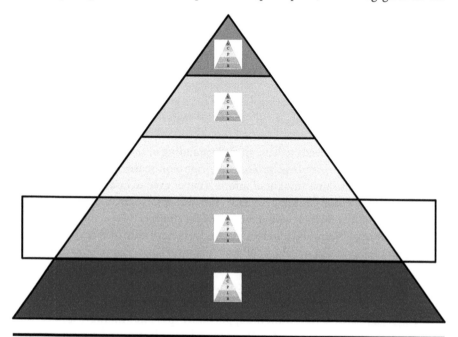

Figure 8.5   The dynamic principle 4: Cultivating Learning.

chance to reflect on our rules of engagement (principle 2) and possibly adjust them to changing circumstances. Fluctuating performance is normal and should be expected. It is important to reflect on how performance can stay on the right course with high productivity and team morale (principle 3). Looking forward, an active learning environment gives ground to creativity and innovation, thus taking performance to an even higher level.

8.2.5 Principle 5: Ensuring Results

A project without results is fruitless. You would not start a project without the hope that at the end of the day it would yield what you desired in the first place. Project success and ensuring results are not only about the quality of the final project deliverables, whatever they may be. The fifth principle is just as alive and dynamic as the other four principles. As such, it is a call for the ongoing activity of practicing this fifth principle. Ensuring results means that you practice this principle from the first day of your project. All project activities should be directed toward the ultimate project vision and contribute to achieving the project objectives. They must also produce tangible results throughout. This keeps the project alive.

Interim results add life to your project. They provide learning opportunities (principle 4) for you and your team, help boost collaboration (principle 2), improve

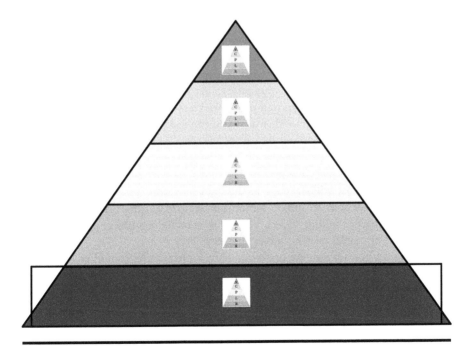

Figure 8.6   The dynamic principle 5: Ensuring Results.

performance (principle 3), give rise to innovation (principle 4), and thus move us closer to realizing the project vision (principle 1).

8.3 A New Definition of Project Success

The project leadership pyramid is dynamic in nature. Its five parts interact with each other. They have to be looked at as one unit. Applying the leadership pyramid in daily project life means that you as the project leader constantly practice all five principles. It is an ongoing exercise. Depending on where you are in a project, there may be a stronger emphasis on one or two principles than on others. But you cannot isolate one from the others.

Think of the picture of the pyramid. If you take out one part of the pyramid, it may still look like a pyramid but it is no longer complete. But why would you want to go for partial success if you could have it all? Holistic leadership comprises all five principles. This is what it means to apply the project leadership pyramid in practice.

The project leadership pyramid principles serve as an orientation to project success. Using the analogy of a journey to the pyramid, we can say that the project leadership pyramid principles help you get your project to the final destination. As with any journey, you plan it and you prepare yourself and your accompanying party for the trip. As much as you plan, however, you know that things can change during your journey. You must stay flexible and adapt to the changing environments. You may need to take detours or you might discover shortcuts. In either case, you have to be willing and courageous to try new unbeaten paths and find new ways of doing things. At the same time, you never lose sight of the final destination, the final delivery of your project. As you begin the trip you may not be able to see the base of the pyramid yet. However, you know that it is reflected in the vision, the top of the pyramid, which you can see from the very beginning of your journey. Applying the other four principles in a consistent manner helps get you closer to the base of the pyramid. This is an ongoing activity. Whenever you hit milestones on your trip (i.e., deliver interim results), it gives you the opportunity to check whether you are still traveling in the right direction. You confirm that your past and planned actions are in sync with the project vision. This brings you back to the first principle of building vision. You are thus including all five project leadership pyramid principles on your project journey.

The project journey you are undertaking as project leader should be a journey to project success. You start with a vision of the pyramid and, with time, move closer to the pyramid base, the final project results. Alas, project success is not solely about the delivery of the final project results, which are in alignment with the project vision. Project success is also about *how* you get to the final project delivery. *Project success is the safe journey from project vision to final project results. Corollary, the project leadership pyramid helps secure a safe and successful project journey which ultimately delivers the project vision.* This is why the five principles are the "leadership principles for project success."

8.4 Simple and Yet Complex: The Five Principles of Effective Leadership

This concludes the first part of the book. I have introduced the project leadership pyramid and delineated each of its five principles. I also explained why it is important to understand the underlying dynamics of the project leadership pyramid. These five principles are straightforward. You can even call them common sense. To no great surprise, you can apply them in your daily project life and thus contribute to project success. If you live by them and internalize them, you too can become a true project leader and effective project manager who doesn't just manage another project but who leads a team to project success.

Note that the project leadership pyramid is not limited to the role of project managers. You can apply its principles no matter what your role in a project. "Regular" team members as well can demonstrate leadership characteristics in any project role. Indeed, if you follow the project leadership pyramid principles by yourself, regardless of your role in a project, you will impact the team and the project performance in a positive manner. Following the five principles will improve your performance in your role.

Part II translates the project leadership pyramid principles into practical examples, showing you how to apply them to set up, execute, and save unaligned projects.

Part III will take you a step further, beyond the world of projects, and attempt to answer the question of how you can use the leadership principles to become a leader yourself.

8.5 Application Suggestions

1. Can you think of a project during which one or more leadership principles were violated and yet the project outcome was still considered a "success"?
2. Can there be project success without following all leadership principles?
3. What kind of project "success" is there when one or more leadership principles is violated?

References

Einstein, A. (1934). On the method of theoretical physics. *Philosophy of Science, 1*(2), 163–169.

THE PROJECT LEADERSHIP PYRAMID IN PRACTICE

II

Chapter 9

Practicing the Principles

> To accomplish great things, we must dream as well as act.

Anatole France (1844–1924),
French author and winner of the Nobel Prize in Literature, 1921[1]

9.1 Purpose and Objective of Part II

The project leadership pyramid and its five leadership principles for project success are more than mere abstract ideas. They serve as guidelines and are based on common sense. As such, you can easily translate them into practical exercises to use in your own project. This second part of the book shows you how to achieve this. It outlines a number of exercises, approaches, ideas, and methods which are all linked with the project leadership pyramid. However, note that by no means do I claim these exercises are complete. The variety of potential projects makes it impossible to list all exercises one might use. The exercises in this book focus on the application of the project leadership pyramid. They are based on best practice and thus give you a general idea of what is possible when you want to apply the project leadership pyramid principles. Still, they remain examples. Whether you want to or can apply them in your own project depends on your specific project setting. Every project is unique. Therefore, you will need to modify the examples to fit the needs of your project.

The second part of the book is outlined as follows. Chapter 10 looks at the project initiation and set-up phase. It includes a number of exercises you can apply when you

---

[1] Quote is a variant from France's introductory speech at a session of the French Academy given on December 24, 1896. (See France, 1896.)

set up your project for success right from the beginning. Chapter 11 dives right into the daily life of project execution. It is not project phase specific. The exercises can be used in any project phase. In addition, Chapter 11 lists possible challenges to the five leadership principles, analyzes the causes, and outlines how to cope with these challenges. Chapter 12 will look at projects in trouble. It proposes different approaches to realign a project gone astray. The first approach outlines actions to engage project stakeholders, the second approach explains how to involve your team, and the third one elaborates on external project rescue missions. Another approach sheds light on what you can do when you are working on a challenged project but are not in charge of leading the project. Last but not least, we will look at situations in which we must cancel a project. Chapter 13 covers exercises you can conduct when you bring your project to a close.

Although the outline follows the project phases of initiation, execution, and closure, this is not meant to imply that projects always run sequentially. They may, but not always. For example, when you initiate a project you also want to account for and plan on specific team-building exercises that you won't conduct until later in your project. At the same time, you want to have a general idea how you might proceed if your project is no longer aligned with its overall vision and project objectives. Just as you have to account for all five leadership principles as one unit, you want to keep in mind the overall picture of the dynamics and challenges of the various project phases. In other words, as project leader you keep a sight on how the various principles and phases work together.

By this token, an exercise listed in Chapter 9 can also turn out to be helpful in project execution or when you need to realign your project. As a matter of fact, some of the exercises outlined resemble each other. For example, you will see a vision-building workshop in Chapter 9 and in Chapter 11. Another example is team-building exercises, which will be covered in all four chapters to come.

Closing each chapter is a summary of the introduced exercises and how they relate to the five principles of the project leadership pyramid. This will clarify once more the interrelatedness of the five leadership principles. And it will show that the same exercise can be applied in different situations.

The possibilities of each project are endless. The exercises in the following chapters aim to trigger your creativity. They serve as a starting point. You must modify them to meet the special needs of your project. I encourage you to be creative in finding new approaches. Try them out, seek feedback, and involve your team in fine-tuning them to your special needs. At the end of the day, you as the project leader are accountable for project success. It is up to you to start on the path to project success and take your team with you.

9.2 Returning "Power" Exercises

Before we dive into the exercises of the project initiation phase, let us introduce a number of exercises that we will return to in every project phase.

9.2.1 *Guided Brainstorming*

This approach is one of my personal favorites. Although it is very simple and straightforward, it produces tangible results in record time.

Most of us know what brainstorming is. Suppose you are the facilitator of a brainstorming session. For a limited time, say 10 minutes or so, a moderator asks a group of people to say out loud anything that comes to their minds when thinking about a certain topic or question, regardless of whether it might make sense to somebody else. For example, the question posed may be, "What can we do to improve team morale?" Any answer counts. You do not allow attendants to comment on or criticize any other responses, thus eliminating the block of analyzing a new idea in its every detail and consequences. The idea is that every expressed input may trigger a new thought process in someone else, generating a new idea that, once expressed out loud, may stimulate another idea by someone else. As the facilitator, you record all responses on a whiteboard or flip chart. At the end of the brainstorming session you sort and discuss the collected input.

Brainstorming has obvious advantages. It helps produce new ideas in a very short time. It stimulates thought processes, almost forcing creative, outside-the-box thinking. In addition, it is a very interactive exercise and can be lots of fun. On the other hand, brainstorming sessions face a number of challenges. Their interactive nature can turn into chaos quickly. As the moderator, you may have a hard time capturing every idea, simply because too many people are talking at the same time and you cannot write fast enough.

A "guided brainstorming" session can overcome these challenges while still utilizing the stated advantages of regular brainstorming sessions.

Similar to a normal brainstorming session, in guided brainstorming a topic or question is presented for discussion. For example, "What can we do to improve team morale?" However, the guided brainstorming approach differs from regular brainstorming in that you do not ask every attendant to shout out his or her thoughts. Instead, you hand out cards and ask the attendants to write down their ideas or thoughts. The trick in this exercise is that you limit the number of cards; that is, one card is good for only one idea. For example, if you give out five cards to each participant, each participant can provide a maximum of five responses. Naturally, this limits the choices. On the other hand, if you conduct a guided brainstorming session with five people you will have 25 responses, which can be a good start for a group discussion.

There are a few things to consider when you give out response cards to the attendants. First, ask everyone to write down what they think is most important. This forces them to prioritize their ideas prior to submitting their responses. Second, limit the time for filling out the cards. Sometimes just 5 to 10 minutes can be enough for this exercise. A good rule to work with is that you want to allow 1 minute for each response card. So, if you have given out five response cards to each participant, give everyone 5 minutes to write down and submit their responses. If they are responding to more than one question or topic, lengthen the duration accordingly. The key is to limit the response time, forcing the participants to focus on their most prominent ideas.

Once everyone has written down his or her feedback, you or the facilitator collect the cards and present them to the whole group. Alternatively, you can ask each individual to present his or her feedback. Beware, though, that this is usually more time consuming. Also, not everyone likes to stand in front of an audience and present his or her opinions. Thus, the preferred choice may be to have a facilitator collect the cards and present the ideas expressed.

Once the facilitator has read the response cards out loud, he or she pins them onto a whiteboard or wall. The group then sorts and categorizes them. You can do this in various ways. First, you can set up categories prior to the brainstorming session and prepare flip charts for each category onto which you can put the response cards. You, the moderator, or the group can do this. Second, the moderator may ask the participants to sort and categorize the cards after the brainstorming. Either way, once you have agreed on the categories, sort the cards accordingly.

My own experience is that it is helpful to plan categories before the brainstorming session and suggest these categories to the participants after they have written down their responses. Whether or not the flip chart or whiteboard is prepared prior to the session depends on the specific situation. If the time for the overall brainstorming session is limited, you definitely need to have everything prepared before the session. If there is sufficient time and you want to have an even higher level of interaction, you may choose to let the participants decide how to sort and categorize their responses.

The idea behind brainstorming is that every response counts. Still, it is impractical to discuss each response. Instead, you want to determine which of the responses is most valuable for the purpose of the topic up for discussion. This is why you, or rather the participants, need to prioritize the cards. For this purpose, each individual has a limited number of votes to cast, say ten votes. Participants can choose to place all their votes on a single card or distribute them, marking the cards with a pen stroke or a sticker for each vote cast. Allow 5 to 10 minutes for this exercise.

Once everyone has cast his or her vote, determine which response cards got the most votes. For example, identify the top three cards and elaborate on each of these responses within the team. Before you open the floor for discussion you must make sure everyone in the group has the same understanding of the responses and their meanings. If this is not the case, you may ask the person who submitted the idea to explain its motivation and purpose or facilitate a group discussion about it.

Personally, I like the guided brainstorming approach a lot and have successfully applied it in many situations. There are obvious advantages to the guided brainstorming approach. Within a relatively short time you collect a lot of input about a given topic, which can be categorized and prioritized with the help of the participants. A guided brainstorming session is highly interactive. Everyone in the group witnesses the process and has a chance to contribute to the final outcome. Chances for consensus on the outcome are very high. Note, however, that the highly interactive character of guided brainstorming sessions can also be a challenge, especially if participants are not used to this format, working in a group. It is especially important to prepare the participants for this kind of exercise before the actual session. My own experience is that skepticism is quickly replaced by astonishment regarding the results, from at least two perspectives: (1) the results on the content level may be surprising and unexpected, and (2) people are oftentimes amazed about the amount of input and how quickly it is categorized and prioritized.

Be aware of other challenges of the guided brainstorming approach. For example, you may not have a meeting room big enough to hang flip charts or wall paper. You may need to limit the number of response cards, use smaller cards, or limit the number of people attending the session. You may also just try to reserve a bigger room. If all else fails, consider recording the input electronically and displaying it on a screen for everyone to see. In other words, use the available space wisely.

I once conducted a guided brainstorming session with a group of about 20 people. In addition to the large group size, the other challenge was that the group was not in the same room but distributed across three locations: Germany, India, and Canada. The meeting room in Germany, where most group members and I attended, was big enough, but this did not necessarily help the other team members. Our solution was to copy the information from all the response cards in Germany onto an electronic whiteboard that the whole team in all three locations could see. The two other teams, in India and Canada, did the same. Together, we compiled the complete list of ideas, which we then categorized and prioritized on a big screen.

Although you may not have the electronic ways and means to set up such a virtual meeting room, the example shows that there is no limit to your creativity. The size of the meeting room is not so important compared to the ability to exchange ideas. There should always be one way or another to capture the ideas in a guided brainstorming session and share them with everyone in the meeting.

Another challenge you may face in a guided brainstorming session is running out of time. This can take shape in different forms. For example, participants may ask for more time to think of and write their ideas on the response cards. There are various ways to respond to this challenge. First, the time allowed to complete the response cards may indeed be too short. In this case, extend it by a few minutes and set a new time limit giving the participants extra time without losing focus. You may also consider collecting the finished response cards and having someone presort them. This may help save time later.

Another reason participants may request additional time is that they simply do not understand the question or the approach. They may find the approach overwhelming. They may not be used to prioritizing their thoughts and ideas. If this happens during a guided brainstorming session it may pose a serious problem. To prevent this from happening, explain the approach before you give out the response cards, ensuring that everyone understands what to do and in what time.

Alternatively, send preparatory material about the agenda and the approach prior to the session.

If you run out of time in the middle of a group discussion following the initial brainstorming round, your response will depend on the value of the discussion. If the discussion is heading in a positive direction, you may want to extend the allotted time. If, however, the discussion is veering off course, you may want to consider interrupting it, capturing the raised issues at hand, and coming back to them at a later time.

Last but not least, running out of time can be a sign that you are trying to accomplish too much in one session. Maybe the topic is too broad or complex to cover in one workshop. If you are caught midstream in a brainstorming session, you must decide quickly whether to (1) adjourn the meeting, (2) continue it and see how far you can get, then cover the remaining agenda points in a follow-up meeting, or (3) agree to cut the scope of the meeting. Again, the best thing to do is to prevent such a scenario from happening in the first place. If you are not sure whether you can cover all planned agenda points, ask your team what they think can be accomplished in the available time slot.

The list of challenges shows us that guided brainstorming sessions, as powerful as they are, require thorough preparation. As with every session, you first need to know the purpose or reason for holding the meeting. Second, you should have a list of objectives you want to achieve in the meeting. Finally, have an idea of the outcome you can expect. Do not send out invitations to a brainstorming session or any other formal meeting without having answers to these three questions. In fact, communicate the answers in your invitation. It would be a pity to have to forgo the potential benefits of a guided brainstorming session because of lack of preparation on your part.

9.2.2 Power Workshop: Breakouts and Plenum

Group discussions can be very informative. On the other hand, the bigger the group the more difficult it can be to come to an agreement on topics discussed. When you are faced with such a situation, consider dividing your group into smaller "breakout" groups of four to six people each. Then continue working with and in these breakouts. The advantage of breakouts is that it is much easier to discuss a topic in a smaller group than in a large one. The breakouts give each individual a much better chance to participate.

Another potential benefit of breakouts is that they allow for multiple topics to be discussed in one big session. For example, you start the meeting with the large group and discuss the purpose and objectives of the meeting. You then divide that group into smaller breakout groups and assign them either the same or different discussion topics. Ask the breakout groups to discuss the assigned topic and then present its results to the others. Limiting the presentation time allows other groups to ask questions and, of course, present their own results to the larger group.

Similar to the guided brainstorming session, when working with the breakout format it is crucial that you come prepared. Think ahead about if and how you want to divide the group. If you have to make such decisions about specific topics in the meeting, invite people with decision-making authority and split the group in a way that there is at least one decision-making authority in each breakout group. Be aware that a meeting with breakouts will require additional room. One way to improve the productivity of the breakouts is to assign someone to each breakout group to facilitate, take notes, or both.

9.2.3 Questionnaires

Interactive sessions can be helpful and productive. Yet, they fall with the amount of time you spend preparing them. In other words, plan on sufficient time for preparation. A one-day workshop usually requires at least one day of preparation time. One way to prepare for an interactive session, or for that matter any session, is to request people's input or opinions on the topic to be discussed *prior* to the session. You can either ask them directly or make use of questionnaires. The responses can be good indicators of the various opinion groups, making it easier to predict certain dynamics in the later meeting.

Once again — what a surprise! — preparation is key. When you set up a questionnaire, make it as easy as possible for respondents to fill it out. Also, explain the value of the questionnaire. Otherwise, it may be considered just another time eater. Tell them whether you plan to share the consolidated feedback, and if so, when and in what format.

References

France, A. (1896). *Discours de réception, Séance De L'académie Française*. Retrieved from http://en.wikiquote.org/wiki/Anatole_France

Chapter 10

Project Initiation and Set-Up

Successful projects don't just happen—they are made to happen.

Neal Whitten,
popular American speaker, mentor, trainer, and consultant

10.1 Identifying and Defining Your Playing Field

10.1.1 Your Own Role

The initiation phase of your project is the most important phase by far. It starts and ends with this phase, so to speak. Whatever you set up in the beginning of your project, it will get back to you one way or another. Project initiation is where you lay the foundation for the success or failure of the project. Of course, there are many other factors that influence the success of your project. However, knowing that now is when you lay the foundation, why not do it right from the beginning?

So, let's start with you. Yes, you. You are at the beginning of your project. This also means that project success starts with you. The project leadership pyramid principles help guide you. But still, you start with yourself. What this means at this early stage is that you have to know your role in the new project. What is going to be your responsibility? What do you expect to deliver, or what do other people expect you to deliver? Your role is not limited to being a project manager. You could work on a project as an expert, a developer, you name it. The role is no limit to practicing leadership. We will come back to this thought later in this part of the book.

10.1.2 Organizational Project Environment

Once you know your role in the upcoming project you need to gain a good understanding of your project environment. What authority will you have in your project? First, is it *your* project or is it somebody else's? Are you simply part of a team or will you form and lead it? You need to know your role, what will be expected from you, and in which environment you will act. For example, is your project part of a bigger program or is it embedded in a line organization? Is it a strategic initiative? If so, is it an isolated endeavor or part of a whole other project with similar goals? When you answer these questions do not focus solely on your project. Look beyond the boundaries of your project. Maybe other similar projects are running at the same time. Will you compete with them? Or will you complement them? Maybe your project is redundant. If so, you had better find out early on or you may end up spending your energies and time in vain. Certainly, that would not be a good start on the path to desired project success. When you identify other projects, do you know what level of influence they will have on your project? Perhaps there are obvious dependencies, such as needing to deliver a product to another project so that it achieves its goals. Or maybe another project needs to finish before yours can start.

As obvious as these questions seem, how often have you asked them at the beginning of your past projects? It is likely that you have. But have you asked them systematically and prior to actually kicking off your project? At the beginning of the journey to the base of the project leadership pyramid — project results and project success — you must know where you stand. Otherwise, how do you determine which way to go to begin? Before you pick a target you need to locate your base.

10.1.3 Stakeholders

The good thing is that you are not alone on your journey. There are others in your world. Now it is time to learn more about them. Yes, there is your team and, yes, the team is at the heart of project work. We will look at the team a bit later when you form it. Before you do that, though, you want to identify the project players. Who will affect the success of your project? Whom do you want to actively involve? Whom do you want to avoid or keep away from the project?

Once you know more about your project boundaries it is easier to identify those who have an interest in the project one way or the other and who can either directly or indirectly influence your project for better or worse. In other words, you have to identify the stakeholders of your project.

The number of stakeholders you need to identify varies, depending on the size, character, or goals of the project. Unless you know your environment inside and out, ask others to help you identify the right stakeholders. A logical start is to ask the project sponsor for a list of potential stakeholders. You want them to share their perspectives on the following set of questions:

- What are the top issues or risks for the project? Why?
- How is the stakeholder affected by these issues or risks? Why?
- Who else is affected and to what extent? Why?
- What are the impacts of the issues or risks (on the stakeholder/on others)?
- What needs to be done to resolve the situation?
- What benefits does the stakeholder expect from the improved situation?
- What do we need to do to achieve this?
- What does the stakeholder expect from you?
- What can you expect from the stakeholder?

It is best if you can meet with stakeholders in person and ask them these questions directly. Ask for a personal meeting. Explain who you are and why it is important to meet; explain why you think it is valuable to *them*. Send them some or all of the questions you want to address, so they have a chance to prepare and get the most out of the meeting. Note, though, that getting the answers to your questions may not be the most important thing in this first meeting. Instead, it is all about personal rapport. Try to get a better understanding of their needs and desires before you tell them about yours. Express a sincere interest in their opinions.

Every stakeholder can become important to your project success. Treat them as such. Win their interest in and support for your project. Once you do, you will have a much better idea about how you want to involve them in your project. Stay in contact with them throughout the life cycle of your project. The extent of contact will vary depending on the significance of the respective stakeholder, and it can change during the project.

Identify your stakeholders early on, meet with them ideally prior to your official project kick-off, win their support, and nurture a healthy relationship throughout your project. No doubt this can be very time consuming. I once spent the first 2–3 weeks of a 5-month project meeting with the various stakeholders, trying to find out about their perspectives, their goals, and their concerns. It helped me gain a better understanding of the overall project situation, environments, project players, and actual project goals. Following up my personal meetings, I summarized the encounters and the conclusions I had drawn from them. In addition, I shared my overall understanding of the project. I consolidated all feedback received on the initial questions and openly shared it with them. This helped gain their trust and support. When individual stakeholders expressed disagreement with the conclusions I had drawn from the consolidated feedback summary, it helped me qualify my findings. This then helped me phrase a project charter statement.

10.1.4 Project Charter: Summarizing Your Understanding of the Project

A project charter is a brief description of the initial situation of the project, its high-level vision and project objectives, constraints and assumptions, as well as a list of key stakeholders. The format you choose is irrelevant. Use whatever is appropriate and sufficient for your project needs. It can be done in PowerPoint, a document or table, or another format. But definitely put it in writing. This forces you to clarify your findings. If you have a hard time doing this, chances are you do not understand the mission of your project. If others disagree with your wording, that may indicate that there are still numerous different opinions about your project. That is definitely not a good start.

You must know which direction the journey will take you. This is why it is important that you, your project sponsor, and the key stakeholders have the same understanding of the project's mission. Hence, I recommend that you have the project charter officially approved by the project sponsor and ideally other key stakeholders. This may not be necessary in all circumstances. It definitely depends on the specific project. In a nonbusiness environment you certainly do not need this formality. Still, you do need to have an understanding of your project's mission.

A couple of years ago when my wife and I and some other parents founded an organization with the goal of building a preschool for kids 1 to 3 years old, we had something like a project charter. It was a document outlining our vision, our objectives for the following months, the people we planned to involve, organizations to contact, and a high-level timeline. The first version of our charter was in the form of an email. We later revised it, creating versions in different formats depending on the target audience; e.g., Word documents for government agencies, PowerPoint presentations for the local town council, and a Website for the general public. The first charter was very short. Later documents included more details. This is typical for any project. Keep your initial project charter short and simple. Its main purpose is to ensure and establish transparency. The more information you get about the project and the more you want to share, the more you want to detail and qualify the charter document. But at the beginning, less is definitely more.

10.2 Vision-Building Workshop

A project charter describes the mission of your project as well as the main constraints and challenges. Alas, it stays on a high level. To build a project vision that is mutually understood and supported, you need to secure a strong foundation. Sending the project charter to all key stakeholders, asking for their approval, consolidating their feedback, then sending out yet another version of it can quickly lead to an endless ping pong. Instead of playing ping pong, invite the key stakeholders to a workshop at which you refine the project's vision and secure mutual understanding and support. Let's have a look at what makes up a vision-building workshop and how to conduct one.

There are various ways to outline this workshop. The following sample agenda serves as a good orientation:

1. Presentation of official project charter
2. Project motivation statement
3. Vision statement
4. SMART project objectives statement
5. Critical success factors
6. Next steps

Notice that we covered the second and third agenda points already in Chapter 3. What differs is the workshop format and that you actively involve the key stakeholders in developing motivation and vision statements rather than doing it by yourself.

Let's look at each one of these agenda points.

10.2.1 Presentation of Official Project Charter

You begin the workshop by reciting the official project charter. Given that it is based on the consolidated input you collected in your meetings with the attending stakeholders, the content of the project charter should not come as a surprise to anyone present. Explain how you developed the project charter, so the stakeholders know how you incorporated their input.

10.2.2 Project Motivation Statement

The project motivation statement is a summary of the answers to the questions you asked your stakeholders in the one-on-one meetings, namely:

1. What are the top issues or risks the project faces?
2. Who (individuals, groups, organizational units, etc.) is affected by these issues or risks and how? Why?
3. What are the impacts of the issues or risks on the stakeholders?

You can vary the questions. The thrust of the questionnaire is that you identify the main driver of the problem, find out who or what is affected by it, and analyze the possible impact. For example, if the motivation to start your project is not problem oriented, but instead you want to create something new, you can modify the questions accordingly. For example:

1. What are the top solutions or opportunities you envision? Why?
2. Who is interested in these solutions or opportunities? Why?
3. What are the effects of these solutions or opportunities? Why?

Rather than posing these questions in an open discussion round, conduct a guided brainstorming session. Give out one to five cards for each response to the questions. Once you have collected all the cards, post them on a wall. The high number of cards and thus responses usually surprises your attendants. It shows them that there are different perspectives of the problem at hand. Next, ask them to categorize and prioritize the cards. You can do this with the whole group or split the group into breakouts and then ask the breakout groups to present their findings. The outcome of the exercise is a written project motivation statement everyone understands and supports.

10.2.3 Project Vision Statement

You now ask those in attendance to take the project motivation statement and juxtapose it with a description of the opposite scenario. Ask them to write down one to three responses to the following questions:

1. What needs to be done to resolve the situation described in the problem statement? Why?
2. What benefits can the affected individuals or groups expect from the improved situation? Why?
3. What benefits do you personally expect from the improved situation? Why?

If the driver of the project is to create something new, the questions may look like these:

1. What needs to be done to bring about the new situation caused by the solutions or opportunities? Why?
2. What disadvantages will the solution have or bring with it? Why?
3. What do we need to do to overcome these disadvantages and obstacles? Why?

As with the development of the project motivation statement, collect responses by conducting a guided brainstorming session. This gives every attendant the chance to contribute to the development of the project vision. Once you have categorized and prioritized the input, ask the whole group to come up with one or two statements addressing the questions posed above. This becomes the project vision statement.

Note that the questions go beyond the strict, one-dimensional definition of a vision. They also address how the vision can be achieved. As such, they cover all five project leadership pyramid principles.

10.2.4 SMART Project Objectives Statement

The project vision statement constitutes an excellent foundation to ask those in attendance about their understanding of project success. Depending on the size of the group, you can do this exercise with the whole audience in a loose group discussion, conduct a brainstorming session, or split the group into breakouts.

Following the discussion of what project success entails, go a step further and ask them what concrete objectives the project should achieve. Ask them to be as specific as possible. Explain the necessity and value of SMART project objectives. Categorize and prioritize the input. Then develop a project objectives statement everybody understands and supports.

10.2.5 Critical Success Factors

The vision-building workshop does not stop there. Stakeholders are important in achieving the project objectives. This is why you want to ask them directly about what they think *they* can contribute to project success. You can post the following guided brainstorming questions:

- ▪ What needs to be done to secure project success?
- ▪ How can I contribute to project success?
- ▪ What do I expect from the project team during the project?
- ▪ What can the project team expect from me?

Categorize and prioritize the responses. Then see how they relate to the project motivation, vision, and objectives statement. Are they in sync? Do they complement each other? Or do you have to modify them to ensure a coherent project vision? If you find that those in attendance have a great desire to discuss this, don't cut the discussion short. It is crucial that the workshop yields a project vision every primary stakeholder can live with. You need a solid starting point for your team to deliver the project. And, as much as you and your team will address the needs of the stakeholders, you need their support and backing of the team. Unless you have already secured this support, now is the time to do so.

10.2.6 Next Steps

Following the workshop, don't forget to summarize the findings. This could be in the form of minutes, a revised project charter, or a "vision document." The format does not matter as much as it is understood and supported by all attending key stakeholders. Explain that the project vision is subject to change but that, if this happens and you must modify the project vision and objectives, you pledge to involve the key stakeholders.

10.2.7 Practical Tips for a Vision-Building Workshop

The vision-building workshop is one of the most important workshops you conduct at the beginning of a project. The outcomes set the direction of the project. They are a foundation of project success. Hence, do not take this workshop lightly. Invest sufficient time to prepare for and conduct the workshop. Experience shows that the minimum duration for this kind of workshop is between 2 and 3 hours. Depending on the complexity of the project and number of stakeholders involved, you may want to plan for more time. Next, invite all key stakeholders to attend, but if at all possible limit the numbers of attendees to 20. This will ensure enough leeway for an effective and results-driven facilitation while staying within the time limit.

The workshop is not just for you as the project leader and the primary stakeholders. Involve your core team in preparing and running the workshop. It sends the right signal that the project requires one big team, which consists of the core team, the key stakeholders, and others. Although you collect the input primarily from the stakeholders about the project motivation, vision, objectives, and critical success factors, your core team can help prepare the workshop and assist you in running it. For example, they may take protocols, serve as facilitators of breakout groups, etc.

For nonbusiness settings, the vision-building workshop will most likely be much smaller in scale. You may actually include only your core team. Still, the questions raised in the workshop are identical, and the outcomes are just as important for a small nonbusiness project as they are for a complex business project or program. Without a commonly agreed upon and supported project vision, your project has no direction. Leadership requires that you help build vision and thus lay the first stone of project success.

10.3 Team Norming Workshop

A project vision statement is extremely helpful. It provides a direction with clear deliverables and a timeline. Using the image of the pyramid, it is the tip of the pyramid. It thus serves as an orientation point for your journey to project success. It is a start.

We learned in Part I that numerous factors must be taken into account to move from the tip of the pyramid down to the base. The project team is at the heart of the project. It serves as one link from the top to the bottom of the pyramid. Furthermore, you don't need just *a* team but a performing team. This is why it is not sufficient to merely form a team, defining roles and responsibilities. You have to actively move your team from the forming stage to the performing stage.

This is where team norming kicks in. A team norming workshop is an exercise for you and your team to jointly define the roles and responsibilities of each individual on the team. You talk about the expectations and motivations on the individual and group level. You define and agree on the rules of engagement that keep the team together. In short, you set the team boundaries and define the rules of the game. As such, you lay a framework for team performance. Consequently, the sooner you conduct this workshop with your team, the greater the chance that you can move your team to the desired performance stage.

Let's take a closer look at how to prepare and conduct this team norming workshop. Once you have an idea of the direction of your project, you should start thinking of forming your team. This includes developing at least a high-level project plan. The accompanying resource plan contains information about the proposed roles and responsibilities of the individual members on the team. Assigning roles and responsibilities to individuals forms the team. At this point the team norming workshop kicks in. The purpose of the workshop is to achieve a mutual understanding among the team members of each individual role and how it relates to the others, forming a whole. In addition, it strives for support of and for each individual role.

This idea distinguishes forming a team from norming a team. Norming means that you secure the understanding and support of everyone on the team for the respective roles and the rules of engagement. As project leader, you do not dictate these rules. Instead, you and your team develop them jointly.

Let's look at a possible agenda for a team norming workshop:

1. Project motivation, vision, objectives, and scope
2. Roles, responsibilities, expectations, and motivations
3. Communication rules on individual and team level (core and extended team)
4. Next steps

10.3.1 Project Motivation, Vision, Objectives, and Scope

Begin the workshop by presenting and discussing the project motivation, vision, objectives, and expected scope. The project charter and the outcomes of the vision-building workshop are key inputs for this agenda point.

It is essential that your team not only understand the project motivation, vision, objectives, and expected scope, but internalize them. After all, the team is responsible for delivering the project. Hence, spend enough time with your team on the first agenda point and do not proceed until you are sure that you and your team are on the same page.

10.3.2 Roles, Responsibilities, Expectations, and Motivations

The second agenda point addresses the expected roles and responsibilities. For each role, prepare one flip chart on which you write the responsibilities and deliverables of this role and the proposed person assigned to it. It saves time when you prepare the flip charts prior to the workshop. Spread them around the meeting room, hanging them, for example, on the wall so that all roles are visible. You or the facilitator briefly describe each role and the key responsibilities and deliverables. You then ask your team to go to each flip chart and write down their understanding of the respective roles on the flip charts. Ask for their input on responsibilities, deliverables, and expected skills as well as what the person in that role can expect from the team in fulfilling its role and vice versa. Every team member is involved in this exercise. Allow at least 20 to 30 minutes for this exercise. Once every team member has had a chance to record their thoughts, each role is discussed individually among the group based on the information captured on the flip chart.

It is important that every team member knows the responsibilities, deliverables, and expectations of each role. Plus, every team member must buy into this role description. If discrepancies or different expectations exist, this is the time to discuss these issues and resolve them.

When you discuss the expectations for and from the individual roles, you may provide the principles of the project leadership pyramid as categories. In other words, what does the team expect from the role with respect to building and achieving the project vision, nurturing collaboration, promoting individual and team performance, cultivating learning, and ensuring results? And what can the individual filling that role expect from the team to help him or her fulfill the role's responsibilities and deliverables?

10.3.3 Engagement Rules on Individual and Team Level

The third part of the workshop addresses the activities and rules of engagement of the team as a unit. The key question to answer is how the team as a whole can help achieve the vision of the project, nurture collaboration, promote team performance, cultivate team learning, and ensure the delivery of expected results. You may want to consider starting this part of the workshop with a guided brainstorming session, asking the team to write down their suggestions on separate moderation cards. Have team members initial their cards with the categories of their response. The categories are V for vision and project objectives and the resulting scope, C for collaboration, P for performance, L for learning, and R for project results. Following the presentation of the results, the team prioritizes the input for each category. The three cards that get the most votes will be discussed by the project team. They become the leading mottos of the daily work of the team in the coming weeks of the project mission.

The leading mottos are not carved in stone. Project circumstances change and so do the mottos. For example, you may develop one motto for the whole project duration and one for the operational work for a limited time of maybe just a couple of weeks. You and your team adjust the latter one to the project requirements at that specific time. We will come back to the idea of creating a leading operational motto in the next two chapters.

10.3.4 Next Steps

The final agenda item (next steps) seems obvious. Decide with the team when you want to revisit the results of the team norming workshop to make necessary adjustments. Trust me, this will become necessary. Every team will go through a storming phase, as explained in the first part of the book. A team norming workshop does not mean that you can skip this storming phase. Although this may be the idea behind conducting a team norming workshop at the beginning of a project, you cannot forgo a storming phase, and there is nothing bad about it. It can be difficult to define and assign roles to individuals, especially at the beginning of a new project. It takes time to find out if the team set-up works as designed. This is why you need to revisit the rules of engagement and make adjustments where necessary. More on this in the next chapter.

10.3.5 The Value of a Team Norming Workshop

Team norming workshops are a powerful exercise, securing the development of performing teams. And they are not limited to the business world. Team normings in a nonbusiness environment may be less formal, but you still must ensure overall agreement of all team members on the rules of engagements. At a minimum, the project leader must make certain that people know their roles and responsibilities, what the team expects from them, and vice versa.

The team norming workshop serves as a great team-building exercise. However, team building does not and must not stop with this workshop. The workshop helps form and norm the team. It is necessary to help build a performing team, but it is not sufficient. Team building is an ongoing activity. It is your responsibility to plan sufficient time for additional team-building activities. This, too, is a team activity. Do not think only the project leader is responsible for coming up with team-building activities. The whole team is responsible. Ask your team for suggestions and let them plan and conduct team-building events.

10.4 Scoping

The vision is clear, you have built your team, roles and responsibilities are defined, agreed, and endorsed, and expectations have been shared. This is great. You are ready to start your project. That is, you are ready to tackle one of the most challenging activities ahead, both for your project in general and the initiation phase in general: the fine-tuning of the scope of the project.

"Now, wait a minute," you may exclaim, "we have already defined the scope. Don't we have a project charter and a vision document that describe the scope?" You are right. Both the project charter and the vision document describe the scope, on a high level. When you ask people about the scope following a vision definition and a team norming workshop, you should get a fairly good description. However, if you dig a bit deeper, chances are that responses will differ. And this should not be a surprise. When you are about to lead and manage a project that will run for, say, 6 to 9 months, how do you want to know all details about the requirements? Just because the overall scope is clear does not mean that you have enough information to plan the rest of the project. Add the factors of uncertainty and complexity and the picture of the scope blurs even more.

This is no reason to panic. Having a mutually agreed upon and supported vision document and having formed your team, you have two prerequisites in your hands that will help you master the challenge of scoping. One thing should be clear to you from the beginning: scoping can be and usually is a time-consuming and complex task. Do not underestimate the effort you need to spend. It is an investment, but the investment pays off well if you do it correctly and from the beginning. It is absolutely crucial for the success of your project that you invest this time. As a matter of fact, you may call the initiation phase of your project the scope or scoping phase. Do not take it lightly. This is when you build the foundation of project success. The project charter, the vision document, and the results of the team norming workshops are part of this foundation. They are also prerequisites for effective scoping right from the beginning. Let's look at how you can proceed.

10.4.1 Part 1: Gathering Requirements

10.4.1.1 Keep the End in Mind

In this first part of scoping you break down the high-level requirements already described in the vision document. Keep in mind what the end solution, the final result of your project, will look and feel like and how you or somebody else will use it. For example, you may look at a specific requirement from the perspective of an end customer and ask yourself, "How do I start this application?" or "Where do I enter my contact information?" If you are building a house, the questions may be, "Where is the door? How do I open it? What do I see first when I open the door?" Founding a preschool for children in your community, you may want to think of the solution from the perspective of parents bringing their children to the preschool: "When can I bring my kids? Who will welcome me and my kids? How does the room look where the kids play? Will there be enough space for my kids to take a nap?"

If the use of the end solution involves processes, describe the requirements from this perspective. For example, the function of a button in a computer program for a call center agent is described in the process "Entering and saving new customer information." The reason for this exercise is to ensure that you are covering all steps and features required by the end customer of your project.

Once you have captured all processes, analyze the requirements that either already exist or still need to be built as part of your project. These requirements can be functional in nature (e.g., clicking the button in a software program saves information just entered by the user sitting in front of the computer). They can also be nonfunctional. For example, you expect your computer to start within 1 minute. The 1-minute time requirement is not linked to a specific functional requirement such as the button in the previous example. Data security or legal requirements are other examples of so-called nonfunctional requirements.

Next to functional and nonfunctional requirements, capture dependencies of requirements. For example, in order to run a new software requirement you need to have a certain operating system or computer.

10.4.1.2 Analyze the Target Infrastructure of the Solution

The infrastructure of the solution needs to be in the background for your solution to work. For example, when you build a house you need to secure access to water and electricity, garbage collection, etc. If you want to operate a preschool you need to have the necessary permits and warrants. When you build new software, you need to know something about the target technical architecture, the data model, etc.

For whatever reasons, these nonfunctional requirements of a project are often neglected. This is not good. Imagine you are about to finish building your new home and maybe even move in when you find out that you forgot to secure water access. Just because these requirements may be less visible at the onset of a project, this does not mean you can ignore them. They are important and require as much attention as all other requirements. Keep the complete picture in mind.

10.4.1.3 Capture Assumptions, Open Issues, and Contributions by Others

There is no way to know every possible detail about your requirements at the beginning of your project. At least this is the case in most projects. If you miss information about a certain requirement and you know that the requirement is essential for the project, you may have to make an assumption about it. For example, you assume that a certain building material for your new house is readily available in the local hardware store. At other times, you may not be sure about a requirement. For example, who will pay for an additional technical expert to develop software?

It is important that you become aware of underlying assumptions and identify open issues. Don't just think about them. Capture and document them just like the details about the requirements and infrastructure. You should also document which activities or deliverables you and your project team cannot handle and instead will assign to somebody else.

10.4.1.4 Bring It All Together

Gathering functional and nonfunctional requirements, analyzing the target infrastructure, and capturing assumptions, open issues, and contributions by others are all distinct activities in the first part of the scoping exercise. Every one of them is important. Still, they stay isolated if you do not bring them together. You are building one solution that accounts for all factors described above. It is good when you understand the requirements. It is useless if you are not aware of the infrastructure necessary for these requirements to be met. And it can be fatal if you neglect underlying assumptions and ignore open issues. Just as a team is made of individuals each fulfilling his or her task, it is the unit of the team that counts and that delivers the project. This is why you need to bring all requirements and assumptions together. When you assign the analysis of functional and nonfunctional requirements on the one hand and the assessment of the target infrastructure on the other hand to different individuals on your team, make sure you synchronize these subteams as well as the whole team.

I highly recommend that you conduct synchronizing meetings with your team at least once a day during the scoping phase. Let everyone share what they are working on that day, what they have accomplished thus far, where they are facing impediments, and where they need help. This ensures open communication and transparency. It also opens doors for team learning. You can read more about the necessity and value of regular sync meetings in the next chapter.

10.4.2 Part 2: Prioritizing Requirements

Adults can sometimes be just like little kids, wanting everything, now and at once. Of course, this is not possible. Having gathered all requirements is good. However, it does not mean that you will be able to realize all requirements. You are bound by time, budget, quality constraints, people available, available skills, you name it. It is easy to say that everything is important. But if you do not set priorities of what you really need right away, you may end up with nothing. You need to know what you really want. This is why you must prioritize your requirements.

There are at least two ways to do this. First, follow your instincts. Use your gut feeling to decide what will be built first. The problem is that in a project with several people involved, it may be difficult to get to a common ground. The probability is close to one that when you ask x number of people what they think is important, you will get x different responses. In short, prioritizing by gut feeling is not the logical choice.

Instead, you need to proceed systematically. I am not calling for the application of a complicated decision science. All you need are two or three categories that help prioritize the requirements of most projects regardless of the nature of your project. The three prioritization categories are as follows:

1. Business or client value
2. Technical complexity
3. Organizational readiness

The first category, "business or client value," asks what a requirement is eventually worth for the business you are in and what value it adds to the ultimate client. For example, a call center agent will appreciate it if the computer screen displays all the contact history information of a customer who is calling. This means customers will not have to explain when and why they called before. The call center agent saves time not looking for this information and can better serve the customer.

The second category, "technical complexity," measures how difficult it will be to realize a given requirement. For example, the technical software feature of listing contact history information can be implemented without additional effort because it is already included in the standard software package and thus does not require any or at least very little customizing effort.

The third category, "organizational readiness," looks at the environment of your project and asks if a given requirement will be supported by this environment. For example, developing a new product that will make other products and therefore organizational departments and hence people obsolete will probably have a low organizational readiness. On the other hand, if a given requirement does not face such obstacles it may come with a medium or high organizational readiness.

The third category may not be applicable to every project. Actually, the first two categories may be sufficient to prioritize the requirements of most projects. Regarding the value of the prioritization categories, three parameters are sufficient in most cases: high, medium, and low. The values are not arbitrary. You and your team must define what "low business or client value" means in comparison to "medium" or "high." Discuss the meaning of the values with your team as well as the key stakeholders. Just as with the vision document, it is important to have a common understanding of and agreement with the prioritization categories and values.

Once you have defined them, use them to prioritize every requirement of your project. Granted, this can be time consuming. In addition, you may easily lose oversight of your requirements and their priorities. This is why I recommend you list all of your requirements in a table and insert columns with the respective priorities.

Using two or three prioritization categories helps simplify selecting the "right" requirements and thus maximizes the value you get out of the overall solution. Suppose you are using two prioritization categories: business or client value and technical complexity. The priority matrix in Table 10.1 will help.

The matrix illustrates why it may not be wise to realize every requirement that has a high business or client value. You can have a requirement with a high business or client value. However, technically it may be very complex to realize

		High	Medium	Low
Technical Complexity	High	2	3	3
	Medium	1	2	3
	Low	1	1	2
		High	Medium	Low

Business or Client Value

it. In this case you may be better off choosing a requirement with a high business or client value and a low or medium technical complexity. As a rule, the requirements that are closest to the origin will have a higher resulting priority than those further away.[1]

There is an important exception to this prioritization rule: Some requirements must be realized in spite of the fact that they have low resulting priority. For example, you may have to build a technical backend for new call center software that is technically highly complex, requires a great amount of effort, and thus induces high costs. The apparent client value of the technical backend is low because the call center is more interested in what it sees on the screen.

Once you have prioritized all requirements this way, you will have a first list of requirements with priority 1. This, however, still need not be the *final* prioritized list. You still have to account for the resource constraints such as available budget, people, and time. The key question you have to ask is if you can realize all prioritized requirements with the available budget and people and within the given time frame. If this is not the case, you have at least two choices:

1. Ask for a larger budget, more people, or more time.
2. Repeat the prioritization exercise and come up with a revised, prioritized list of requirements that make up the scope of your project.

---

[1] Of course, if you arrange the parameters differently, this rule does not hold. For example, if you sort the parameters business or client value in the order "Low – Medium – High," the requirements in the bottom right corner of the matrix will receive the highest priority.

Needless to say, in most cases you probably do not have the luxury of option 1. If, however, the final prioritized list of requirements is still too long and cannot be realized with the given budget, people, and time frame, this is the time to talk to your project sponsor and key stakeholders.

It depends on the project to which extent you want to involve key stakeholders in the prioritization exercise. In my own personal experience, it is best to prepare a preliminary, prioritized list of requirements that can be realized and then present the suggested scope with the key stakeholders.

Next to the scope you also want to discuss and agree on how you plan to proceed. On the one hand, you all may agree to freeze the presented scope and realize it as it is. On the other hand, you may be asked to start work on the requirements with the resulting priority of 1, present an interim result, and then decide how to proceed.

In either case, you do need to agree on the scope and how to proceed. Regarding the latter, you also need to discuss how to handle expected or unexpected changes in scope. This is especially important when the scope is officially "frozen." The longer and more complex a project is, the greater the probability that the scope will be changing. Projects with "frozen scope" are no exception to this rule. Once changes are inevitable, it is good to have a prioritized list of requirements — a scope matrix — available.

10.4.3 Part 3: Building the Plan

The definition of and agreement on the scope are like the filling of the top part of the project leadership pyramid. Without the definition and agreement, the project vision remains shallow. If you do not have an agreement, you could compare it by trying to fill the top of the pyramid but the content (sand or whatever you use to fill the pyramid) does not get where it belongs. The scope — or shall we say the content of the vision or the top of the pyramid — is one important element of the pyramid. Still, in order to get down to the next lower levels of the pyramid there is something else you need to do. Once you have defined and agreed on the scope you have to build a project plan. In addition, you have to revisit the roles and responsibilities within your teams and make any necessary changes. The same applies to the rules of engagement the team agreed on during the initial team norming. Last but not least, you must make sure that the scope, the project plan, the team set-up, as well as the rules of engagement are all in sync with the overall vision as documented in the project charter and vision document. You may also consider summarizing all results of the project phase in one scope document.

10.4.4 A Word on Documentation

There are no doubt projects where documentation is exhaustive and mandatory. Other projects may not need any documentation whatsoever. I am not in the position to tell you what level of documentation is the right one. It is project specific. You must determine what level of documentation is necessary and sufficient. Documentation helps clarify things, ensure transparency, and thus may serve as orientation. On the other hand, it may prevent you and your team from doing the actual work. It is up to you what level of documentation you choose as appropriate. Do not exaggerate documentation and do not neglect it. Find the right way and do what is best for your project. The minimum documentation I recommend — regardless of the chosen format — is the project charter, vision document, scope matrix, and high-level project plan.

10.4.5 Timing

No doubt, scoping can be time consuming. If done right, however, it helps save you and your team a lot of time. This is one reason why it is so crucial to do it correctly right at the beginning of the project. Scoping is not limited to the initiation phase of a project. The longer a project runs, the more likely the scope will change over time. This does not mean that the scoping phase lasts forever. You and a performing team can conduct a scoping phase within 1 to 4 weeks. This may be ambitious for some projects, but it is possible. If you still have doubts, look at the sample plan in Appendix C and see which parts you can apply in your next project.

10.5 Summary

Table 10.2 provides an overview of the proposed exercises and how they relate to the five principles of the project leadership pyramid. At the bottom of the column of the five project leadership pyramid principles, I list the key activities as they relate to the respective leadership principle. Namely:

- Principle 1. Build vision: Prepare and conduct a vision-building workshop with the key stakeholders. If possible, involve your core team, too.
- Principle 2. Nurture collaboration: Prepare and conduct a team norming workshop.

Table 10.2 Overview of Project Initiation and Set-Up Activities and How They Relate to the Project Leadership Pyramid Principles

INITIATION & SET-UP	Vision	Collaboration	Performance	Learning	Results
Identifying and defining your playing field					
assessing own role	X	X			
assessing project environment		X			
stakeholder analysis including questionnaires, personal meetings, etc.		X			
project charter	X				
Vision building workshop	X	X	X	X	X
project motivation statement	X		X	X	
project vision statement	X				X
definition of "project success"	X	X	X	X	X
project objectives statement	X				
critical success factors		X	X	X	X
Team norming workshop	X	X	X	X	X
project motivation, vision, objectives, and scope	X				

(continued)

Table 10.2 Overview of Project Initiation and Set-Up Activities and How They Relate to the Project Leadership Pyramid Principles (Continued)

INITIATION & SET-UP	Vision	Collaboration	Performance	Learning	Results
roles and responsibilities		x	x		
expectations in and by role(s)		x	x		x
motivations (on individual and group level)		x	x	x	
team activities/rules to nurture communication		x			
team activities/rules to promote performance			x		
team activities/rules to cultivate learning				x	
team activities/rules to ensure results					x
team-building events & activities		x			
Scoping					
1. Requirements gathering	x				
identifying requirements from end user perspective(s)	x				x
analyzing target infrastructure of the solution	x				
capturing assumptions, open issues, contributions by others	x				

	Vision-Building Workshop	Team Norming Workshop	Team Norming Workshop	Team Norming Workshop	Scoping
consolidating results of requirements gathering in scope/requirements matrix	x				
2. Prioritizing requirements					
estimating high-level realization effort of requirements	x				
prioritizing criteria (value, level of complexity to realize requirement(s), organizational readiness)	x				
prioritization workshop	x				
prioritized scope/requirements matrix, project scope	x				x
3. Building the plan	x				
adjusting results of team norming		x			
consistency check with vision and project objectives	x				

Key

- Principle 3. Promote performance: Prepare and conduct a team norming workshop.
- Principle 4. Cultivate learning: Prepare and conduct a team norming workshop.
- Principle 5. Ensure results: Scoping. In other words, assess the expected scope of the project.

References

Whitten, N. (2005). *Neal Whitten's No-Nonsense Advice for Successful Projects*. Vienna, VA: Management Concepts, p. xv.

Chapter 11

Project Execution

Life has no rehearsals, only performances.

Unknown

11.1 Empower Your Team and Let It Deliver

Project execution is about delivery. And delivery is about team. Your team. As project leader, therefore, it is your responsibility to build and empower a team that delivers. This brings us back to the heart and core of project delivery: your team. Building and empowering a team goes beyond forming a team, where you assign roles and responsibilities. The team norming workshop described in Chapter 10 yields rules of engagement. They apply to the whole team, including you as the project leader. Every team member is responsible for living by the team rules. This applies especially to you as a project leader.

As project leader you must create an environment in which your team can prosper. You assign roles to those individuals who can best meet the responsibilities of those roles. Having addressed and accounted for personal and team expectations in the team norming workshop, you make sure that they are not forgotten. It is certainly not possible to please everyone. This is not your job. However, you do need to make sure you help meet those expectations that serve the purpose of the project. Helping does not mean that you are the only one taking care of individual expectations. Helping does mean that you empower your team to do so.

In one-to-one personal meetings with team members, find out how they are progressing in their tasks. Is anything blocking them from achieving their goals? If they are dealing with something they should be able to take care of by themselves,

119

help them find avenues to do so. If you can help, go ahead. If they need help from somebody else or the team as a whole, ask them to address the impediments in the next team meeting or to approach the right person by themselves.

Empowering your team on the individual and group levels does not mean that you micromanage your team. Instead, help your team identify ways and means to address issues by themselves. One of the prerequisites for this to happen is an open information flow. Project-related information is openly shared.

One strategy for generating and securing an open information flow is to post all project-related information on walls in a room that is reserved solely for the team. Project-related information includes the following: project motivation and vision statements, project objectives statement, project plan, list of achieved milestones and delivered results, list of open milestones and results to be delivered, open issues or impediments, risks, assumptions, etc. You may refer to this room as the "project room" or "war room," or whatever you like. It should be a permanent meeting room, reserved solely for the team. It is not a room for individuals to work. It is a room to share information with and among team members.

If your entire team is not working in the same location, you can create a virtual team room in the form of a Website or a file you share over the Internet. It should include the same information you would find in a project or war room. Appendix E contains a sample structure of a virtual team room.

Another great way to share information among team members is daily stand-up meetings. These stand-up meetings offer all team members the chance to summarize their main accomplishments of the previous day, outline their next steps, address any issues or impediments they face and need help with, or sketch new ideas they want to elaborate with the team after the meeting. Limit the individual speaking time so that these stand-up meetings do not last longer than 10 to 15 minutes. This should be sufficient to identify any topics that need clarification after the meeting. Make attendance of the stand-ups mandatory for every core team member. After all, the main purpose is to synchronize the team effort. It is quite possible that team members will complain about the mandatory character of the stand-ups. The good thing is that it eliminates other meetings. It promotes quick decision making and improves everyone's project knowledge. It thus actually saves time and is a great investment in collaboration, performance, learning, and results.

You may argue that holding stand-up meetings on a daily basis is overkill. This may be true. Again, it is up to you, based on your project situation, to judge if daily stand-ups are necessary and helpful or not. If your team works on a daily basis, 10 to 15 minutes should not be difficult to find. It helps secure information flow and thus serves as an investment in effective collaboration. Hence, claiming you would not have this time is a pretty lame excuse. In other nonbusiness settings, where you are not daily working with your team, it may be sufficient to meet every other week. I suggest a minimum iteration of 2 to 3 weeks. Again, the key is to share information and to secure that the team's activities are in sync with the project vision and directed toward achieving the project objectives. The bottom line is that you as project leader need to ensure that information is shared freely, openly, and directly.

Creating an environment in which your team can prosper does not mean micromanaging. Just the opposite is the case. Defining and assigning roles and responsibilities jointly with your team is a step toward building trust, to let your team show its talents. Empower your team as a group and each individual team member. Give them a chance to develop and live up to their potentials. See where you can help without micromanaging your team. For example, it is not your responsibility to develop solutions to every issue raised by your team. There is no way that you can know everything. The individual team member should be the best person to say what needs to be done to fix an issue or should know the right person to ask for help if this is not the case. You want your team members to understand that raising issues is great, but it is not sufficient. At a minimum, you can expect team members to suggest how to fix their own issues. If all else fails, team members must ask the team for help rather than waiting for a miracle to happen or expecting the project leader to solve it. Keep this in mind when you and your team define and assign roles and responsibilities and when you develop and agree on the rules of engagement for your team.

If there is one ongoing activity for a project leader, it is team building. The team is the base of power for the project manager. A weak team will make it difficult for the project manager to manage the project to success. A strong, performing team, on the other hand, yields synergy effects that allow the seemingly impossible to become possible. We noted earlier that a team doesn't fall from heaven or develop overnight. You as the project leader have to form it and build it. This is an ongoing task and, yes, it can be quite time consuming. The results of a performing team yield returns on this investment multifold.

As project leader you must make sure that your team can perform. Create the environment most fruitful for individuals and the team as a whole to prosper. Team-building events should have a stable place in your plans. The same applies to celebrating accomplishments with your team. Don't forget that we are all human and want to be treated as such. Working on a great team starts with you as the project leader. You have to take the first step and make it happen.

11.2 Involve and Add Value to the Extended Team

The rules of active collaboration and open communication are not limited to your core team. Extend the same rules to the extended project team. As much as you need your core project team, you need the extended team. The extended team basically consists of all primary stakeholders. Some are more active than others. But you definitely want to involve all of them. If you depend on their help, one of the first things you should do is show them how *you* can help *them*.

Adding value starts with sharing project-relevant information. Tell them about your project, its objectives, and its progress. Tell them about the key challenges and what you are doing to manage them. Send out newsletters about past accomplishments and next steps. If at all possible, deliver interim results. These can be documents, prototypes, demonstrations, you name it. Chapter 7 elaborated on the many benefits regular interim results generate. They tell your stakeholders about project progress. They show that the project is alive and that you are producing results. They may help clarify requirements. They create a sense of accomplishment within your team. They also animate you and your team to think in terms of solutions rather than working on abstract ideas and a far-fetched project objective. Celebrating the successful delivery of interim results helps bring your team closer together. It thus helps nurture collaboration. Regular deliverables provide excellent learning opportunities. Feedback on interim results will give you information to determine whether your project is still on track or if you need to make adjustments. Actively soliciting feedback contributes to promoting collaboration beyond the boundaries of your core team. You involve the extended team and thus make them feel like part of the project team. For example, when you need to specify the requirements of a new Website, show them a prototype and ask for their feedback and input way before the final delivery date. Then show them how you incorporated their feedback in the next version of the prototype and final deliverable. When extended team members perceive this level of involvement as an added value, chances are much higher that they will be willing to support you when you need their help.

Although it is your team delivering interim results, you as project leader have to ensure that it becomes possible. Plan for it and ensure that information is shared through the right channels and arrives to the right people at the right time. This means empower your core and extended team and let magic evolve.

11.3 Project Reviews

The longer term the project, the greater chance there is that the scope and maybe even the overall direction may change. You must be aware of these changes as they are taking place. If you realize a change too late, it may also be too late for your project and it may fail. One of the best ways to prevent this from happening is by conducting project reviews. They are merely another form of learning.

There are two forms of project reviews: internal and external. Both types help you determine if you and your project are still on track, what is working, and what you and your team need to improve. Let's look at internal project reviews first.

11.3.1 Internal Project Reviews

Internal project reviews can come in many different forms. Daily stand-up meetings with your team are a form of project review. Team members tell what they are working on, what the main issues are, and what they are doing to solve them. The information provided helps you determine whether your project is on track. At a minimum, it gives you a good starting point to probe deeper on if and to which extent the project is still in sync with the overall project vision, if collaboration is practiced, performance, and the quality requirements are met.

Once a week, or at least once every 2 weeks, conduct a team meeting that is longer than the usual stand-up meetings. "Longer" does not mean an endless meeting; it means longer than 15 minutes. Time-box this team meeting to 1 to 2 hours, depending on how often you conduct it. The purpose of this regular team meeting is to review and assess past performance, present issues, and possible solutions. To be more concrete, you ask each team member the following questions:

- What has gone well thus far? Why?
- What has not gone well? Why?
- What can we do better, and how?

To save time, it is best to make use of a guided brainstorming session, with each person writing one answer per card. Provide the project leadership pyramid principles as a framework to categorize the answers. Team members initial their response cards in the top right corner to denote the principles of the project leadership pyramid (V, C, P, L, or R):

- V: Vision/project objective(s). Sample guiding question: Does everyone have the same understanding of the project objectives and live by them?
- C: Collaboration (in team, with management or sponsor, with customer, etc.). Sample guiding questions: How do you rate our teamwork, communication with stakeholders and customers, etc.? Are we abiding by our own team rules? Do our team rules meet the requirements of our project? If not, what do we have to adjust?
- P: Performance of individuals and/or team. Sample guiding question: How do you evaluate our team performance?
- L: Learning or feedback culture within team and project environment. Sample guiding question: How much do we value open and constructive feedback in our team?
- R: Results/solution quality. Sample guiding question: How do you rate our quality of work?

Within a few minutes the guided brainstorming session will produce a wide array of input. The least it yields is a starting point for asking additional probing questions on issues and impediments presented.

Once you have collected all cards, ask your team to prioritize the input. Elaborate on the three cards that get the most votes. Derive appropriate action items from them and let them become leading mottos of the daily work of the team in the coming week till the next regular team meeting. Do not neglect the other feedback cards. You can assign them to individuals or park them until the next meeting.

In one of my past projects, we conducted weekly team meetings that followed this format (Juli, 2003). At an earlier team meeting we had developed the weekly motto "work smart, not hard." That weekly motto was extended every week until the project closed. It became a guiding principle for the daily work and every issue we faced on the individual and team level.

Identifying impediments and risks and actually making mistakes can be great learning opportunities. When you have just found out that there is a serious technical problem causing a slip in your project plan, analyze the root causes of the problem. A practical approach to find the root cause of a problem is to ask *why* this impediment or risk has arisen. You ask this *why?* question up to five times, until you have identified the core of the problem. You then develop action items that help resolve the core source of the problem.

For example, in a former project of mine the user acceptance test (UAT) of a new software application did not pass. Eventually all technical errors were fixed. However, the question loomed how to improve quality during the next release cycle. Applying the five *why?* questions yielded the following answers:

- Step 1: Why did the UAT not pass? Because there were too many technical errors in the backend.
- Step 2: Why were there too many errors in the backend? Because they were not tested and fixed prior to the UAT.
- Step 3: Why were they not tested and fixed prior to the UAT? Because the responsible technical manager did not plan and spend sufficient time for the technical system test that preceded the UAT.
- Step 4: Why did the technical manager not plan and spend sufficient time for the technical system test? Because he knew that technical development could not be finished prior to the final testing and he thus decided to use the time originally reserved for testing for the late development effort.
- Step 5: Why did technical development take longer than expected and communicated? Because developers were working on other projects with a higher priority.

The answer to step 5 revealed one of the core causes of the missing quality. It was not the lack of technical skills one might have assumed. The real reason was not technical in nature at all. It was that the project did not get the necessary attention by the technical manager and its team because other projects had a higher priority. Hence, to prevent similar quality issues in the future, the project leader was well advised to check if his own team was committed to the vision and objectives as well as the timeline in the first place.

In another example, a prestigious, private French school in Germany wanted to relocate its school building and campus to a neighboring community. School officials talked to the local mayor of that community, who welcomed the idea of having a private school there. The community had old ties with a town in France and the population was very open to French culture. Interestingly, the public mood turned negative, even hostile toward the project of relocating the private school into its community. What went wrong? Again, applying the five *why?* questions yielded the following responses:

■ Step 1: Why was the public hostile toward the relocation of the school into its community? Because the school would cause a significant traffic problem due to the parents taking their kids to school.
■ Step 2: Why would this have caused a significant traffic problem? Because the roads leading to the school were too narrow to handle increased traffic, causing congestion and making it less safe for schoolchildren to cross the roads.
■ Step 3: Why were the roads too narrow? Because they led through a residential area with parking spaces along the road, narrowing the streets.
■ Step 4: Why did the parking spaces narrow the street? Because there were no other parking spaces available for the residents living along the street.
■ Step 5: Why were there no parking spaces available for the residents living along the street? Because the community lacked a traffic concept to handle the increased traffic while at the same time providing ample parking spaces for the cars of the local residents.

The answer to the final *why?* question revealed one of the main shortcomings of the private school's plan to relocate its campus to the neighboring community. Although the public as well as the local town council were principally open to a private school, they opposed the plans because they lacked an adequate concept to cope with the increased traffic.

Both examples show that the core cause for a problem, impediment, or risk may be less apparent than originally assumed. However, to solve or mitigate an issue you have to address its core cause. Otherwise, you may only treat symptoms and the issue or risk will reoccur. This would restrict the potential value of learning from past mistakes. On the other hand, identifying and solving the root causes of issues can unleash the true power of learning and innovation.

11.3.2 External Project Reviews

External project reviews need not be much different in their structure than internal ones. The auditor wants to learn where the project is in comparison to the plan, what the top issues and risks are, and what the team is doing to resolve them. The main difference from an internal project review, of course, is that it is facilitated by an external third party. This is not bad. Having a fresh, outside perspective can turn out to be a blessing. Oftentimes we develop tunnel vision when we are working for a long time on a project. This is not ideal and yet it is way too common. After all, we are human. It is ok if we welcome the chance to have somebody from the outside assess our project. We may think that everything is working great.

But because we may have developed tunnel vision we may miss other "obvious" obstacles.

Another difference between an internal and external project review may be the audience. Whereas in internal project reviews the complete core project team is participating, external reviews are oftentimes limited to the auditor and the project manager and possibly one or two other members of the team. This is not a requirement. The opposite may be true. Involving the complete core team in external project reviews can give the review the character of a lessons-learned workshop.

This is exactly one of the key purposes of a project review — external or internal: to identify lessons and show that you have learned from them. In addition, you want to identify ways to improve your performance, increase efficiency and productivity, and improve collaboration and quality.

External project reviews usually take more time to prepare and conduct. Consequently, they are less frequent. Unless they are mandatory in your project environment, plan them before the close of a project phase. This may still give you enough time to put some of the advice from the review into practice. If you find out about a mistake or shortcoming after a project phase, it may be too late. In this case, you may learn a lesson, but it may be useless if you do not have a chance to apply it. You might just as well skip such a project review altogether.

There is one exception to this conclusion. When you follow a client-driven iterative approach where you deliver a functioning part of a product or service after each iteration, the project review may actually take place with the delivery or shortly thereafter. The key difference from a "regular" project review is that it incorporates the identified lessons learned directly in the plan of the coming iteration. It thus secures the learning character and value of a project review.

11.4 Status Reporting

Most projects require you to prepare and deliver a regular status report to the project sponsor and other primary stakeholders. The frequency and format vary from project to project. Regardless of the frequency and format, I suggest you cover the following points:

- *Executive summary*: In one or two sentences, describe where the project stands. What is relevant is how the project progresses with respect to achieving the project vision and objectives.
- *Accomplishments*: List the top three accomplishments of the past reporting period. Focus on actual, tangible results that add value to the project organization and show that you and your team are moving in the right direction.
- *Upcoming milestones*: List the top three milestones of the next reporting period. Similar to the listed accomplishments, report expected results rather

than ongoing activities. Note that when you report upcoming milestones you make a commitment to deliver them in the mentioned time period. Thus you want to make sure prior to the report that you and your team can deliver them. If you cannot commit to a delivery date, state this. Raising the wrong expectations will eventually hurt you. If you and your team face impediments, explain them.

▪ *Impediments*: Spell out the top three impediments you and your team are dealing with at present and explain how you plan to solve or at least mitigate them. Don't describe a problem without pointing out its source and suggesting a resolution. If you need help from the outside, state that and suggest a resolution. An alternative to listing the top three impediments is to distinguish between existing problems and potential risks. Again, limit the list to the top three problems and risks and be explicit about how you plan to solve and mitigate them.

A status report is not a scientific paper. It is a snapshot of your project. Even if you do not have to prepare a formal report, say in a nonbusiness setting, you always want to have the above information available. This does not need to be volumes of information. Keep it simple and straightforward. As a matter of fact, for most projects a one-page status report suffices. The important thing is that you share *correct* project information with the primary stakeholders. "Correct" means that you do not slant the project information to make it look or sound good. If you face a serious challenge in your project, state this and explain what you plan to do next. Listing the top three accomplishments, upcoming milestones, and impediments forces you to prioritize and focus. Do so with your team.

Identifying the top three accomplishments, upcoming milestones, and impediments of your complete project implies that not every issue on the operational level of your team will make it to the front page of your status report. And this is not necessary. Operational issues are best solved on the operational level. What most stakeholders are interested in is how the project overall is doing with respect to the vision and the expected results. If the recipients of the status report request additional information about the project on a lower, operational level, share it. Alternatively, you may want to consider inviting them to attend and listen to a stand-up meeting or team meeting. The bottom line is that you want to ensure transparency and an open information flow. This requires openness, honesty, and integrity on your part. These are qualities you also expect from your own team and your primary stakeholders. And, as always, it starts with you.

11.5 Project Pyramid Assessment Guidelines

You can summarize the structure of the probing questions you answer in the project reviews and status reports in the project pyramid assessment guidelines. These guidelines consist of two main parts.

Part 1: Assessing the quality of vision, collaboration, performance, learning, and results. Sample guiding questions for each of the principles are:

1. Vision:
    a. What are the motivation, vision, and objectives statement of the project? To which extent are they mutually understood and supported by the core and extended teams?
    b. Is the scope of the project defined and mutually understood by the core and extended teams? If not, what are the gaps? What prevents these gaps from being filled? Why? What has been done or is planned to fill the gaps?
2. Collaboration:
    How do you rate the teamwork, communication with stakeholders and customers, etc.? Is the team abiding by its own team rules? Do the team rules meet the requirements of the project? If not, what has to be adjusted?
3. Performance:
    a. Is the team given the opportunity to excel? How does the project leader empower the team?
    b. Does the team as a whole perform as expected and required to meet the project objectives? If there are any gaps in individual performance, how does the project cope with this challenge?
4. Learning:
    a. How much do(es) the team(s) value open and constructive feedback?
    b. What rules are in place that promote and cultivate learning and innovation?
5. Results:
    a. Does the project team deliver regular, interim results? How is the quality of these deliverables?
    b. How does the project ensure the quality of regular, interim, as well as final results?

Part 2: Assessing the top three impediments to the project leadership pyramid principles. Sample questions include:

1. From the first part of the project assessment, what are the top three impediments to each principle in the project leadership pyramid?
2. What causes these impediments? You may want to apply the five *why?* questions, as explained in Section 11.3.1, to identify the real cause.
3. What needs to be done to solve and/or mitigate the impediments? To what extent does the team follow this strategy?

The advantage of the project pyramid assessment guidelines is that they assess the critical factors for project success reflected in the five principles of the project leadership pyramid. Depending on the nature and complexity of a project, you can add to, modify, or delete some of the sampling questions. The important thing is that you cover all five principles.

11.6 Secure Ongoing Learning and Promote Innovation

Learning is important. It is crucial for project success. This is why you as project leader must create a learning environment. Establish clear and unmistakable learning and feedback rules, such as conducting weekly team meetings to reflect on what is going well and what needs to be improved. Plan regular external project reviews before the end of each major project phase or milestone. At the same time, review the rules of engagement, including roles and responsibilities, and make necessary adjustments. Following a major project phase, you may even want to conduct a complete team re-norming workshop. Preparation for and conduct of this workshop is similar to an initial team norming session. Once again, if possible, ask a third party to facilitate it, allowing you to actively participate in the team norming exercises.

You may even want to consider setting aside 10 to 20% of your time for innovation. This is what Google is practicing. Google team members work 4 days a week on the assigned project. The fifth day is reserved for innovative activities, when everyone is working on either an innovative approach related to a specific work package of the project or something completely different. Whether or not you have the luxury of building in 20% for innovation is project specific. But think of how much time you do want to reserve for innovation. This includes reflecting on lessons learned and trying out new and innovative ways of work. The potential payoffs of learning can be great. Not only can you and your team improve efficiency and productivity, but it will also strengthen team morale, boost performance, improve collaboration, and improve delivery quality.

Create an environment in which mistakes are not punished, but instead, team members admit mistakes, fix them quickly, learn from them, and continue to improve the other project-related innovations. Do not let mistakes question or even stop your innovation. Innovation without making mistakes does not and cannot exist.

Don't keep lessons learned to yourself. Share them within your team and with others outside the team. For example, you can use wikis. Not only does it allow you to share your experience, it also constitutes a great opportunity to market your project and its accomplishments.

Making learning a stable part of your project serves as an investment and insurance for quality and project results. The longer your project, the more time you will need to plan on for learning and innovation. As things change over time, you will have to make the necessary adjustments. As project leader it is your responsibility to ensure project results that are in sync with the project vision. Learning is the element that links vision, collaboration, and performance with results. This is why learning is so important to project success and why it is one of the principles of effective project leadership.

11.7 Coping with Challenges to the Project Leadership Pyramid

I started this book with a hypothesis: *Effective project management needs to have a solid foundation based in project leadership. Without project leadership there is no direction for project management. Leadership is the decisive factor in improving the chance for a project to succeed. Without leadership, chances are that a project will be "just another project."* Leadership is a decisive factor for project success. The project leadership pyramid lays out the principles of effective leadership. The principles serve as a strong guideline. Do not be fooled, however, that these five leadership principles are set in stone; i.e., once you have followed them during project initiation you do not have to modify them. The principles themselves are dynamic and complex. You need to be flexible when applying the principles in practice without compromising the overall theme of project leadership. Just as you can expect challenges to the project, you can anticipate tests to the five project leadership pyramid principles set out in this book. The question is how do you cope with these challenges and overcome them?

Let's look at some common challenges, identify likely sources, and sketch possible solutions and mitigations. Note that it is impossible to list all possible challenges. Nor can we outline all possible solutions. The aim is to show that solution strategies to challenges often lie in the application of other project leadership pyramid principles. This is where the concept of the 5×5 pyramid comes into play once more. The project leadership pyramid principles are not isolated from each other. Combining them adds a new level of dynamics to the project leadership pyramid. You need to have an understanding of these dynamics to cope with and overcome challenges to the project leadership pyramid principles. Let's look at some typical challenges.

11.7.1 Challenges to Principle 1: Build Vision

Trust me, building vision is the most important activity at the beginning of every project. Actually, you want to build vision before the actual start of the project. It is important and it is time consuming. And it is an investment in project success you do not want to forgo. As project leader you must plan for sufficient time to build vision. Make sure that everyone in the project knows the direction of the project from day 1.

What can be really frustrating is when you understand the importance of vision building and work on a project where things do not work out as described in this book. Three typical challenges are detailed here.

11.7.1.1 No Leverage or Control to Build Vision

Challenge(s):

- You are the *assigned* project manager and come aboard the new project when the project vision and objectives have already been defined. They have been predetermined and you do not have the authority to question and/or modify them even though you realize that the objectives do not fulfill the SMART criteria.

■ Neither the project vision nor the project objectives are clear or mutually understood and endorsed by the key stakeholders. However, you are expected to start the project anyway.

Likely Sources:

■ Option 1: The project sponsor may lack an understanding of the significance of a clear vision and SMART project objectives that are mutually understood and developed jointly with the key stakeholders and the project manager.

■ Option 2: The project sponsor or project authorizing organization is unwilling to modify the project objectives. It rejects any changes because it believes that would signal organizational weakness.

■ Option 3: The project sponsor or the project authorizing organization does not want to qualify the project vision and project objectives because they, too, do not know the answers.

Possible Solutions/Mitigations:

You may be only the *assigned* project manager, but this does not imply that you need not speak up for good and effective project management and leadership principles. A project leader does not just swallow whatever is served without questioning it. This is especially so when the new project leader identifies that the project vision and objectives are not clearly defined and mutually understood. Not stepping up to the occasion is a lack of leadership. It takes effective leadership to lead a project to success. And it starts the very first day of the project. Now is the time to act.

Regarding the three options of likely sources, the following mitigations may help clarify the situation for the better:

■ Option 1: Explain to the project sponsor or project authorizing organization the significance and value of a clear and mutually understood project vision and objectives. Outline their benefits to the sponsor and the whole organization. The ideal scenario would be to conduct a vision workshop with the key stakeholders. If the sponsor does not want to get involved in clarifying the vision, it is your responsibility to do so as the project leader. Meet with the key stakeholders and find out about their needs and understanding of the vision. Consolidate the findings and present them to the stakeholders and the sponsor. Lay out your understanding of the situation and how you plan to move forward.

■ Option 2: A project and a project team require a clear direction. This is reflected in the project vision and objectives. If both the official project vision and objectives allow too much room for interpretation, you have to find out what the project sponsor had in mind. Knowing that the sponsor does not want to change the wording of the vision or objectives, you may want to consider building a prototype with the purpose of clarifying your understanding of the situation. Present the prototype to the sponsor and the key stakeholders. At some point they have to tell you what they expect you and your team to deliver. Once you receive feedback on the prototype, the direction and requirements become clearer. You may not even have to change the official wording of the project vision or objectives. You thus help the sponsor save face.

■ Option 3: If the sponsor does not know what the project vision and objectives are, a vision workshop or building a prototype are two examples of what could help clarify the situation. Explain the value of a joint approach to building the vision. In some situations, the project sponsor may have only a faint idea about a project vision and objectives and no expertise to qualify them. This is what the team is for. Offer to coordinate the effort of defining the vision and objectives.

11.7.1.2 Project Environment Not Open to New Ideas

Challenge(s):

The challenge of leading a project in an environment that is not open to new ideas is at least twofold: the environment is hostile to new content or the organization rejects any new forms of leading and managing a project.

Likely Sources:

■ Option 1: There is a lack of understanding about the negative impact of hostility to new ideas on the project and its environment.
■ Option 2: People are skeptical about new ideas because they are afraid of them.
■ Option 3: People resist new ideas because they want to keep the status quo for personal reasons.

Possible Solutions/Mitigations:

■ Option 1: Develop first a project motivation and then a vision statement. This addresses the impact of the absence of change and identifies the potential benefits of change. Pay special attention to the added value of project results. Then contrast the findings with the status quo. The greater this gap is, the more obvious it should be to embrace change.
■ Option 2: The first thing to do when you are dealing with people who are afraid of new ideas is take their concerns seriously. You want to know where their fears are coming from and try to understand them. Developing a project motivation statement should help you identify the most prominent ones. Building the vision statement then is a process of developing a way to control and overcome the key concerns and letting the benefits outweigh the disadvantages.

■ Option 3: It is simply not possible to please everyone in your larger project environment. You just cannot do it. And it would be futile to try to prove otherwise. This calls for prioritizing the stakeholders and their needs and how they relate to the project vision and objectives. Similar to option 2, pay special attention to those you find to be most important to the success of your project. Involve them in your project effort and win the support of these skeptics. The key is to show them the potential value of the project. If you identify obvious disadvantages of the project to them, identify ways to overcome them.

11.7.1.3 Superficial, Not-Thought-Through Vision

Challenge(s):

The vision of the project is vague at best. It is not concrete with respect to a clear direction for the project. As such, it leaves plenty of room for interpretation. Not too surprisingly, there is neither a mutual understanding nor support of the project vision and project objectives among the key stakeholders of the project. Consequently, the project objectives do not meet the SMART criteria.

Likely Sources:

■ Option 1: You did not spend enough time to define the project vision.
■ Option 2: Stakeholders do not understand the significance and value of a commonly agreed-upon vision and objectives.
■ Option 3: There is a lack of an overall vision beyond the project.

Possible Solutions/Mitigations:

■ Option 1: Given that building project vision is the most important activity at the beginning of a project, you should plan sufficient time to qualify it. This should be self-explanatory by now. Building vision usually cannot be accomplished overnight. It takes time and a joint team effort. If possible and adequate for your project setting, invite the key stakeholders to a vision workshop and define the project vision and objectives. It is an investment with great returns.
■ Option 2:
  – You need to show to the key stakeholders the negative impact of a project vision that is only vaguely defined and not understood or supported by all key stakeholders. You and your team are expected to deliver and meet the project requirements. This is difficult if not virtually impossible to do if the project vision and objectives are too vague. Especially with respect to the project objectives, you want to meet the SMART criteria and leave little room for interpretation.

- You may also consider digging a bit deeper into the real reason for the lack of understanding of the significance and value of a commonly agreed upon vision and objectives. Are the key stakeholders not used to a clear vision and project objectives, do they simply not *want* to be concrete about the project vision and objectives? If the latter is the case, find out the drivers behind this motivation. They could become severe stumbling blocks if you do not recognize and deal with them early.

■ Option 3: You may think that if there is no vision beyond the project you are in trouble right from the beginning. It is a difficult situation. Your job, however, is not to save the world but to help secure project success. Every project has an end date. If there is no vision of what is going to happen once you have delivered the project it is not good, but is it really your first and foremost responsibility to solve this issue? No. Stay focused on your project. Explain to the project sponsor and key stakeholders the value of following a vision that goes beyond the immediate project. It provides a framework and orientation point for the project.

11.7.2 Challenges to Principle 2: Nurture Collaboration

Promoting and nurturing collaboration can be quite complex and difficult. It is even more so when you are working in an environment that is not used to open collaboration. Working in and with virtual teams adds another dimension of complexity. The same applies to large teams, executing projects in an environment of mistrust and politics. Let's have a closer look at three exemplary challenges.

11.7.2.1 Line Organization Too Strong

Challenge(s):

A weak project organization is characterized by a strong line organization. You have a project budget and people working on the project, but not all, if any, team members are available full time to work on the project because they continue to fulfill regular line activities. As project leader, you do not have any discretionary authority over your own team members. Whenever a line activity takes more time than planned, it costs your project. Your project suffers rather than the line organization. It may even come down to seemingly little things, such as planned absences. The line managers approve or disapprove vacation requests. Consequently, team members go to their line managers for planned absence requests rather than to you as the accountable project leader. In short, your project exists and is acknowledged by others, but you do not really have the necessary organizational influence or authority to direct your own team. Instead, you rely on the good will of others.

Likely Sources:

- The organization is not used to projects.
- The line organizations do not see the value of projects to their own line organizations and/or the company.
- The line organizations feel threatened by your project. They are afraid of losing control to you over their own people.

Possible Solutions/Mitigations:

Project leadership starts with building project vision. The resulting activities include a thorough analysis of the project environment. From this perspective it must not come as a surprise that you are leading a project in an environment where the line organization enjoys a greater attention than your project.

Involve all key stakeholders in your project. This is especially important with respect to those line managers who could undermine your project. Project involvement starts with identifying and acknowledging their concerns. From this understanding outline ways and means to mitigate their concerns. Show how the project adds value to each respective line organization. Don't just talk about transparency. Create and practice it on a daily basis. Hence, share all project information that may affect the respective line organizations. Treat them as part of the extended project team and make them feel it. In return you can ask for their support for your project.

If your efforts to reach out to the line managers do not yield the desired results, ask the project sponsor for specific help. Ideally, the project sponsor supports you in your role. On the other hand, the project sponsor may acknowledges the challenge but not really do anything about it. It is a blessing without any leverage. If the project sponsor does not see the challenge and is not willing to back you, all you can do is explain the resulting risks and issues and how they could be mitigated. However, given that you do not have the sufficient organizational leverage, you cannot take on accountability to solve these risks or issues. Instead, accountability lies with the project sponsor. Continue to do your best and update the project sponsor as well as the rest of the extended project team on the project progress.

The extreme case would be that the project sponsor does not back you and the line organizations continue to undermine your sincere project effort, making project success impossible. If this is the case and there is no way out, the last resort may be to cancel the project altogether, thus saving time and resources.

11.7.2.2 Virtual Teams vs. Co-Location

Challenge(s):

Your project team is not working from the same location but is distributed across several workplaces. You may work in the same location but in different buildings. Part of the team may be working in different geographic locations nationally or even internationally.

Likely Sources:

- This could be common practice in a large, international organization.
- There is not enough office space for the project team.
- There is no common time to bring in the complete team to one table because people are working in different time zones or are not available full time.

Possible Solutions/Mitigations:

- Set the expectation that you want your team to come together on a regular basis. If this is physically not possible, make use of the phone, email, or other collaboration tools.
- Use modern communication technology tools such as phone, email, and even better, a professional collaboration tool.
- If team members have reservations about a regular get-together, at a minimum you must insist on a free, open, and proactive flow of all project-related information. If this minimum requirement cannot be met, it raises the question of whether you have recruited the right team in the first place.
- Rotate team members geographically, sending them to work in different team locations for an agreed period of time. They get to know the other team members better and can better identify, understand, and resolve possible impediments to collaboration (Sutherland et al., 2008).

11.7.2.3 Project Environment Not Open to Active Collaboration

Challenge(s):

You may operate in a project environment that is not open to any form of active collaboration and where information sharing is limited to a bare minimum. This could happen outside your core team or even within your team. For example, a team member may resist working with or helping other team members.

Likely Sources:

- This could be a reflection of the organizational culture.
- Some people may have had bad experiences sharing information too freely because it was used against them.
- Information cannot be shared freely because it is classified.

Possible Solutions/Mitigations:

- Reach out to the skeptics of open collaboration. Find out what causes them to think this way. Acknowledge their concerns and develop solutions to cope with them.

- Be a role model. Practice free and open collaboration by sharing information, involving extended team members, and helping other team members if it supports the purpose of the project vision and objectives.
- Plan and conduct a social event that brings people together.
- Convince skeptics with the results of collaboration in your own team.
- If you are working in an environment that deals with classified information, it is no automatism to give up on the idea of nurturing collaboration. Such organizations have been around for a long time. Hence, there is a form of collaboration even though it may look different from common practice. Find out what information can be shared with whom and when. Understand how people work together, help each other.

11.7.3 Challenges to Principle 3: Promote Performance

Having a performing team is great, especially when all of your activities promoting performance turn out to be successful. Unfortunately, projects seldom run as smoothly as desired. Let's look at some common challenges to performance and how we can overcome them.

11.7.3.1 Lack of Skills

Challenge(s):

Lack of skills means you, individual team members, or the whole project team do not possess the required skills, expertise, and/or experience to conduct the necessary work. Without these skills you may not be able to achieve the project objectives.

Likely Sources:

- Experts are not available when needed.
- You are dealing with a new technology with which there is little if any prior experience.
- You do not have the budget to bring the right experts aboard.

Possible Solutions/Mitigations:

- Determine the required skill sets before you recruit your team.
- Find out if any formal training may fill the knowledge gaps. Plan for and secure the necessary training funds and times.
- Discuss with your team if knowledge gaps can be filled by informal training; for example, in the form of coaching or teaching by more experienced team members.

11.7.3.2 Nonperforming Team Member

Challenge(s):

A team member does not fulfill the expectations set out in his or her project role.

Likely Sources:

- Option 1: The team member may lack the necessary skills and/or experience.
- Option 2: The team member may be missing necessary input to conduct his or her work.
- Option 3: The rest of the team isolates the team member; for example, by withholding project-relevant information.

Possible Solutions/Mitigations:

First, you need to find out the core reasons why a team member is not performing as expected. This determines your next steps:

- Option 1: If the team member is missing skills and/or experience:
  - Train the individual in the missing skills and empower the individual to accomplish the work package. Training can be formal or in the form of coaching by a more experienced team member.
  - Evaluate the work package distribution among your team. Modify it to utilize the strengths of each individual team member.
  - If none of the mitigations work, you may have to replace the nonperforming team member with someone who can live up to the expectations set for this role.
  - If as project leader you cannot replace a nonperforming team member because, for example, you are not endowed with the organizational authority to do so, you have to escalate it to the responsible, organizational supervisor. If the supervisor does not react, escalate the issue further to the project sponsor, who has to make the ultimate decision. At that point the ownership of the issue and its resulting risks is being transferred to the project sponsor.
- Option 2: If the team member is missing necessary input to conduct the work:
  - Identify missing link and address it with people involved. Discuss impediments in daily stand-up meetings and work on a solution with the complete team.
- Option 3: If the team member is being isolated by the rest of the team:
  - Review team norming results with the complete team. Make necessary adjustments to integrate every team member into the group and form a coherent and performing team.

11.7.3.3 Team Absence

Challenge(s):

Working with and for a team that actually is not a team can be challenging. In this environment individual performance counts more than the performance of the whole team. Team members care primarily about their own work and results. They focus on their own activities and interests. The team does not constitute a coherent unit but an accumulation of egoistical individuals.

Likely Sources:

- Mistrust of coworkers for personal or other reasons.
- Personal chemistry in team is not working.
- Project organization does not honor group performance and accomplishments. Line organizations value individual performance higher than contributions to the performance and accomplishments of a project team.
- Lack of true team experience. People are not used to working in teams, sharing information freely, and openly and actively working with others toward a common goal.
- Individual team members lack the motivation to work with the team or for the project because they wanted to do something different.

Possible Solutions/Mitigations:

- Conduct a team norming workshop with the team. Engage in team-building activities.
- Evaluate work package assignments within the team.
- Find out why team performance is valued less than individual performance. What impedes honoring team performance and accomplishments?
- Actively market the project progress and accomplishments in your project environment.
- Show to the critical stakeholders the actual value the project is contributing to the greater project organization.

11.7.4 Challenges to Principle 4: Cultivate Learning

Earlier I mentioned an example of a project manager who obstructed the free flow of lessons learned. The results were devastating. It created an environment of distrust. Instead of teamwork, the "team" worked in isolated groups. The project was delivered late and quality standards were not met.

Unfortunately, this is not the only possible obstacle you may face in cultivating learning. Let's look at some other possible scenarios and see how you can overcome them.

11.7.4.1 No Time for Learning

Challenge(s):

"I don't have enough time." This is one of the most mentioned excuses whenever I encourage people to plan for and spend sufficient time to learn, to reflect on the past, and to create new ideas.

Likely Sources:

- People have busy schedules, run from one meeting to another, and conduct their work in between.
- The project schedule may not allow any time buffer for learning.

Possible Solutions/Mitigations:

- There may indeed be times when there is no time to lean back a little and reflect on our past doings, our accomplishments, and our lessons learned in our projects. However, there are usually also times that are less hectic and that leave room for active learning. Use these quiet times with your team to nurture learning.
- Set expectations that learning is a key part of your project and that you expect every team member to share lessons learned, contribute to the team knowledge, and help each other.
- Combine feedback sessions with other events team members attend or don't want to escape from, such as lunch or coffee breaks.
- Revisit the project schedule and determine whether it is too tight, leaving no time for learning. Not having and taking sufficient time to reflect and adjust our actions may haunt us when we have to live with the consequences of potential mistakes. The longer it takes you to correct a mistake, the costlier it usually is, *if* you still have the chance to correct it.

11.7.4.2 No Feedback Culture

Challenge(s):

- Team members are not used to openly sharing constructive feedback.
- Feedback is not constructive but focuses on blaming individuals.

Likely Sources:

- Team members do not share feedback becausee they fear it could be used against them.
- Team members take any form of constructive feedback as a personal assault. *Or* people phrase feedback in a personally assaulting way.

- Team members are not receptive to any feedback except praise.
- Team members are afraid of receiving "negative" feedback. Hence, they too do not give feedback to others.
- Team members are afraid their feedback is belittled and not taken seriously.

Possible Solutions/Mitigations:

- Set the expectation with your team right from the beginning that all feedback counts, regardless of the hierarchical position of the individual.
- Conduct one-on-one meetings with each team member in which you solicit and give constructive feedback.
- Conduct regular feedback sessions with your team. Bring in a third facilitator or rotate the role of the facilitator on your team.
- Instead of "negative" feedback, ask the team members to phrase their observations in delta statements, explaining what needs to be done differently.

11.7.4.3 Mistakes Are Punished

Challenge(s):

It is very difficult to cultivate learning when you operate in a project environment that has no tolerance for mistakes or errors and in which the individuals committing them are punished.

Likely Sources:

- No feedback culture.
- Expectation that everything can be planned and executed accordingly to plan.

Possible Solutions/Mitigations:

- Explain that mistakes will be made. The key is to admit and fix them quickly and, even more important, to learn from them.
- Find out about possible mistakes and impediments in one-on-one meetings with your team members rather than in a bigger group.
- Engage the team in risk management activities, from identifying till mitigating them. Share and celebrate successful mitigation. Analyze failed mitigations with your team and derive lessons learned.
- Embrace a client-driven iterative approach to project delivery. This gives the customer the chance to share feedback.

11.7.5 Challenges to Principle 5: Ensure Results

If you are not producing ongoing results, your project is ailing and possibly on the best way to failure. In this case there may not be much you can do about it. If you find out only at the end that the results do not meet the initially defined and agreed requirements, it is too late. The question is how you can prevent this from happening. There are a lot of challenges on the way. And there are also blocks that may hinder you in fulfilling your leadership responsibility to ensure results. Let's look at some of them and see how you can overcome them.

11.7.5.1 No Interim Results Possible

Challenge(s):

There may be projects for which it is not possible to deliver interim results.

Likely Sources:

- Option 1: The project contract prescribes the delivery of the final product. The time and scope are fixed, with no room for discussion or possible modifications.
- Option 2: The project vision and objectives are in total flux.

Possible Solutions/Mitigations:

- Option 1: Plan for and conduct regular internal and external project reviews to find out if your project is still on track. Present findings to your extended project team and client.
- Option 2:
  - Conduct a vision definition workshop with the client.
  - Develop a prototype to clarify vision and objectives.

11.7.5.2 Lack of Commitment for Ongoing Results

Challenge(s):

Lack of commitment for ongoing results can come from within your team or from the client. In the first case, parts of the team are unwilling to deliver results during the project and instead focus on the final delivery. In the second case, the client does not want to spend time reviewing interim results.

Likely Sources:

- Option 1: Lack of team-internal commitment:
  - Insecurity and nontransparency about own progress.
  - Fear of having to reveal shortcomings.
- Option 2: Lack of client commitment:
  - Lack of interest in project.
  - The client doesn't see necessity or value of interim results because the final product is stable and predictable.
  - Fear of having to modify requirements.

Possible Solutions/Mitigations:

In both cases, explain the necessity and value of ongoing interim results to the team and to the client.

- Option 1: Lack of team-internal commitment:
  - Set expectation of results-driven project activities.
  - Create an open feedback culture. Encourage mistakes for the purpose of individual and team learning.
  - Let the team decide what can be done in each iteration.
- Option 2: Lack of client commitment:
  - Develop and demonstrate a prototype to show the value of ongoing results.
  - Ensure ongoing results internally; assign a team member to act as a proxy representative of the client.
  - Conduct regular internal project reviews; share findings with the project team.

11.7.5.3 Poor Quality

Challenge(s):

It is fatal for your project if you do not find out until the project is over that the final product or service does not have the required quality. It is equally worrying when quality assurance is neglected during the project.

Likely Sources:

- No commonly agreed upon quality requirements.
- Quality not tested until the end of the project.
- Quality requirements compromised for speed of delivery; there is no time for ongoing quality assurance activities.

Possible Solutions/Mitigations:

- Define quality requirements from the beginning of your project. Translate them into individual project requirements from the end-customer perspective.
- Plan for and conduct regular internal and external project reviews. Share and act on findings with your team and the client.
- Plan for and deliver interim results in regular iterations: Deliver most important requirements first to the client, and let other requirements follow in subsequent iterations.

11.8 Summary

Table 11.1 provides an overview of the proposed exercises and how they relate to the five principles of the project leadership pyramid.

Table 11.1 Overview of Project Execution Activities and How They Relate to the Project Leadership Pyramid Principles

EXECUTION	Vision	Collaboration	Performance	Learning	Results
Empower your team and let it deliver		×	×	×	
productive work environment			×		
empowering team		×	×		
1:1 meetings (status, motivations, expectations)				×	×
team building events		×	×	×	
celebrate team accomplishments		×	×	×	×
open information flow		×			
1:1 meetings (status, motivations, expectations)				×	×
project room		×		×	
virtual team room		×		×	
daily stand-up meetings		×		×	
regular team meetings (weekly/biweekly)	×	×		×	×
let team deliver		×	×	×	×

Involve and add value to the extended team			X		
1:1 meetings (status, motivations, expectations)			X	X	X
newsletters			X		X
delivery of interim results	X		X	X	X
Status reporting	X		X		X
Project reviews	X			X	X
internal project reviews	X		X	X	X
daily stand-up meetings			X	X	
regular team meetings w/ focus on lessons learned (weekly/biweekly)	X		X	X	X
using project leadership pyramid principles as categories to capture lessons learned	X	X	X	X	X
5 why's				X	X
leading team motto	X		X	X	X
external project review	X				X

(continued)

Table 11.1 Overview of Project Execution Activities and How They Relate to the Project Leadership Pyramid Principles (Continued)

EXECUTION	Vision	Collaboration	Performance	Learning	Results
lessons learned workshop	X	X	X	X	X
Project pyramid assessment guidelines	X	X	X	X	X
Secure ongoing learning and promote innovation		X	X	X	
learning and feedback rules		X		X	
reviews and updates of rules of engagement		X		X	
reserved time for innovation	X		X	X	X
sharing lessons learned		X		X	
mistakes are part of innovation			X	X	X
Coping with challenges to project leadership pyramid	X	X	X	X	X
Challenges to Principle 1: Build Vision	X	X		X	X
no leverage or control to build vision	X			X	X
project environment not open for any new ideas	X	X			

	Col1	Col2	Col3	Col4	Col5
superficial, not-thought-through vision	X				X
Challenges to Principle 2: Nurture Collaboration		X			X
line organization too strong		X			
virtual teams vs. co-location		X			
project environment not open for open collaboration		X			X
Challenges to Principle 3: Promote Performance	X	X	X	X	X
lack of skills		X		X	
nonperforming team member	X	X		X	
team absence	X	X	X		X
Challenges to Principle 4: Cultivate Learning	X	X		X	X
no time for learning	X			X	
no feedback culture		X		X	

(continued)

Table 11.1 Overview of Project Execution Activities and How They Relate to the Project Leadership Pyramid Principles (Continued)

EXECUTION	Vision	Collaboration	Performance	Learning	Results
errors are punished		x		x	x
Challenges to Principle 5: Ensure Results	x	x		x	x
no interim results possible	x			x	x
lack of commitment for ongoing results	x	x		x	x
Poor quality	x			x	x
KEY	regular interim results to check if project is moving into the right direction	open communication flow	team empowerment	project reviews; secured learning and innovation	regular interim results

At the bottom of the column of the five project leadership pyramid principles, I list the key activities as they relate to the respective leadership principle. Namely:

- Principle 1. Build vision: Regular interim results to check if project is moving in the right direction.
- Principle 2. Nurture collaboration: Open communication flow.
- Principle 3. Promote performance: Team empowerment.
- Principle 4. Cultivate learning: Project reviews.
- Principle 5. Ensure results: Regular interim results.

References

Juli, T. (2003). Work smart, not hard! An approach to time-sensitive project management. In *2003 PMI Global Congress Proceedings*. The Hague, Netherlands: Project Management Institute. Retrieved from http://www.thomasjuli.com/work_smart_not_hard.pdf

Sutherland, J., Schoonheim, G., Rustenburg, E., & Rijk, M. (2008). Fully distributed scrum: The secret sauce for hyperproductive offshored development teams. Paper presented at the Agile Conference 2008. Retrieved from http://www.stevedenning.com/Documents/XebiaAgile08.pdf

Chapter 12

Projects in Trouble

> Leaders are made, not born. Leadership is forged in times of crisis. It's easy to sit there with your feet up on the desk and talk theory. Or send someone else's kids off to war when you've never seen a battlefield yourself. It's another thing to lead when your world comes tumbling down.

> **Lee Iacocca (1924–),**
> *American businessman*

12.1 Expect the Unexpected

There cannot be any doubt: Nobody wants to be in a project that is in trouble and may even be doomed to fail. And yet, oftentimes there is not much you can do to avoid it. The project leadership pyramid and its principles serve as an excellent guideline for project success. Alas, they are no guarantees. So many things can go wrong along the way. You as project leader cannot control everything. If there is one thing that is certain it is that there is a great amount of uncertainty in virtually every project.

Let's face it. You may be better off expecting the unexpected. What counts is that you realize early enough that your project is in trouble or that there are dark clouds on the horizon. The earlier you recognize it, the better the chances that you can get your project back on track. I am assuming that this is what you want.

And, there is good news. Just as the project leadership pyramid helped you set up and execute your project, you can apply the same principles to realign your project or rescue another project. Let's look at how to proceed.

First, as project leader you need to know where your project stands. In the last chapter we talked about the significance and value of status meetings. They come in different forms: informal stand-ups, regular team meetings, lessons learned workshops, and project reviews, be they internal or external. The project pyramid assessment guidelines outlined in the previous chapter can help you determine fairly clearly where your project stands at the moment and in which direction it is going. This is the first step to get your project back on track. The real problem would be if you as project leader did not conduct regular reviews. Note that it may not even be necessary to conduct formal status meetings. The minimum you must do is go through the questionnaire by yourself. Again, you as project leader have to know where your project stands.

If the outcome of this analysis is that your project is indeed no longer aligned with its vision, collaboration rules, performance principles/values, learning culture, and quality standards, there is no reason to despair. You cannot control every factor responsible for project success. Trouble at one point may be inevitable due to internal or external influences. However, this is no excuse for inaction. The previous chapters listed a number of challenges to the project leadership pyramid principles during project execution. Table 12.1 presents some of these internal and external influences. The section in the chapter where each topic was discussed is provided in parentheses.

No matter how great the challenge, as project leader there is always something you can do. Every challenge also poses an opportunity to excel — for you as the project leader, for individual team members, or for the team as a whole. And not every challenge causes the entire project to be in trouble.

Let's define what we mean by dealing with a project in trouble. There are at least two scenarios. First, your project is no longer aligned to one or more principles of the project leadership pyramid. The good news is that the assessment showed there is a good chance that it can be realigned and brought back on track. The second scenario is not as positive. Your project is beyond repair. There is not much that you or anybody else can do to get the project back on track. The project is doomed to fail. As we will see later in this chapter, such projects are not always automatically terminated.

A project in trouble is not necessarily a bad thing though. At least there is no automatism. Take for example a project where the team atmosphere is poisoned. After an initial good start, the team has split into various factions. There is no teamwork. Instead, antagonism and distrust are widespread, isolated and insular work practices dominate, and deliverables are late and/or of poor quality. This is truly a horror scenario. But it could also be simply a sign that your team is in its storming phase. If you have not conducted a team norming yet, do not wait any longer. Now is the time to do so. If you have already done so, review the results of the team norming and adjust them to master the present situation. A team norming, or the evaluation and adjustment of the initial one, can help align the team, get it back on track and help develop a performing team. Although the crisis was highly stressful, mastering it together as a team brought all team members closer together. The team now forms a unit and performs on a high level. Team synergy

Table 12.1   Internal and External Influences on Project Success

Internal Influences	Project Leadership Pyramid Principles	External Influences
- Superficial, not-thought-through vision (11.7.1.3)	Vision	- No leverage or control to build vision (11.7.1.1) - Project environment not open to new ideas (11.7.1.2)
- Virtual teams vs. co-location (11.7.2.2) - Project environment not open to active collaboration (11.7.2.3)	Collaboration	- Line organization too strong (11.7.2.1) - Project environment not open to active collaboration (11.7.2.3)
- Lack of skills (11.7.3.1) - Nonperforming team member (11.7.3.2) - Team absence (7.3.3)	Performance	- Performing team members leave team - Computer fail-out
- No time for learning (11.7.4.1)	Learning	- No feedback culture (11.7.4.2) - Mistakes are punished (11.7.4.3)
- No interim results possible (11.7.5.1) - Lack of (team or individual) commitment for ongoing results (11.7.5.2) - Poor quality (11.7.5.3)	Results	- No interim results possible (11.7.5.1) - Lack of (stakeholder) commitment for ongoing results (11.7.5.2)

effects take place, performance levels are at a peak, information sharing is daily business, and the quality of the regular deliverables has improved significantly and meets all requirements.

In this example, the troubled project was actually turned around into a performing project. Without the obvious team crisis the necessary alignment activities may have never been conducted. The project could have failed.

The key to this turnaround was a thorough assessment of the present situation. It is absolutely crucial that you know where your project and your team stand and in which direction you are moving. Furthermore, you need to be able to decide if you can solve the situation by yourself or if you need help from the outside. If you think you can do it by yourself or with the help of your team, project realignment measures are in order. If, on the other hand, you cannot do it by yourself and somebody else comes in to help, project rescue missions are necessary.

Let's turn to the first scenario, where project realignment is a viable approach. We look at two examples. In the first example in Section 12.2 the project is behind schedule and over budget. You gather the stakeholders and align the project objectives and stakeholders' expectations. The second example in Section 12.3 outlines how you can involve your team in realigning your project.

12.2 Realigning Project Objectives and Stakeholders' Expectations in a Project behind Schedule and over Budget[1]

Let me tell you a story about a project that had a good start but slipped into trouble soon thereafter. The CEO of the company and every department head agreed that it was time to replace the proprietary call center and promotion management applications with a new customer relationship management (CRM) system. The project was estimated to run for 9 months. The motivation of everyone involved was high and everyone was certain that this project would be a success. After all, it was not the first project of this size and complexity that the company had managed successfully.

Two months later, initial enthusiasm has given way to cruel reality. During the first 2 months, the key requirements of the marketing department have been captured and documented. However, the call center and the billing departments have not concluded documenting their requirements due to different opinions about the scope and level of project involvement of their subject matter experts. Consequently, the project is behind schedule and not within budget.

The sponsor is not willing to accept this situation any longer and has decided to replace the part-time project manager with an external, full-time, and more experienced project manager who will report directly to her. She is asking you to take over. Your mission: Do whatever is necessary to get the project back on track and finish it on time and within budget.

You start by interviewing the department chairs about the situation. Quickly you learn that expectations about the project vary significantly. There is anything but a common understanding of the project objective. You decide to invite all department chairs (i.e., marketing, customer care, call center, accounting/billing, IT), the sponsor, and business and technical track leaders of the project team to a mutual workshop. The workshop is scheduled to run for 3 hours. The question is, can this workshop become the foundation of success and, if so, how?

---

[1] This section is largely based on a paper I presented at the PMI Global Congress North America in Denver, Colorado (Juli, 2008).

12.2.1 Workshop Set-Up

The morning of the workshop, you introduce the objective of the workshop: To achieve a mutual understanding of each other's expectations about the project, revisiting the official project objectives statement and aligning it with (a) the present situation and (b) the stated expectations of attendants. The expected outcome is a refined project objective statement that meets the SMART criteria — specific, measurable, achievable, relevant, and time-boxed. This objective statement is mutually understood and supported.

You divide the workshop into three distinct parts. Following the introduction, the group of 20 people (two track leads of the project team plus two to three representatives each of marketing, customer care, call center, accounting, and IT) will be split into five groups of two to three individuals each. They will meet in parallel breakout sessions of 30 to 45 minutes to discuss and summarize their needs and their expectations of the project and its deliverables. A prepared set of questions serves as a guideline for this fact-finding session. Following the breakout session, each group will present the documented responses to the attendees and answer any questions about the presented results. During the second part of the workshop, participants will prioritize the presented results of the group sessions based on the SMART and other predefined prioritization criteria. The aim is to qualify the existing project objective so that it is better aligned with stakeholders' expectations and meets previously set criteria. A review of remaining open questions and an outlook of the next steps will conclude the workshop.

Everyone agrees with the agenda of the workshop. The groups split up into breakout groups and start work.

12.2.2 Breakouts

Each breakout group is made up of representatives of the various departments involved in the project. They all have decision-making authority. This is important, because otherwise the workshop results may have to go through yet another round of management approval, which could prove time consuming and detrimental to the achieved consensus of the workshop, calling into question the overall purpose of the workshop in the first place.

At the beginning of the breakout session, you give each group a set of questions. The goal is to guide the group discussion toward tangible results that they will share later with the other groups.

The questions address the group's present understanding and evaluation of the project, their expectations, and their definition of the project objective. In our example, you hand out the following questions and ask them to write each answer on a separate moderation card:

1. Purpose: Why do you and your organization need a new CRM system? List the most important reasons.
2. Value: On a scale of 1 to 5 (with 5 being highest), what level of priority does a new CRM system have for you and your organization?
3. Other projects: What other project(s) is (are) more important to you and why? (Please list up to three other projects.) On a scale of 1 to 5 (with 5 being highest), what level of priority does each have?
4. Impact of delay: What impact would it have on you and your organization if the project were delayed and/or does not meet your expectations (e.g., limited scope)? How do you measure (i.e., quantify) this impact? List the three most important impacts and quantify them.
5. Fallback plan: Do you have a fallback plan/solution in place? How much would it cost? Limit your response to three options and quantify them.
6. SMART project objective(s): Based on your answers to the previous questions, phrase the project objective(s), making sure that it is (a) specific, (b) measurable, (c) achievable, (d) relevant, and (e) time-boxed.
7. Critical success factors: What are the top three most important factors that have to be met for the project to be successful?

Following the 30- to 45-minute breakout session, each group presents its responses to the whole group. Each response card is pinned onto a whiteboard or wall under headings for the various categories (e.g., purpose, value, other projects). Limit each group's presentation time, including Q&A, to 10 minutes. A short break of 15 minutes gives everyone a chance to read the various responses once more. This concludes the first part of the workshop.

12.2.3 Prioritization

After the short break, the whole group meets to prioritize the collected input. To meet this purpose, every attendant has three votes for each category. The votes can be split evenly or allocated to one or more entries in each category. Although every category is important, you ask the attendants to cast their votes first for the categories' purpose, other projects, and impact of delay. You explain that following this prioritization exercise the whole group will discuss the top two entries in each category that receive the most votes. The objective is to agree on a single entry and phrase that everyone or at least the majority can support. You facilitate this discussion. In case of a tie, the sponsor will have the last word.

To a certain extent, this voting exercise can be tricky. It can be argued that one department should have more votes than another. On the other hand, giving each department the same number of votes yields a more realistic picture of the overall perspective of all stakeholders involved. Accounting for all involved is a critical success factor in defining a foundation of mutual agreement and support. After all, you need to get the project back on track.

Based on the result of the first voting exercise, the group now casts their votes on the collected SMART project objectives. In case submitted objective statements do not meet the SMART criteria, you help qualify and rephrase the statements until they do. As in the first voting round, the two statements with the most votes are discussed with the whole group. The goal is to come up with a definition of SMART project objectives that enjoys the support of all attendants. Once more, in the event of a tie or deadlock, the sponsor casts the final vote.

Keeping the results of the first and second voting rounds in mind, the group casts their votes on the critical success factors. This time, the top three factors that receive the most votes are discussed in the group. They will be accounted for in future requirements gathering and evaluation, project planning, executing, monitoring, and closing of the project. As an alternative to the breakout session, you can elaborate on the question about critical success factors in the whole group following the first two voting rounds.

Last but not least, you summarize the prioritized project objectives and stakeholders' expectations. Any open issues and/or action items are captured, owners assigned, and solution dates agreed. The next concrete steps depend to a great extent on the actual outcomes of the prioritization exercise. For example, you may want to revisit the functional and nonfunctional requirements of the CRM solution, review the project governance structure, and adjust the project plan to meet the qualified and realigned project objectives and stakeholders' expectations.

12.2.4 Workshop Benefits

The workshop serves as a starting point to get the project back on track. It yields a common definition and understanding of the project objectives. This builds a foundation for all consecutive project work. It also serves as a prioritization guideline for any remaining requirements gathering and evaluation as well as for project planning, executing, monitoring, and closing activities.

At the same time, the workshop brings the key stakeholders together. It thus serves as a simple and effective team-building exercise. It constructs a learning environment that promotes a better understanding of the expectations of the other departments and individuals without constraints and assumptions.

Do not jump to the conclusion that the workshop itself and its outcomes are sufficient to realign the project objectives and stakeholders' expectations. They are a starting point. They help build a solid foundation to get the project back on track. The list of open issues and action items collected during the workshop indicate that the workshop is a mere starting point, albeit a good one. It is now up to you to lead the project team and everyone else involved to a successful finish. The project leadership pyramid principles provide you with an excellent orientation to do so.

12.2.5 Practical Tips

Having conducted similar workshops for numerous projects myself, I can testify that such workshops are critical in realigning project objectives and stakeholders' expectations. Every project is different and unique. Although the project scenario and workshop described in the previous section may not be applied to others in a one-to-one fashion, the general idea certainly is applicable.

Experience shows that the minimum duration for this kind of workshop is between 2 and 3 hours. Depending on the complexity of the project and number of stakeholders involved, you may want to plan on more time. Next, limit the number of attendees to 20. This will ensure you enough leeway for an effective and results-driven facilitation while staying within the time limit. Invite all key stakeholders to attend. It is crucial that all attendees be decision-making authorities. In addition, I recommend that you interview the stakeholders prior to the workshop. Although this is not absolutely necessary, it will help you build personal rapport and trust with them.

Last but not least, every workshop has its own dynamics. To a certain extent you can control these dynamics: come prepared and ask your team for help and support. This last thought takes us to the next section. Namely, how else can you involve your own project team to realign your project?

12.3 Realignment with Team Involvement[2]

Being faced with your own project gone astray is probably one of the most difficult challenges you can come up against as a project leader. You cannot handle such a situation alone. Where do you start? Who should drive the effort and who else should be involved?

I analyzed a number of prominent approaches to project recovery (Aiyer et al., 2005; Bailey, 2000; Block, 1998; Ludwig, 2008; Ward, 2007). Most of the approaches to project realignment have the following steps in common:

- Admit there is a problem.
- Analyze the problem.
- Develop a recovery plan and execute it.
- Ensure sustainable and long-lasting results.

The approaches differ in their responses to the question, *Who drives the realignment effort?* In most cases it is either the project manager alone (a top-down approach) or an external person or team conducting the recovery.

---

[2] This section is largely based on a paper I presented at the PMI Global Congress North America in Orlando, Florida (Juli, 2009a).

What are the most effective approaches to re-align a project?

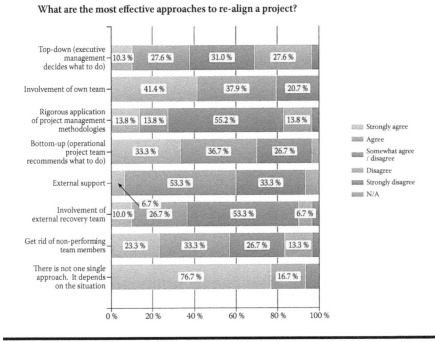

Figure 12.1   Most effective approaches to realigning a project.

In July of 2009 I conducted a survey on project realignment (Juli, 2009b). Although the survey was from a scientific point of view not representative, it still revealed some common threads about the importance of involving your team in realigning your project. One of the questions I asked was what the most effective approaches to realigning a project were. The results speak for themselves (Figure 12.1).

Greater than 93% of those surveyed explained that there is no such thing as the ultimate approach. It more or less depends on the current situation, your team members, executive management, and your customers. In second and third place were responses that actively call for team involvement: 78% believed that you have to involve your own team, whereas 70% called for a bottom-up approach, in which the project team first assesses the situation and then communicates the results to higher management levels. Interestingly, less than a third of the respondents thought that rigorous application of project management methodologies was the most effective approach to realign a project.

What we can conclude from the survey results is that it definitely makes sense to involve your team in project realignment.

In the next question of the survey, I asked how the respondents involved their own team in realigning a project. Figure 12.2 summarizes the responses. Eighty-six percent chose the answer "problem assessment." This was in sync with the other

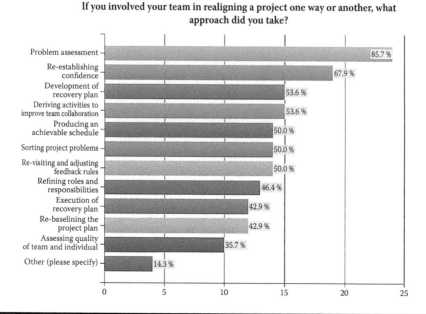

If you involved your team in realigning a project one way or another, what approach did you take?

Figure 12.2   Approaches taken when realigning a project.

approaches I reviewed (Aiyer et al., 2005; Bailey, 2000; Block, 1998; Ludwig, 2008; Ward, 2007), except that in this case the whole team is involved rather than only one person.

This is not necessarily contrary to other prominent recovery approaches that stress the importance of regaining control. One of the most important foundations of control that you have as a project leader is your own team. You are surely not the only person on the project who is performing, save for a single-person project. The team as a whole realizes the problem. As the project leader you lead and manage the project. At the same time, you are a member of the team. Corollary, if you do not have a functioning team, you are acting without a solid foundation of control. Team building helps establish this foundation of control.

In the case of a project in trouble, you can try to realign it and gain control by yourself. Still, it will be easier and more effective to involve your team right from the beginning rather than at the end. Good leadership, team building, teamwork, project control, and hence project realignment go hand in hand. The *Guide to the Project Management Body of Knowledge* states, "Team building is the process of helping a group of individuals, bound by a common sense of purpose, to work independently with each other, the leader, external stakeholders, and the organization. The result of good leadership and good team building is teamwork. ... Outcomes of team building include mutual trust, high quality of information exchange, better decision making, and effective project control" (Project Management Institute,

2008, p. 418). There is no doubt that for a project in trouble you do need to regain control over the project. But you cannot do it by yourself or solely from the top down. If you want to succeed you need to involve your team in the process. This is why *it takes a team to realign a project*.

12.3.1 Workshop Set-Up

There are numerous ways to involve your team in realigning your project. A simple yet very effective start is to conduct a project realignment workshop with your team. Plan at least 2 hours for this workshop. Depending on the complexity of the project, I recommend 3 to 4 hours, possibly even longer. It is best if you can find a neutral facilitator to lead the workshop. This allows you as the project leader to actively participate. After all, you are a member of the team.

Whether you limit the circle of participants to the core project team or extended team, including some stakeholders, depends on the situation. The number of participants should not exceed 20 people altogether. If your team is bigger, you may want to consider exercises for subgroups of five to eight people and then have the subgroups present their results to the whole group. For illustration purposes, I assume a project team size of 10 to 12 individuals.

The project realignment workshop is split into three parts: first, you revisit the past; second, you assess the present; and third, you build the foundation of the future. The purpose of the first part is to gain a common understanding of where you and your team have come from. The results of this first part are a list of categorized and prioritized lessons learned. The purpose of the second part is the need to admit that there is a problem and we as a team are capable of resolving it. The outcomes of this part are a problem and solution statement and a project recovery objectives statement. Finally, in the third part of the workshop, we build a common ground and direction on how to move forward to succeed. The results of the third part are refined roles and responsibilities and a list of activities that secure mutual understanding of the project objectives and project recovery objectives statements. This will also boost team collaboration, performance, learning, and project results. Let's take a closer look at each of these parts.

12.3.2 Workshop Step 1: Revisiting the Past

In this part of the workshop you and your team review what has happened in the past. The outline is identical to the internal project review presented in Chapter 11. Team members are given five to ten cards each, on which they will write their answers to the questions:

1. What has gone well thus far? Why?
2. What has not gone well? Why?
3. What can we do better and how?

Each person may write one answer per card. This means, if each person has five cards, each can give five answers, regardless if it is a response to the first, second, or third question.

To sort the answers, ask each team member to mark his or her response card in the top right corner with the initial of the following categories (V, C, P, L, or R):

- V: Vision/project objective(s). Sample guiding question: Does everyone have the same understanding of the project objectives and live by them?
- C: Collaboration (in team, with management or sponsor, with customer, etc.). Sample guiding questions: How do you rate our teamwork, communication with stakeholders, and customers, etc.? Are we abiding by our own team rules? Do our team rules meet the requirements of our project? If not, what do we have to adjust?
- P: Performance of individuals and/or team. Sample guiding question: How do you evaluate our team performance?
- L: Learning or feedback culture within team and project environment. Sample guiding question: How much do we value open and constructive feedback in our team?
- R: Results/solution quality. Sample guiding question: How do you rate our quality of work?

Once everyone has recorded his or her feedback, the workshop facilitator collects the cards and presents them to the whole group, reading each one aloud and then pinning it onto a whiteboard or wall. The whiteboard may look like the example in Figure 12.3.

	Vision	Collaboration	Performance	Learning	Results
☺	...	...		...	...
	...	...		...	...
	...	...		...	...

☹	...	...		...	...
	...	...		...	...
	...	...		...	...

Figure 12.3   Whiteboard example.

Alternatively, you can ask each individual to present his or her feedback. Beware though that this could be much more time consuming. Not everyone likes to stand in front of an audience and present his or her results. This is why making use of a facilitator is the logical choice.

Once all cards have been posted, the team prioritizes the input. For this purpose each individual has a limited number of votes to cast, say ten votes. Participants can choose to place all votes onto a single card or distribute them. They place either a mark or a sticker on the cards for each vote cast. Allow 5 to 10 minutes for this exercise.

Once everyone has cast his or her vote the team discusses the response cards with the most votes for each question. The facilitator needs to make sure that the whole team has the same understanding of the responses and their meanings. Things that went well thus far you definitely want to continue. Things that did not go well need special attention. They will form the basis for the next exercise, in part two of the realignment workshop.

12.3.3 Workshop Step 2: Assessing the Present

In the second part of the workshop, the team drills down the top issues and risks of the project and comes up with a project recovery objectives statement. For the first exercise you may want to split your team into groups of two or three people. Each group answers the following questions:

1. What are the top issues or risks identified in part one of the workshop? Why?
2. Who is affected by these issues or risks? Why?
3. What are the impacts of the issues or risks? Why?
4. What needs to be done to resolve the situation? Why?
5. What benefits can we expect from the improved situation? Why?
6. What critical success factors need to be met to achieve this? Why?

Responses are recorded on a flip chart. Each group then presents its answers to the whole team. Next, the complete team discusses the various responses and agrees on a summary statement that describes the issues at stake and outlines the solutions. Limit the actual discussion time to 10 to 30 minutes, depending on the project situation.

Once you have achieved this, go back to the small teams you formed for the prior exercise and develop a project recovery objectives statement. This is based on the commonly agreed upon problem and solution statement in the previous exercise. Once more break into smaller groups and ask each group to build a SMART recovery objectives statement. SMART means that the recovery objectives need to be specific, measurable, achievable, relevant, and time-boxed.

Following the breakouts, the small teams present their suggestions to the whole team. The complete team then discusses the various responses and agrees on a common wording for the project recovery objectives statement.

Note that it is absolutely critical that everyone on the team understands and buys into this project recovery objectives statement, its scope, and its implications. The objectives statement sets the direction of the project and teamwork. You as the project leader are the skipper, who ensures that your boat is and stays on the right course to its ultimate destination. This destination is described in the project vision and objectives statements. This is why you must make sure that the project recovery objectives statement is in sync with the overall project vision and objectives statements.

12.3.4 Workshop Step 3: Building the Future

Having a project recovery objectives statement is extremely helpful. It provides a direction to the team with clear deliverables and a timeline. It is a start. For the project recovery objectives statement to become alive you have to put it into the perspective of your imminent environment; i.e., your own team. For this purpose, you revisit the roles and responsibilities of each team member and identify areas where each individual can contribute to achieving the recovery objectives. In other words, you conduct a team norming with the focus on defining roles and responsibilities and rules of engagement that best fit the project recovery objectives. Unless you already have a description of each role on your team, identify each role, its responsibilities, and its deliverables and then capture it on a flip chart. Use one flip chart per role.

The description should address two aspects: (1) the role in the project in general and (2) the role in the recovery mission in particular. Once you have spread the flip charts around the meeting room, ask team members to add their expectations of this role, writing them onto the respective flip charts. In reverse, ask each team member what the person in each respective role can expect from the team to fulfill it. Allow 15 to 25 minutes for this exercise.

The facilitator presents the final flip charts to the whole team. It checks that every single team member understands the responsibilities, deliverables, and expectation of each role. Plus, every team member must buy into the respective role description. If there are any discrepancies or different expectations, this is the time to discuss these issues and resolve them.

Once you have revisited and refined the individual project roles and responsibilities for the project realignment, list the activities that boost team collaboration, team performance, team learning, and project results. This will ensure the whole team lives up to these activities and consequently the project and recovery objectives.

For this second exercise the facilitator hands out a limited number of cards and asks each team member to write down his or her suggestions. Have team members initiali their cards with the categories of their response: as before, V for vision and project objectives and the resulting scope, C for collaboration, P for performance, L for learning, and R for project results.

The facilitator collects and presents the cards to the group. Similar to the first exercise of part one of the workshop, it is useful to have a prepared flip chart showing the various categories.

Following the presentation of the results, the team prioritizes the input. Use the same voting rules as in the first exercise of part one of the workshop. The three cards that get the most votes will be discussed and elaborated on by the project team. They become the leading mottos of the daily work of the team in the coming weeks of the project recovery mission.

12.3.5 Lessons Learned from Project Realignments

The workshop setup is simple. At the same time, it yields powerful results: The team develops a project recovery objectives statement, revisits and refines project roles and responsibilities to support project realignment, and collects a list of activities to secure living up to the project objectives and project *recovery* objectives statements. It also boosts team collaboration, team learning, and team performance, as well as gaining tangible project results. At the same time, the workshop is a strong team-building exercise. The team jointly reviews the past, assesses the present situation, identifies and categorizes problems, and develops resolutions to the most pressing issues and risks. This is a joint team effort. It secures team commitment and accountability. This is a powerful foundation for project realignment.

Still, do not jump to the conclusion that the realignment workshop automatically guarantees successful rescue missions. It does not. It is a stepping stone, although an important one. After a realignment workshop, it is up to you as the project leader and your team to execute its team-created recovery plan and live up to its guiding principles. The workshop is a start; team performance comes next.

A project gone astray usually cannot be realigned overnight. It takes time. Team involvement and team building are ongoing activities. You, as the project leader, have a special and important responsibility at this stage. The workshop empowers the team as a whole as well as each individual team member.

Involving your team is one of the smartest things to do to master such a complex task. It is not sufficient though. Take, for example, project situations where the existing project team is part of or even the source of the problem. In this case, it may not make a lot of sense to continue work with the present team. Instead, you may want to consider replacing the team or individual nonperforming team members or choose a top-down approach, where executive management dictates what to do and how to recover the project in trouble. Ultimately, however, you have to involve your existing or newly formed project team.

Now let me tell you a story of a project where a single nonperforming team member threatened the success of the overall project. The project consisted of several subprojects. Most of them were running smoothly; i.e., milestones were met and deliverables were generally of good quality. Unfortunately, there was one project that continually was running late. The project objectives were clearly defined, but there was a work breakdown structure the subproject manager helped create and bought into. In short, the set-up looked promising but, in reality looked different. Deliverables were incomplete, late, and of poor quality.

Colleagues and consultants helped the subproject manager in his work. Still, performance remained dismal. Adding to the complexity, the subproject manager became sick for 3 weeks. The designated stand-in attended weekly project meetings but explained that he was not able to fill in for the sick project manager because this would have meant neglecting his other work. What a stand-in! What good does it do to have someone standing in for you in case you become sick if this person cannot really replace you? The bottom line was that work in this subproject laid still for 4 weeks.

Once the subproject manager returned, the project manager and consultants met with him to lay out a road map to recover the late subproject. Again, the subproject manager actively participated in this exercise, committing to the newly planned deliverables and milestones. Did anything change? Unfortunately not.

What went wrong? Colleagues and consultants pointed out to the responsible project managers that there were evident signs that the subproject manager was simply not up to his task. He had lots of practical experience in his field of expertise, but this was the first time he had been asked to manage a project. The organizational supervisors believed that, given his experience and academic training, he had to be qualified to manage and lead a project. Sound familiar? It makes me wonder what drives this faulty conclusion. Project management can be learned, there is no doubt. But it also takes a certain mindset and attitude. Strong project managers are solution and results oriented. They have the drive to finish things. They know their limits, when to ask for help, when to raise an issue, and how to identify risks. In the previous example, this was not the case.

So what could have been done? If all else fails, replace the subproject manager. Leadership involves making decisions, even when they are not pleasant. In the case of a nonperforming team member who is endangering the success of an entire project, the project leader must act. In the situation described above this would have meant to "sack" the subproject manager and replace him with someone else or distribute the workload to other team members capable of managing it. If the project leader cannot make this decision because, for example, he or she is not endowed with the organizational authority to do so, the issue needs to be escalated to the organizational supervisor. If the supervisor does not react either, the issue has to be escalated to the project sponsor, who must make the ultimate decision. At that point the ownership of the issue and its resulting risks are being transferred to the project sponsor.

Not taking any action, downplaying an obvious problem, or not actively mitigating a risk is not leadership. It is true that some issues may be resolved by inaction, letting the dynamics take care of it. If done so on purpose and for good reasons, fine. Principally, I think this is the wrong approach. One of the pillars of effective leadership is ensuring delivery and results. If that requires sacking a nonperforming team member, so be it.

You may have noticed that the project realignment workshops with the stakeholders and your team are made up of exercises discussed in Chapter 10. This is no coincidence. The best way to align your project for success is to set it up right from the beginning. In my own survey (Juli, 2009b), I asked what lessons learned from project rescue missions can be applied to setting up and managing a project. The vast majority (88.9%) of the survey respondents answered that it is to plan and conduct a vision/project objective definition workshop with your own team. Having the same understanding of the project objectives and the general direction of your project and its environment (i.e., the vision of your project) is a critical factor to project success. Second, having a list of short-term (e.g., weekly or biweekly) deliverables and measurable results ensures that the project stays on track. Third, setting up quality standards for each project phase, such as entry and exit criteria, is another critical success factor.

It is up to you as the project leader to practice true leadership and follow this advice. Do not try to accomplish the challenge of aligning or realigning your project by yourself. Build, involve, and empower a team right from the beginning. It is an investment that serves as your insurance for project success. And it can yield great payoffs. It takes a team to align and realign a project. And it takes effective project leadership to empower the team to do so. It is up to you to be or become this leader.

12.4 External Project Rescue

There may be situations in which you as the project leader have reached the end of your possibilities. You realize that you and your team cannot realign your project by yourselves. You need help from the outside. Or you may be asked to help rescue another project. In either case, the approach is the same and very similar to the realignment efforts.

Every project rescue mission starts with a thorough assessment of the present project situation. Assessment approaches differ. Not too surprisingly, however, I recommend that the rescuer or the rescue team uses the same project pyramid assessment guidelines as a starting point. The assessment results will tell the rescue team whether the project can be realigned with the help of part of or the whole existing team, or whether an external team should take over the rescue mission altogether. It is not possible to say which option is better. There is no automatism.

In cases where the existing project team was part of or the main reason for causing the project to run off track, it may indeed be better to bring in a new rescue team. If this is not the case, it may make sense to involve the existing team in one way or another because it knows, or at least it should know, the project situation best. It is up to the rescue leader to make this decision.

The actions the rescue team takes to realign the project depend on the specific project situation. Whereas the project pyramid assessment guidelines follow a strict order, starting with looking at the vision and working down to analyzing results, the best rescue strategy may be to address results first, then collaboration, followed by performance, the learning culture, and last refining the project vision. What counts is that the rescue mission establishes all five principles. The exercises for this effort are similar to the ones used in the project initiation and execution phases. This is no coincidence. Rescuing or realigning a project puts it back onto a solid foundation. This foundation is based on the five leadership principles. Ideally, every project is set up and executed this way. If not, you need to go back a step or two and do your homework before you proceed. Otherwise, there is a much greater chance for project failure.

By this token, the objectives of external project rescue missions are the same as in the project realignment efforts described above: to get the project back on track *and* to align it with all the principles of the project leadership pyramid. The short-run solution may be to get the project back on track and turn it back over to the existing project team. However, rescue missions must not fall short of realigning the project with the five leadership principles for project success. If they do, chances are that the project will fall off track again within a short time. The objectives of both rescue and realignment efforts are to secure that the project leadership pyramid principles are followed and thus help secure project success.

12.5 Canceling a Project

We still have to talk about the situation where a project cannot be saved. There are a number of things that can happen. The first possibility is that the project continues its path to failure. Not possible? Yes, it is. Actually, one can find quite a few project failures where it was clear early on that they were doomed to fail and still nothing or little was done to save them. Take, for example, the attempt by the first Clinton administration to reform the U.S. healthcare system. Opposition in Congress was too strong to win its support. The well-meant initiative ended in a political fiasco for the Clinton administration. Another example is when the project sponsor decides to continue a project in spite of the fact that it is clear it would not reach its objectives and fail. The reason for this decision may be social, because the sponsor does not want to dismiss the people working on this project and become unemployed. This, too, can be the right choice. In yet another example, the objective of a project is to build a new product. The project team solely focuses on the technical solution, leaving issues of selling the product totally out of the equation. On the other hand, the marketing and sales teams are not even aware of the new product development project. The project team fails to recognize that the marketing and sales teams have recently changed their going-to-market strategy. At the end of the day, the project team delivers the final product on time and within budget. Unfortunately, it does not add any value because no one is ready for it. The project failed.

The second possibility is that the project is indeed canceled. In other words, the team is disseminated and all project actions come to a close, although not the originally intended close. This is not necessarily a bad choice. If your project assessment shows that the project is beyond repair, for whatever reason, why would you want to continue spending time and resources and waste your team's time and effort for a futile effort? In this case, canceling the project may be the best choice and definitely better than project failure.

It could actually be your responsibility to call this shot and either cancel the project by yourself if you can or request that the project sponsor terminate it. Having to make a decision whether to terminate the project or continue it until it fails is a difficult one. No doubt, this is a difficult calling and certainly not a situation we strive for. We probably all want to avoid such a situation. Sometimes, however, we cannot. Then it is important to weigh all factors and make the right decision. If you or somebody else decides to cancel the project, do not just stop all project actions at once. Canceling a project due to insurmountable difficulties closes the project. As such, it calls for a clean project closure, which is described in the next chapter.

12.6 Working on a Troubled Project — Without Being in Control

> Real integrity is doing the right thing, knowing that nobody's going to know whether you did it or not.
>
> **Oprah Winfrey (1954–),**
> *U.S. actress & television talk show host*

The previous sections described situations of troubled projects for which you were the acting project manager, the person in charge. Now let's turn to the question of what you can do in a project that is obviously in trouble but you are *not* the responsible project manager. Do the project leadership pyramid principles still hold? Or, asked differently, can you still apply the principles and thus help realign the project, and if so, how?

Some time ago I was faced with exactly this situation. I was working on a 6-month project, the goal of which was to develop and introduce a new, legally mandatory technical product. The client's industry was traditional in nature, with little if any project culture and even less experience in software integration projects, which happened to be the present project. I was not the project manager but the quality manager. In this role I was responsible for setting up policies and processes that helped secure quality requirements to be met. It was not the first time that I filled such a role. The scope and complexity of the project appeared manageable and the role not overly challenging. Soon after I started my new role, I was proven wrong. It appeared that the project manager violated all principles of the project leadership pyramid. Six months later the project was still not finished. The final delivery date was postponed three times. Eventually, the 6-month project was 6 months overdue. The new product was delivered. From this perspective the project was a success. However, not all product requirements were realized. Furthermore, the path to the final delivery date was anything but smooth.

The project had a bad start. The sponsors, the steering committee, and the project manager talked about a product vision and there even seemed to be a consensus about the overall direction. Not so, however, regarding the understanding of the strategy for how to get to the vision. For a fairly long time the various stakeholders discussed the scope of the project. But, the first delivery date was set without having achieved a common understanding of the scope. Hence, it was not really surprising that the first project objectives statement was rather vague. This was done "for political reasons," I was told.

As time went by it became clear that the first delivery date was no longer viable. It was postponed another 2 months. Again, there was no real consensus of the scope of the first release of the new product. Six weeks later it was déjà vu. The project manager told the steering committee that the delivery date had to be moved once more. This time he was more careful about the scope and the delivery date. It was agreed to specify the scope within the first 2 months of this new extension. Once this was achieved everyone agreed to move the deadline a last time. The project, which was originally scheduled to run for 6 months, became a 12-month project with limited scope. Wow, what a feat!

The project team consisted of technical and functional experts from the line organization of the company. Most of them continued to work in their normal line role. Only a few team members could focus 100% of their time on the project. Interestingly, the project manager was not among those few lucky ones. The project team met on a weekly basis to discuss the status of the various subprojects. Later in the project, daily stand-up meetings were organized. Unfortunately, attendance was sporadic at best, reflecting the dismal quality of collaboration on this project. Information sharing was held to a minimum. Known problems or risks were not proactively shared with the whole team. Team members hesitated to take on ownership of known problems and rather delegated tasks to others without telling them or following up. The team was not a team but a group of individuals having to work together. They were experts in their field; that is, some of them were. Early on in the project it became obvious that one team member was overwhelmed by the tasks assigned to him. The project manager knew about it. He discussed the issue with the affected person, his line managers, and the project sponsor. No solution was found and the team member stayed. It turned out to be a major problem. The mentioned team member was responsible for planning, developing, and running a prototype that was crucial for the development of the complete product. The quality of the prototype turned out to be so bad that it proved of no value to the project. It caused the delay of the first two deadlines, yet said individual stayed on board.

The rest of the team was aware of this problem and expressed concern in a lessons learned workshop early on during the project. Team members also complained about the unclear scope of the project and missing information. We shared the minutes of this workshop with the project manager. The constructive feedback and suggestions were obvious. Less obvious was the reaction of the project manager. He took the expressed feedback of his own team as a personal assault against him. As a consequence, he banned any future lessons learned sessions.

The morale in the team deteriorated. Fortunately, all team members were professional enough to continue work and finally helped deliver the final product, 6 months after the original set date. The project was proclaimed a huge success and the project sponsor was happy.

Looking back at this project, I admit that a project that seemed like an easy ride in the beginning turned out to be a nightmare. The sad thing was that I was in the middle of it. There were quite a few times when I was close to quitting and leaving this project. I am glad that I did not. This project turned out to be a valuable lesson. Let me tell you why.

One of the first questions that comes to mind is whether I contributed to this mess, or if and how I tried to realign the project. The latter is the case. In my role as quality manager I set up a number of policies and procedures that were aimed to secure and improve the quality of the project and the product to be developed. It was not a problem of the quality management plan that addressed all aspects of the project. The project manager read and officially approved the quality plan. The dilemma was that only a very few followed the advice outlined in this plan. Unfortunately, the project manager was not one of them.

When it became clear that the key stakeholders had different opinions of the objectives of the project and the new product, I helped the project manager fine-tune the project objectives. The resulting project objectives statement was better. Alas, it did not fully meet the requirements of a good project objectives statement insofar as it had to be specific, measurable, achievable, relevant, and time-boxed. I pointed this out to the project manager. Unfortunately, he resisted any additional fine-tuning, calling it an academic exercise. Granted, this could have been argued. The real problem was that there was no common understanding and support of the project objectives. This was one of the main reasons for the project being delayed and not meeting its original requirements.

The team morale was low throughout the project. Communication was held to a minimum. I did not want to participate in this. I created a virtual team room in which I stated all of my past, present, and planned activities and deliverables. This file was openly shared with everyone. Soon the project office joined in. We agreed to conduct one-on-one meetings with all subproject leads, which gave us a chance to talk about their status, issues, and risks. The project office consolidated the information and created a report. The communication flow among the team members improved, no doubt. However, it was still not the desired proactive communication flow we were after. This became evident when we set up daily stand-ups toward the end of the project, during the so-called hot phase. The attendance at the stand-ups was dismal. Whenever we met it turned out to be valuable. But again, information had to be pulled out of individuals. There was no proactive information sharing.

As quality manager, I suggested ways out of this dilemma and discussed my recommendations with the project manager and the project sponsor on a weekly basis. It was not that the responsible parties were not aware of the obvious problems and risks. Indeed, the open and direct nature of my reports was acknowledged and appreciated. However, the recommendations were either alleged as not being true or neglected altogether. This was a truly frustrating experience.

The big question is whether it would have been the right thing to leave this ailing project. The answer is a clear "no." Working on a troubled project is not a nice experience. It can be extremely stressful and causes a lot of frustration. However, running away from a project like this is no solution. Rather than complaining about obvious dilemmas, the question we need to ask ourselves is what we can do to improve the overall situation.

It starts with you. You have to understand your role and how it fits in the bigger picture. You need to know where, when, and how you can make a difference and thus contribute to realigning the project. Assessing the project and finding out it is in trouble is one aspect. Another aspect is to analyze your own role in this puzzle. If this analysis reveals that you, too, caused some of the trouble, you better do something about it. If, on the other hand, there is not much for which you can be blamed, ask how else you can help the project. In the project example described here, I helped fine-tune the project objectives statement, reviewed and corrected the project plan, coached the project office, and established a virtual team room and other communication rules. When you understand the project leadership pyramid principles, you know what it takes to realign and lead a project to success. If you are not the responsible project manager for a project in trouble, you can still apply the project leadership principles for your own role. This applies to all five principles. You want to know what the objectives of your role are and how they fit in with the other roles and activities in the project (principle 1: build vision). The project manager may not nurture collaboration, but this is no excuse for you to remain passive. Establish open communication channels with those you are working with on a daily basis (principle 2: nurture collaboration). Regarding performance, deliver what is expected from you (principle 3: promote performance).

If you are missing required input and cannot deliver, talk with the respective individuals, finding a solution or workaround. If it still does not get worked out, escalate it to the next level in your project. Problems are not bad. They are the first step to finding a solution. The problem is when you identify a problem or risk and do nothing about it. When working within a team, you must use the talents and expertise of the team. The fact that other team members do not practice this is no excuse for you to do the same. In a previous chapter we talked about the value of lessons learned workshops. Recall that there are several ways to share experiences in a group and learn, and thus cultivate learning. Talking with your immediate team members, sharing your concerns and recommendations, shall give you sufficient feedback to proceed. There may not be formal lessons learned workshops initiated by the project manager. But there are so many other possibilities for you to learn from others and at the same time share your own lessons learned. You can create and cultivate a learning environment for yourself (principle 4: cultivate learning).

The fifth principle, ensuring results, applies to you and your role too. When you are involved in a troubled project and are not the project manager responsible for realigning it, you have an extra incentive to ensure your own results, whatever they may be. Now, when you find out that it will be difficult and maybe even impossible to deliver for reasons you cannot control, you have to talk about it. For example, explain it in your status report. It has to be sincere, truthful, and solution and results oriented. Do not just describe the problem. Suggest a solution and explain how you can contribute to it. If necessary, escalate the issues at hand to a higher authority.

Holding back the facts and the recommendations for possible solutions is definitely the worst thing you can do in a situation like this. If you do, you are compromising your own integrity. This is the last resort. You definitely do not want to give up, ever. By the same token, if you are asked to withhold information or, for example, to slant your status report that points out the issues at hand (i.e., if you are asked to compromise your integrity), you have to escalate it. Do not do this behind the back of the project manager. Involve him or her; inviting him or her to join you when you escalate the issue to the next higher person in the hierarchy. If this is not possible, or the escalation does not yield a resolution and there is no solution in sight, you may need to consider turning to the very last resort: leaving the project. Leadership comes with integrity. If you want to practice the project leadership pyramid principles, integrity is the last thing you want to give up.

The project described here did not come to this end. From the perspective of the project leadership pyramid, the project was a complete failure. The sponsor was happy with the result. But, again, the project result is only one factor in assessing the success or failure of a project. It is the whole project, the process that leads to project results, that matters. This was flawed in virtually every aspect imaginable.

It was tough and at times highly frustrating to work and stay on this project. Still, it would have been a mistake to walk away from it. I could still do my job as quality manager. This allowed me to help secure quality standards at a minimum and not the level recommended by best practice. Leaving the role of quality manager would have added even more risks to the project, something I could not account for, especially not as a quality manager. If I had left I would have compromised my own integrity. It would have been a mistake.

In a nutshell, if you are working on a troubled project and you are not in charge of realigning the project, find ways to apply the principles of the project leadership pyramid in your role. Be a role model and make a difference. Show integrity and true leadership.

12.7 Summary

Dealing with projects in trouble is probably one of the most difficult challenges we face as project leaders. No one likes realizing that their project is not aligned and is on a path to failure. It is not possible to plan for all uncertainties and avoid all possible trouble. We can, however, soothe it and take the necessary steps that reduce the chance of falling off the track. What is important for you as project leader is to know what to do when project trouble is imminent. Do not wait till the end. Project success is not defined solely by meeting the project requirements at the end of the project. The path to the end results matters, too. This is why you constantly need to have an eye on the completeness and coherence of the project vision, the effectiveness of ongoing collaboration, adequate levels of performance and productivity, and the culture of learning in your project. This is in addition to securing ongoing results.

When you realize that your project is no longer aligned with one or more of the five leadership principles, you have to act. Blaming someone and finding a scapegoat does not solve the problem. It has nothing to do with effective leadership. The questions you have to answer are what you and your team can do to help realign the project, what you can learn from it, and how you can help prevent this from happening. Identify what causes the problems of your project on the individual and group level using the pyramid assessment guidelines. Then take action.

Make no compromises. If you are dealing with an ailing project, follow a clear-cut strategy of realigning the project; regardless if you choose a top-down or bottom-up approach. This is not the time to make compromises but to act. You, as the project or recovery leader, must follow through, lead the pack, and set the direction. Personally, I believe it is best to involve the project team in realigning the project. However, sometimes the team is the core source of the problem. In this case, follow a top-down approach.

Be aware that compromises almost always yield compromised outcomes and result in mediocrity. Make up your mind what you really want to achieve. Then follow through. For example, if you want to introduce Agile software development into your project as a means to resolve underlying problems, do so, but do not do it halfhearted. As noted by Michele Sliger (2008): "While continuing to grow, the state of Agile adoption seems to be plucked straight out of an Ayn Rand novel, where the acceptance of mediocrity has infected the masses like a plague. Half-hearted adoptions have led to half-hearted results (as in 'we suck less') that in turn are leaving these organizations straddling a tipping point from which they more often than not slide backwards, rather than making the push over the top to high performance and exponential growth in ROI."

Corollary, if you want to leave the path of mediocrity and enter the way to performance and excellence, you have to act. Compromising is not the answer to problems. Leadership requires courage and action, not compromises.

The actions you or the rescue team take to realign the project depend on the specific project situation. The goal is to realign the project with all five principles of the project leadership pyramid. If you are working on a troubled project and you are not the responsible project manager, apply the project leadership pyramid principles in your own immediate environment. Make a difference in your role and thus contribute to stabilizing the troubled project. Project success and project realignment start with you.

If, however, along the way it becomes obvious that your project is beyond repair and doomed to fail no matter what you do, it is your responsibility as project leader to call for termination.

Concluding this chapter, Table 12.2 provides an overview of the proposed activities and exercises and how they relate to the five project leadership pyramid principles.

At the bottom of each column of the five project leadership pyramid principles I list the key activities as they relate to the respective leadership principle. Namely:

- Principle 1. Build vision: Prepare and conduct project realignment workshops with your stakeholders and your team.
- Principle 2. Nurture collaboration: Prepare and conduct project realignment workshops with your stakeholders and your team.
- Principle 3. Promote performance: Prepare and conduct a project realignment workshop with your team.
- Principle 4. Cultivate learning: Prepare and conduct project realignment workshops with your stakeholders and your team.
- Principle 5. Ensure results: Plan activities and exercises to reestablish the project leadership pyramid principles in your daily project life.

Table 12.2 Overview of Activities in Projects in Trouble and How They Relate to the Project Leadership Pyramid Principles

TROUBLED PROJECTS	Vision	Collaboration	Performance	Learning	Results
Project pyramid assessment guidelines	X	X	X	X	X
Realignment workshop with stakeholders	X	X		X	
mutual understanding of expectations	X	X		X	
adjusting SMART project objectives with respect to situation and expectations	X			X	
critical success factors	X	X	X	X	
Realignment workshop with team	X	X	X	X	
1. revisiting the past				X	X
2. assessing the present	X	X	X	X	X
3. building the future	X	X	X	X	X
External project rescue	X	X	X	X	X
assessment	X	X	X	X	X
exercises of initiation phase	X	X	X	X	X

KEY	Project Realignment Workshops	Project Realignment Workshops	Project Realignment Workshop with your team	Project Realignment Workshops	"Exercises to reestablish PLP principles"
exercises of execution phase	x	x	x	x	x
Canceling a project	x			x	x
continue to failure	x			x	x
stop and "close" project	x			x	x
Lonely warrior on troubled project	x	x	x	x	x
assess own role	x	x	x	x	x
apply PLP principles to own role	x	x	x	x	x

Note: PLP = project leadership pyramid.

References

Aiyer, J., Rajkumar, T. M., & Havelka, D. (2005). A staged framework for the recovery and rehabilitation of troubled IS development projects. *Project Management Journal, 36*(4), 32–43.

Bailey, II, R. W. (2000). Six steps to project recovery. *PM Network, 14*(5), 33–38.

Block, T. R. (1998). Project recovery: Short- and long-term solutions. In *Proceedings of the 29th Annual Project Management Institute 1998 Seminars & Symposium.* Long Beach, CA:.Project Management Institute.

Iacocca, L. (2007). *Where Have All The Leaders Gone?* New York: Simon and Schuster, p. 11.

Juli, T. (2008). Realigning project objectives and stakeholders' expectations in a project behind schedule. In *2008 PMI Global Congress Proceedings.* Denver, CO: Project Management Institute. Retrieved from http://www.thomasjuli.com/Realigning_Project_Objectives_by_Thomas_Juli,Ph.D._v1.0.pdf.

Juli, T. (2009a). *It Takes a Team to Realign a Project: Lessons from Rescue Missions.* Orlando, FL: Project Management Institute. Retrieved from http://www.thomasjuli.com/It takes a team to realign a project_ Article_by Thomas Juli, Ph.D..pdf.

Juli, T. (2009b). *Online Survey: Team Involvement in Re-Aligning a Project.* Edingen, Germany. Retrieved from http://www.thomasjuli.com/Team Involvement and Project Re-Alignment - Results of Online Survey - Spring 2009.pdf.

Ludwig, E. (2008). Your project is spiraling out of control. Now what? The road to recovery. *PM Network, 22*(11), 46–53.

Project Management Institute. (2008). *A Guide to the Project Management Body of Knowledge* (4th ed.). Newtown Square, PA: Project Management Institute.

Sliger, M. (2008). Little scrum pigs and the big, bad wolf. *Stickyminds.com Weekly Column.* Retrieved from http://www.stickyminds.com/sitewide.asp?ObjectId=14404&Function=DETAILBROWSE&ObjectType=COL&sqry=*Z(SM)*J(MIXED)*R(relevance)*K(simplesite)*F(sliger)*&sidx=6&sopp=10&sitewide.asp?sid=1&sqry=*Z(SM)*J(MIXED)*R(relevance)*K(simplesite)*F(sliger)*&sidx=6&sopp=10.

Ward, J. L. (2007). Five critical first steps in recovering troubled projects. In *2007 PMI Global Congress Proceedings.* Hong Kong: Project Management Institute.

Chapter 13

Closing a Project

The closing years of life are like the end of a masquerade party when the masks are dropped.

Arthur Schopenhauer (1788–1860),
German philosopher

13.1 Necessary and Sufficient Conditions for Project Success and Closure

The delivery of the required results is the culmination of every project. This is so by definition. For many if not most people this is what project success is all about. When a team wins a championship, say the soccer world cup, who asks about the path to the final and how they played? The bottom line and most important thing to the team is winning this championship. Years of hard work paid off after all. And it is true, if this has been the one and only objective we could call this a project success.

Well, we know better. There is more to a project and project success than the mere end result. In the case of winning the soccer world cup, everyone is happy about the result. But what about the overall project? Was it a success too? Was the way the team managed to win this championship all in all successful? Would it work again the next time? How about the overall project vision? If the answer is yes to every question, indeed, the project can be considered a success.

Previous discussions in this book showed that project success is not merely about results. Take the image of the pyramid once more. It is not the base that makes up the pyramid. It is the combination of each stone forming one unit that makes the pyramid complete. The same applies to a project. A project is not where you can say that the end result justifies the means to get there. This is not what project leadership is about. You have to look at the overall picture and then conclude whether the project was a success or not. A project is a process, with a beginning and an end. If you care only about the end result, you may not even need a project in the first place.

This is why I have stated that delivering results that meet the project objectives and are in sync with the project vision is a necessary condition for success. It is not sufficient though. The sufficient condition for project success is that the remaining principles — collaboration, performance, and learning — are lived by and contribute to the final results. The same conditions apply for closing a project.

13.2 Delivering Results and Making Sure They Arrive at Their Right Destination

Delivering project results is important, of course. Project results must meet the project objectives and be in sync with the project vision. This last part, consistency with the project vision, indicates that project success and project closure are not limited to merely fulfilling the minimum requirements outlined in a scope document. Being in sync with the project vision means that it has to fit in with the overall vision set forth at the beginning of the project. For example, if the project is about the development of a new product that will be further improved in future projects, it would be your responsibility as project leader to ensure a smooth transition to the next project. You may not be accountable for this transition, but it falls into your area of responsibility for pursuing the project vision.

A project is seldom isolated. At the beginning we saw the necessity and the value of understanding the project environment, seeing our own project as part of a whole organism. In closing a project, we are doing the same again. Throughout the project we have to be aware of our changing surroundings. Officially, this may not be in the scope of the project. However, if you neglect your own immediate surroundings, you may be surprised by changes taking place that can have direct or indirect impacts on your project. Keeping the overall project vision in mind accounts for this expanded view of your project world.

Corollary, when you communicate the results of the project, you do not limit the audience to only the project sponsor, your project team, and a number of key stakeholders. The audience varies from project to project. You may also include those who are part of the project vision — those who have a stake in the project vision and who have influenced it in the past one way or the other, are doing it now, or may do so in the near future. This is the audience to whom you want to communicate the results. The ways and means to communicate results are project specific. For example, it may be appropriate to share the information regarding delivery of the results by writing and publishing articles. It depends on the needs of the project. In addition, chances are great that the composition of this group may have changed during the life cycle of your project.

13.3 Conducting and Sharing Sunset Reviews

The information you share is most likely about the project results. Results are obvious. You can see or touch them. They are tangible and are most likely easy to measure. But how do you find out if you have also met the sufficient condition of project success? Simple: You ask your own team. It is the team after all that delivered the results. The team knows best how successfully collaboration, performance, and learning were practiced. One way to gather this feedback is to conduct a sunset review (also known as a postmortem or post-project review). The set-up is similar to that used for a lessons learned workshop. It is best to have a third person facilitating this session, allowing you as the project leader the chance to actively participate. The key questions to ask your team are as follows:

■ What worked out well in our project? Why?
■ What could we have done better and how? Why?

Again, ask people to relate their answers to the five leadership principles of vision, collaboration, performance, learning, and results. If you want to be more specific with these two questions, use the project pyramid assessment guidelines for additional and much more detailed questions.

Sunset reviews are a great exercise. Now that the project is over they oftentimes bring a lot of dark secrets to life. This is normal. During the guided brainstorming session you may be overwhelmed by the amount of feedback received. The question is what are the three most important lessons learned that the team as a whole and each individual can take away from this project. In other words, have the team prioritize the collected lessons learned. Then ask them to share them with others, by presenting them to peers, posting them on wikis, writing articles, you name it. The key is to share these lessons learned and apply them next time around. If you keep a lesson learned to yourself and perhaps even forget, it is useless. The same applies to the sunset review.

Sharing lessons learned is critical to becoming an expert and proving leadership. By sharing your experience you are exposing your findings to the outside world. They may be accepted or challenged. Either way, if you seek feedback from your audience you can learn more about the viability of your lessons than by holding them to yourself. In this sense, sharing lessons learned serves as a sanity and reality check. This is vital if you want to excel in your profession. Phrased differently, you cannot excel in your profession unless you share your knowledge and expertise with a wider audience. It is one thing to know a lot, being an expert on a certain topic or craft. It is another thing to communicate your knowledge to the outside world. When you are able to talk about your expertise and share it with others you open the doors to a unique learning opportunity which, as a consequence, strengthens your expertise even further.

Setting aside 20% of your time for innovation without asking your team members to share their insights leads the whole exercise ad absurdum. It becomes useless. The same applies to project closure. Looking at only one factor out of five (namely, results) is one dimensional and portrays not even half the truth of successful project leadership and leadership principles for project success.

The mandate to share lessons learned is not limited to the core project team. Involve the extended team. It is up to you if you want to invite key stakeholders to the sunset review of the core project team. Unless there were fluid boundaries between the core and extended team, I advise against it. You can involve key stakeholders by holding a separate sunset review and, of course, by meeting with them on a one-on-one basis. This may be your last chance to find out if you managed their expectations successfully. It is not that you are trying to please everyone. You cannot. You should, however, find out if you met the originally communicated, shared, and supported expectations from the vision development workshop, for example. What can they tell you about their perceptions of the project and if it was a success? If neither a joint workshop nor one-on-one meetings is possible, send feedback forms to solicit their feedback. Give yourself the chance to prove that you have fulfilled their expectations and added value to them.

Once more, involve the primary stakeholders and make them feel part of the team. Stakeholder management does not stop with having identified them. It is an ongoing activity and it ends with the official project closure.

13.4 Celebrating and Giving Out Rewards

There is one last element of the sufficient condition of project closure: Celebrate the success with your team. Show your team your appreciation. Give out awards for great performance on the team and individual level. Recognize the achievement of the team. Remember that it was the team delivering the project. Without your team you cannot realize a project.

An easy way to celebrate with your team is to combine the sunset review with a closing team event. For example, the sunset review may be conducted in a location off-site where you celebrate with your team following the sunset review workshop. It is the end of your project journey. You have led a long trip, mastered challenges, and managed unexpected surprises. You helped build vision, nurtured collaboration, promoted performance, cultivated learning, and ensured results. Now relax, celebrate, and enjoy the moment.

Table 13.1 Overview of Project Closure Activities and How They Relate to the Project Leadership Pyramid Principles

CLOSURE	Vision	Collaboration	Performance	Learning	Results
Final project results	X				X
delivering final project results	X				X
communicating results	X				X
Sunset reviews	X	X		X	X
conduct sunset review with team	X	X		X	X
sharing results of sunset reviews	X	X		X	X
feedback rounds with stakeholders	X	X		X	X
1:1 meetings	X	X			
feedback workshops	X	X		X	
Celebrate success		X	X	X	
give out awards/signs of appreciation		X	X		
team closing event		X	X		

KEY	show why and how they fulfill the project vision and objectives	celebrate success	reward performance	sunset reviews	communicate results

13.5 Summary

Project closure is not solely about the delivery of results. It is also an activity where you review the journey to the final stage of delivering project results. You look at each step and how it fits together with all the others, building a whole unit and thus making project success complete.

At the beginning of the book, I compared a project with a journey to a pyramid that we see in the far distance. We want to explore and understand. To get to the bottom of the pyramid we have to understand and live through the other stages and steps on the way. You realized the importance of nurturing collaboration, promoting performance, cultivating learning, and eventually ensuring results. Conducting a sunset review at the end of your project reveals what worked well on the path to the base of the pyramid and what needs to be improved next time around. This final analysis comprises all stages of the journey and includes all leadership principles. It is not the isolated stages that led to project success; it is the combination of them all. By the same token, you have to understand and live the leadership principles as one unit. This is the dynamic project leadership pyramid. The pyramid is not solely for you as project leader. It also serves as a guideline for your team and everyone else involved. Your task and responsibility as leader is to be a role model and empower your team to follow the same principles. It takes a team to deliver a project to success, but it starts with you as the project leader and it closes with you.

Table 13.1 summarizes the activities and exercises mentioned in this chapter and shows how they relate to the five principles of the project leadership pyramid.

Again at the bottom of each column of the project leadership pyramid principles, I list the key activities as they relate to the respective leadership principle. Namely:

- Principle 1. Build vision: Show why and how the project team fulfills the project vision and objectives.
- Principle 2. Nurture collaboration: Celebrate project success with your team.
- Principle 3. Promote performance: Reward individual and team performance.
- Principle 4. Cultivate learning: Conduct and share the results of sunset reviews.
- Principle 5. Ensure results: Communicate project results.

Chapter 14

Summary

Practice, the master of all things.

Augustus Octavius (63 BC–AD 14),
first emperor of the Roman Empire

14.1 Key Exercises of the Project Leadership Pyramid

Let's conclude Part II with a summary of the key activities and exercises proposed in the previous chapters. In Table 14.1, at the bottom of each column of the five project leadership pyramid principles, I list the key activities as they relate to the respective leadership principle. Let's look at them one by one.

14.1.1 Key Exercise of Principle 1 (Building Vision): Vision-Building Workshops

The key exercise of the first principle of the project leadership pyramid is the vision-building workshop described in Chapter 10. The workshop provides an excellent opportunity for you to bring in all key stakeholders and build a common understanding of the vision of the project. Begin by developing the project motivation statement, which describes the purpose of the project. It answers the question of why you want to start your project in the first place. From the project motivation statement you work out the project vision statement. It sets the direction of the project. From this statement you derive the project objectives, requirements, and timeline.

Table 14.1 Key Exercises of the Project Leadership Pyramid Principles

	Vision	Collaboration	Performance	Learning	Results
Project Initiation	Vision-Building Workshop	Team Norming Workshop	Team Norming Workshop	Team Norming Workshop	Scoping
Project Execution	regular interim results to check if project is moving in the right direction	open communication flow	team empowerment	project reviews; secured learning and innovation	regular interim results
Projects in Trouble	Project Realignment Workshops	Project Realignment Workshops	Project Realignment Workshop with your team	Project Realignment Workshops	Exercises to reestablish PLP principles
Project Closure	show why and how they fulfill the project vision and objectives	celebrate success	reward performance	sunset reviews	communicate results
KEY EXERCISES	Vision-Building Workshops	Team Norming Workshops Team-building activities	Team empowerment	Regular project reviews; secured learning and innovation	Regular, interim results

Whether you can actually conduct such a workshop is less important than answering the questions that lead to the motivation and vision statements. As such, the structure of the vision-building workshop is applicable to projects inside and outside of business alike.

14.1.2 Key Exercises of Principle 2 (Nurturing Collaboration): Team Norming Workshops and Team-Building Activities

Similar to the key exercise of the first principle, you may not have the chance to actually conduct a formal workshop with your team. The key is to gather your team around you and agree on the various roles and responsibilities, expectations, and motivations. This is your chance to secure a common understanding of the project vision within your own team. It is absolutely crucial. Because you rely on each other, you want to make sure that you are traveling in the same direction.

Ongoing team-building activities remind us that teamwork does not just happen. It evolves. It takes your initiative as well as that of the complete team. Nurture collaboration on every level possible. It is a critical success factor for teamwork to grow. Remember that you are as strong as your team. The team is the base of your power in a project. Grow this leverage and nourish it. As much as effective project leadership affects project success, it is the team that delivers the project. The team is the heart and soul of the project.

14.1.3 Key Exercise of Principle 3 (Promoting Performance): Team Empowerment

Team performance is no figment of your imagination. You can build and promote it. The best and most effective way to do so is by empowering your team. This is the common denominator of all exercises of the third principle. "Give people the information to act, then look for magic to happen" (Blanchard et al., 1998, p. 77). Build your team, be an active part of your team, contribute to teamwork, and build confidence within your team. Trust your team and let team synergy unfold. Provide your team the opportunity to excel and contribute to project success.

Project success is not limited to the final delivery of the project. Earlier I defined project success as the safe journey from project vision to final project results. Do not lose sight of the final project objectives. At the same time, do not neglect the accomplishments on your way to the final project results. Rewarding performance is not constrained to project closure. Acknowledge individual as well as team accomplishments, as little as they may be, throughout the life of your project. Celebrate them and refresh the joy and passion in your team. You need it to lead the project to success.

14.1.4 *Key Exercise of Principle 4 (Cultivating Learning): Regular Project Reviews and Continuous Learning and Self-Improvement*

If there is one sure thing it is the uncertainty you will have to cope with in more or less every project. You can plan but you cannot forecast the future. Planning without reviewing and adjusting your plans is shortsighted. It ignores reality and is a ticket to project failure. Regular project reviews provide the chance to keep your project on track or realign it if it has gone astray. They are one of the key exercises of the fourth leadership principle.

Continuous learning and self-improvement is not a call for drifting off into academic exercises. They should be solution and results oriented. A solution orientation is one of the foundations of innovation. A results orientation channels energies toward tangible project results. Cultivating learning means that you create an environment of joy of continuous and results-oriented innovation. It is guided and directed learning. It benefits the project purpose and contributes to project success.

14.1.5 *Key Exercise of Principle 5 (Ensuring Results): Regular, Interim Results*

Results are what a lot of people and organizations care most about. This can be a huge constraint. And it can be a good one, too, because "boundaries have the capacity to channel energy in a certain direction" (Blanchard, 1998, p. 41). It is a call for results orientation in our daily project work.

You know that project success is more than the delivery of final project results. At the end of the day you have to deliver. However, it does not restrain you from delivering on an ongoing basis. Therefore, the key exercise of the fifth principle is to deliver results regularly and iteratively. Remember that the fifth principle calls on you to keep the project vision in mind in all your activities and to produce results that benefit the purpose of the project. Ensuring ongoing results builds the base of the pyramid until it is complete. Project success is not defined by a single product or service delivered at the completion of a project. It is the accumulation of the many results yielded from each and every project leadership pyramid principle.

14.2 A Call for Action and Creativity

We are at the end of the second part of the book. This does not mean that we are at the end of animating the project leadership pyramid. It is the beginning. I started this part of the book explaining that the exercises and activities proposed can only be a starting point. They give you an orientation to what is possible.

You may be overwhelmed by the variety of possible situations to which you can apply the principles of the pyramid. Or you may be underwhelmed because this part of the book lists only a few examples. In either case you are right. Every project is different and unique. We cope with endless scenarios as project leaders. You may even call it dealing with chaos. Often this is exactly what we are managing or at least trying to manage: chaos. If you want to lead projects to success in this world, you need a simple, yet powerful structure that gives you a form of guidance and orientation. The five principles of the project leadership pyramid provide this. It is up to you to apply them to the best of your abilities. The structure of the pyramid does not restrain you; the opposite is the case. Best-selling author Stephen Denning (2010) aptly summarizes the meaning of structure:

> The living part of the organization thus coexists with the structures because they enable creativity. We see examples of this phenomenon everywhere. In nature, we see the fantastic diversity generated by a few basic structural elements: no more than a hundred varieties of atoms and a couple of primary colors lead to a universe of infinite beauty and diversity. In the 12 notes of the musical scale, in the 26 letters of our alphabet, we see how these rigid structures have enabled the creativity of music and literature. Without structure, there is nothing for creativity to build on.

The good news is that the leadership principles for project success described in this book provide this structure. Now it is your turn to use this structure and apply the five principles of the project leadership pyramid. Project success starts with project leadership. It starts with you. Be creative in your approach, involve and empower your team, and let magic happen.

References

Blanchard, K. H., Carlos, J. P., & Randolph, A. (1998). *Empowerment Takes More Than a Minute*. San Francisco: Berret-Koehler Publishers.

Denning, S. (2010). *The Leader's Guide to Radical Management: Re-Inventing the Workplace for the 21st Century* (to be published: 10/24/10). San Francisco: Jossey-Bass. p. 217.

THE PERSONAL
LEADERSHIP
PYRAMID

Chapter 15

How to Become an Effective Project Leader

Leaders are neither born nor made — meaning environmentally trained and nurtured. They are self-made through chosen responses, and if they choose based on principles and develop increasingly greater discipline, their freedom to choose increases.

Stephen Covey (1932–),
U.S. author and speaker

15.1 Leadership Perspectives

The principles of the project leadership pyramid are general principles of leadership. They are not limited to the world of projects. You can apply them in any situation that calls for leadership. They are common sense. Hence, they are applicable to a wide array of situations.

The principles are not project role specific. In other words, their application is not limited to the role of project manager. On a given project you may be working as the central project manager, as a subproject manager in a large program, or as a team lead. You could be a team member or someone looking at a project that is affecting your daily work. There are many project roles with different levels of influence on project success. Still, whenever we are talking about influencing project success, we are also talking about the project leadership pyramid principles. This means regardless of your role in a project, by following and practicing the principles, you can contribute to project success and become an effective leader in your role.

This chapter summarizes how you can apply the principles and become an effective leader. We will look at various perspectives often found in project situations. First, the top-down perspective is where you serve as either the project manager or project sponsor and have the greatest control over the project. The second perspective is probably most common in projects. This is when you are assigned to the role of project manager by someone above you in the organizational ranking. Last but not least, we will look at a situation where you are filling any role but that of the project manager. Let's look at the various perspectives one by one and see how you can become an effective leader by applying the project leadership pyramid principles.

15.2 Top-Down Leadership

It is tempting to say that this is the easiest role in a project to have. You are sitting at the very top of the project. You define the direction, set up the project, give out the requirements, and form the team. Alternatively, you may be the sponsor of an initiative leading to a project. As the official sponsor and main leader of the project, you have the greatest power over the project. You can start and stop the project any time you like. This is called a top-down leadership position.

The high and influential position itself does not guarantee project success. The project leadership pyramid principles hold true and need to be applied. You are the one who is probably most interested in project success. In such a situation it is first and foremost important to set the direction of the project. You have to build vision. It is not that you merely define the project objectives; this can be so. What is more important is that you describe the bigger picture of the project. For example, you do not define a project of "laying bricks" or "build a wall"; you tell your team that your project is "part of building a cathedral." Remember, a project vision goes beyond the boundaries of strict project objectives. It sets the tone of the overall project environment. It is the very top of the project pyramid that you see first from the distance, on the journey to project success. For example, it is not about founding a preschool; it is about developing a reliable childcare organization for families in your community. It is not about integrating a new call center software application; it is about providing good customer service and setting a new standard in service excellence. The vision drives the project. Everything else is derived from it. The vision addresses the utmost desires and needs at the same time. This is what you want your team to be passionate about. This is what creates enthusiasm in your team. Hence, building vision comes first.

Second, you need to understand that team, performance, and learning go hand in hand and are Prerequisites for project success. Let's look at each of these elements once more and start with the heart of a project: the team. It is not about you as the project leader alone. By now you know that a project leader without a team is worth nothing. If you want your project to succeed you have to build, norm, and empower a team. You have to form it and create an environment where it can prosper. You inspire your team with the vision. You involve your team in specifying the project objectives and requirements. The work atmosphere is such that the team can prosper and quickly move to a true performance stage. This is when both individual and team performance is practiced every day. You cover your team's back and the team covers yours. This is where you want to move your team, because this is where team synergy effects take place. It is the vehicle that carries your team closer to project success.

The project culture you create for your team and its environment is crucial. Culture can turn out to be *the* critical success factor. If the project culture is ailing, you can have the best project strategy and it is not going to fly. Project culture is important. Invest enough time to create a solid and powerful culture. This is a culture where everyone on your team believes in the project vision. Everyone understands and believes in the project objectives and its requirements. Why? Because the complete team helped specify them. Collaboration is not just a term on a piece of paper. The team actively works together. It is not about individual performance alone. It is the sum of all individuals performing together which forms a whole. It is team synergy and team performance. This is the culture you want to create. Team performance means that team members do not work alone and isolated. They work together and they help each other. They know they can succeed only together as a team. The team reflects on its performance regularly, seeking ways and means to improve. It is open for feedback from the outside, knowing that it helps improve work and performance. One way to solicit feedback is to deliver interim results on a regular and iterative basis. The team provides feedback and generates a sense of accomplishment. Everyone on the team knows what it means to deliver on time. It is fun to deliver.

You also know that in order to deliver project results you and your team will make mistakes along the way. This is normal and inevitable. Knowing this, it is your responsibility to set the expectation that it is okay to make mistakes. They are necessary to learn and can be beneficial if we learn from them. Not a single team member should be afraid of making mistakes. Make sure everyone on your team contributes to the purpose of the project. Do not micromanage them to do so. Empower them. In most cases they know better than you how to get there. Micromanagement blocks the free flow of learning. Do not fall into that trap. Instead, encourage your team to find new ideas and ways of doing things. Let the team unravel the power of innovation and utilize it for the benefit of the project. Plan sufficient time for innovation. A previous chapter included the example of Google reserving 20% of the work week for innovative activities. It could be argued whether 20% should mandatory; 10% may be sufficient for your project. No matter what amount of time you allot for innovation, do it because it pays off. It can help carry your project to new levels and thus make it a true success.

In a nutshell, when you are in the position of leading your project from the top down, it is most important to build the right vision. Set the direction of the project. Build a culture of active and open collaboration, performance, and learning, and empower your team to achieve its mission.

15.3 Bottom-Up Leadership

The second perspective is probably one of the most common situations in the project world. Someone assigns you to the role of project manager. Now it is up to you to move from the project manager to true project leadership. Remember the difference between managing a project and leading a project to success. Leaders act, managers react. This is your chance to prove your leadership skills. Following the principles of the project leadership pyramid will help you achieve this.

Alone you cannot achieve it. When you are in a position with limited influence, your team becomes even more important. The team is the most important base of power you have as a project manager. Build it and use it, not for you but for the sake of the project. First and foremost you have to build a performing team. Do whatever you can to achieve this. It is not about leading a team. It is about empowering your team to do its job and excel.

One of the first things you and your team need to do in a joint effort is specify the project objectives and requirements. If they have been predetermined by others, make sure you and your team have the same understanding of them. This relates to the overall vision, the project objectives, requirements, and critical success factors. Clarify the direction and the scope of the project in case there is any chance of misunderstandings. This is not limited to your core team. Identify the key people and organizations influencing your project. Work with them and ensure that they too have the same understanding of the direction and the scope of the project. Analyze the needs of your stakeholders and how they relate to your project and your daily work. Work with and for the stakeholders as far as it benefits your project. Be clear about your purpose. Let them take part in project success. You should not need to conceal information from them. Open communication is a key success factor in achieving effective collaboration throughout the project. One of the best ways to secure the support of your stakeholders is to deliver results that add value to them. Show them how your work contributes to their benefit. There will come a time when you will need their help and support. It will be much easier to receive it if you have given them something in return *before* it is their time to deliver.

In short, the road to effective project leadership is through your team. The team is the foundation of power of every effective leader. Form it and build it and empower it to perform. Ensure a common project vision within your team. Extend the support of your own team to the key stakeholders of the project. Involve them in your project to the benefit of the project.

15.4 The Lonely Warrior Leadership

The third situation may at first sight seem like the most difficult starting point to becoming an effective leader. You understand the principles of the project leadership pyramid, but you are not the assigned project manager. For example, you are an external consultant. Alas, this situation can be quite helpful in developing leadership characteristics and thus you becoming an effective leader in your role. The bottom line is that the principles of the project leadership pyramid still hold true. Following them is the best way to do your part in contributing to project success.

The first step is to use the project leadership pyramid assessment guide to obtain a better understanding of the project in general and your specific role in particular. The second step is to practice the principles of the project leadership pyramid as they relate to your role.

Let's turn to the first step and start looking at the vision of the project. Even though you may not be the responsible project manager, you have to know what the project vision is and how the project fits into the overall vision. A step further down, you want to learn about the project objectives, requirements, and known critical success factors. If you find out that neither the vision nor the objectives or requirements are defined, this helps you gain a better understanding of the environment you are about to enter. Once you have a better understanding of the project environment, take a closer look at your own role and see how it fits in.

What is the scope of your role? What do you have to deliver? What do you need to do so? In addition, you need to know why and to what extent your role is important to project success. What were the initial expectations in setting up and filling this role? Have these expectations changed in the meantime? Next, think about how your role fits in with the other roles. With whom are you working? Whom do you need to do your job? What do others need from you to do their jobs, and when? In return, what do you need from them to fulfill your role and the team's expectations?

Answering these questions gives you a better idea of the scope of your own role. At the same time it helps you understand the culture of the project and the overall environment in which you are working. This is very important because culture affects daily project work a great deal. For example, you may find out that the organization in which you are working is not used to running projects. Maybe no one expects projects to be finished on time and within budget. Or you find out that project information is generally not shared across project boundaries and that you are not allowed to speak to anyone outside the core project team without first asking the project manager for permission. Review Chapter 11, where we described a number of challenges to the principles of the project leadership pyramid and how to cope with them. In addition, Chapter 12 included a case study of a lonely warrior in a project where the project manager violated virtually every leadership principle.

With respect to the third principle of the project leadership pyramid, promoting performance, it boils down to your own expected performance. You may not be responsible for the overall success of the project, but you are responsible for your own deliverables. You want to make a difference in your role and thus contribute to the success of the project. This is not a call for solely focusing on your own performance without looking left or right. You know that active collaboration cherishes team performance. If you can contribute to the development of team performance, do so. This is in your own interest and in the interest of the project. It is an investment on your part and will be most likely paid back to you. It will improve your own performance which in turn can have ripple effects on team performance and thus project success.

The fourth principle, cultivating learning, ought to be practiced by the project leader as well as everybody else on the project. This includes you. Even if nothing comes close to an active learning environment for the team (e.g., there is no open feedback culture or the project manager blocks the exchange of lessons learned), there are always learning opportunities for you. Solicit feedback about your deliverables. Find new ways of delivering. Ask others about their feedback. See how you can improve the quality of your own deliverables. Maybe there are other and better ways to do your job. If you are working on a project where the project manager blocks official lessons learned workshops, there is no law that prohibits you from exchanging your own lessons with other colleagues in an informal matter. Remember that you are not the person calling the shots in the project. You have to fill your own role and stick to it. Be a team player and show leadership in your own role.

The final principle of ensuring results is a call for your own action. You need to know what results are expected from you and the rest of the team, when and how. This affects your own activities in the most direct way. Are you expected to deliver by yourself? Or are your deliverables input to somebody else's?

The project leadership pyramid assessment guide helps you gain a quick understanding of the project and where it is headed. You can also apply it to understand your own role better. This is the first step. The second step is to apply the project leadership pyramid principles by yourself. In other words, you translate the principles to the needs of your own role. To a certain extent you may describe your role as a project you want to master and lead to success. Starting with vision, you have to make sure you know what is expected from you. You have taken care of this during the assessment. What you may not have done yet is ensure that other members of the team understand this, too. In other words, you want to make sure that everyone involved in your job knows what your role is and how you contribute to the bigger picture/project. With respect to collaboration, seek out working with and for others as it relates to your job and contributes to the project. Ensure that you live up to the expectations of your role. Seek feedback from others and ensure results.

Perceiving and living your own role as a project in itself is not contradictory to the call for collaboration as long as it is consistent with the overall direction of the project. You are delivering your own project, fulfilling your own role, and thus contributing to the success of the overall project. The key is to understand how your role fits in with the greater unit of the project and how you can actively and constructively contribute to project success. Thus the project leadership pyramid principles serve as a guideline to project success on the level of project leader as well as on the level of every individual role. This works as long as the principles are practiced in a way that complements each other. If this is not the case, it may lead to undesirable results. The overall project vision defines the overall direction of the project and hence every role. Yours is no exception.

15.5 Follow the Principles of the Project Leadership Pyramid

A project is like a journey. At the end we want to see results. However, it is not the results alone that constitute the success of the project. It is the process leading to the results that matters. This process is the actual project. In Chapter 8, I defined project success as the safe journey from project vision to final project results. The project leadership pyramid helps secure a safe and successful project journey that ultimately delivers what has been described in the project vision. Hence, you cannot limit your idea of project success to the mere results. You must look at the whole project life cycle, starting with the vision and objectives of the project. They set the direction of the project. To get to the results we have to look at how we get there. This is when the team comes in. Collaboration, performance, as well as learning matter. The combination of all five principles constitutes the core of project success.

I have introduced the image of a pyramid and the description of a long journey to project results. Initially, you may have no idea which way to go. The top of the pyramid can serve as a guide. In the project world, this is the vision. The closer you get to the pyramid the better idea you have of the size of the pyramid and what it is made of.

The project leadership pyramid principles are not limited in their application to the role of project manager. You can apply them in any project role. Every principle is important. If you have the luxury of leading a project from the top down, make sure that you clarify the vision of the project and build a culture of open collaboration. Empower your team to perform and deliver results. When you come from the bottom up, for example, having been assigned as a project manager without much leverage from the top down, it is crucial that you build a strong team. This team is your foundation of influence on project success. Last but not least, if you are not a project manager, but simply working on a project as a team member, apply the project leadership pyramid principles in your own role. Fulfilling your own role thus contributes to the success of the overall project.

The project leadership pyramid principles serve as a guideline to effective leadership and how it contributes to project success. Following and practicing them is no guarantee for project success, but they make it more likely. They address the core of project success and thus improve the chances for success significantly. Understanding the principles can be the first step toward project success. Modify the principles to the needs of your project. Practice the principles in real life; fill them with content. This book has provided numerous examples of how to do so. Finally, know that the principles are not carved in stone. They serve as an orientation. No more, no less. Develop them further and fine-tune them. Share your experiences with your own team and the greater community.

The project leadership pyramid gives you a powerful tool to lead your project to success. We know that as project leaders, we cannot succeed by ourselves. We need the help and support of our teams. It is a joint effort. This is why it is important to build teams and empower them to perform and deliver. We are nothing without our teams. Yet, we have to take the first step of building our teams. It still starts with you taking the first step. It starts and ends with project leadership. It is up to you to take this step and lead your team to project success. I wish you a happy and prosperous journey.

References

Covey, S. R. (2004). *The 8th Habit: From Effectiveness to Greatness.* New York: Free Press p. 62.

APPENDICES

The appendices provide a number of the project templates that have been mentioned in the book. I hope that you will find them useful in your own projects. These templates are by no means complete. They are simply meant to give you an idea of what is possible. All are in sync with the leadership principles described in this book. All of them have been proven to work. Still, because every project is different and unique, modify and improve them to suit your specific needs.

In addition to these appendices, you are invited to visit the Website www.TheProjectLeadershipPyramid.net, where you can download the templates after registration and entering the code L8P2f4Px. The Website also includes valuable references to other resources and organizations you may find useful on your journey to project leadership and project success.

Appendix A: The Project Vision Document

A.1 Introduction

A.1.1 Purpose of the Project Vision Document

The purpose of this document is to collect, analyze, and define high-level requirements and aspects of ... *[Project Name]*. It focuses on key requirements and aspects of the strategy, which come from the top needs of the customers and key stakeholders. These will form the basis for the more detailed requirements described in ... *[e.g., the scope matrix and/or corresponding document and/or presentation]*.

A.1.2 Definitions, Acronyms, and Abbreviations

[Provide the definitions of all terms, acronyms, and abbreviations required to properly interpret the project vision document. This information may be provided by reference to a project glossary.]
...

A.1.3 References

[Provide a complete list of all documents referenced elsewhere in the project vision document.]
...

A.2 Solution Overview

A.2.1 Project Motivation Statement

[Provide a statement summarizing the motivation of the project. This can be a problem that needs to be solved or something you want to create or develop. In the first case,

you can use the following format:

1. *What are the top issues or risks the project is dealing with? Why have they emerged?*
2. *Who (individuals, groups, organizational units, etc.) is affected by these issues or risks and how? Why?*
3. *What are the impacts of these issues or risks on them?*

Summarize the answers to the questions above in one or two statements. A format may look like the following:]

The **issue(s)** *of ... [describe the issue(s)]*
affect(s) *... [the stakeholders affected by the problem, if applicable].*
The **impact(s)** *of which is (are) ... [what is (are) the impact(s) of the problem(s)].*

[If your project is to create something new, answer the following questions:

1. *What are the top solutions or opportunities you envision? Why?*
2. *Who is interested in these solutions or opportunities; who benefits from them? Why?*
3. *What are the effects of the solutions or opportunities? Why?*

Phrase the statements as follows:]

The **solution(s)** *or* **opportunity(ies)** *of ... [describe the solution(s) or opportunity(ies)]*
interest(s) *... [the stakeholders interested in the solution(s) or opportunity(ies), if applicable].*
The **effect(s)** *of which is (are) ... [what is (are) the effect(s) of the solution(s) or opportunity(ies)].*

A.2.2 Project Vision Statement

[Once you have written the project motivation statement, phrase a project vision statement by answering the questions below. If the project aims to resolve a problem, the questions are:

1. *What needs to be done to resolve the situation? Why?*
2. *What benefits can we expect from the improved situation? Why?*
3. *What do we need to do to achieve this? Why?*

If you want to create, develop, or build something new, the questions are:

1. *What needs to be done to bring about the new situation caused by the solutions or opportunities? Why?*
2. *What disadvantages will the solution have or bring with it? Why?*
3. *What do we need to do to overcome these disadvantages and obstacles? Why?*

Summarize the answers in a project vision statement. The following format serves as an example:]

> The **successful project** will (help) … *[describe the solution(s) or opportunity(ies)].*
> It will **benefit** … *[list the key benefits of a successful project outcome].*
> In order to achieve the solution we have to … *[list the* **critical success factors** *of the project].*

A.2.3 Product or Solution Perspective

[This subsection of the project vision document should put the product or solution in perspective with regard to other related products or solutions and the user's environment. If the product or solution is independent and totally self-contained, state it here. If the product or solution is a component of a larger system, then this subsection should relate how these systems interact and should identify the relevant interfaces between the systems.

You may describe the product or solution perspective in words, tables, or diagrams.]
…

A.2.4 Product or Solution Position Statement

[A product or solution position statement communicates the intent of the solution and the importance of the project to everyone involved in the project plus the customer of the project. Provide an overall statement summarizing, at the highest level, the unique value position of the product. The product or solution position statement serves as an elevator pitch of the final product or solution. Possible format:]

> For … *[target customer],*
> who … *[statement of the need or opportunity].*
> The … *[product/solution name] is a …* *[product category].*
> This … *[statement of key benefit(s) that is a compelling reason to buy or use the product or solution].*
> Our product or solution … *[statement of primary differentiation].*

A.2.5 SMART Project Objectives

[List the commonly agreed upon objectives of the project here. Make sure the objectives meet the SMART criteria; i.e., they have to be

> **S — Specific**, *i.e., the goals are clearly defined*
> **M — Measurable**, *i.e., the objectives and the results are measured quantitatively or at least can be evaluated qualitatively*

A — Achievable, *i.e., humanly possible, and the project has all the required resources*

R — Relevant, *i.e., avoid the temptation of defining a goal just because it fits nicely to the previous three criteria*

T — Time-boxed, *i.e., the objectives must be achieved by (a) certain deadline(s)*

Note: At the very beginning of a project the SMART objectives are often at a high level. For example, you may know that you need to achieve improved operational efficiency. However, you may not know the areas on which changes will be focused. As the project progresses you will get a better idea of the project requirements and henceforth can qualify the project objectives statement accordingly. If you do, don't forget to communicate any changes with the key stakeholders and ensure their endorsement of the qualified project objectives statement.]

…

A.2.6 Key Features and Benefits

[Summarize the expected key features and benefits the solution will provide.]

…

A.2.7 Assumptions, Dependencies, and Constraints

[List any underlying assumptions, dependencies, and constraints the project team needs to be aware of and account for.]

…

Table A.1 Key Stakeholders

ID	Stakeholder Group	Role	Key Individuals	Group Needs	Group Objections or Concerns
	[Name the stakeholder group/type]	[Briefly describe the role (e.g., providing requirements, testing, reviewing) they are playing in the project]	[Name the key individuals of the stakeholder group]	[If groups have a particular point of view, then it may be worth storing it here]	

A.3 Project Environment Description

A.3.1 Stakeholder Profiles

[Briefly describe the stakeholders of the project's internal and external environment including the customer of the project.] (see Table A.1)
…

A.3.2 Customer and End-User Environment

[Describe the customer and end-user environment. For example, if the project objective is to integrate new call center software, describe the work environment of the present call center agent, such as applications and platforms in use, external interfaces the solution (system) will integrate with, etc.]

Appendix B: Scope Matrix

B.1 The Scope Matrix

The scope matrix is a table that lists all requirements the project team must deliver as part of the project. It helps categorize and prioritize the requirements in a systematic manner. It breaks down and describes all project requirements to an appropriate level of detail. Although this level of detail depends on the needs of your project, the approach taken from extreme programming can be very handy. It suggests that you assess whether a functional requirement is well formed using the "INVEST" acronym:[1]

Independent — Requirements should be independent of each other as much as possible.

Negotiable — Requirements are negotiable in the sense that they do not describe every little detail but leave room for creativity in their design and implementation.

Valuable — Requirements have to add actual value to the customer(s).

Estimatable — Requirements should be broken down to a level where you and your team can estimate the effort to specify and implement or realize them.

Small — Requirements must be small enough to be specified, implemented, or realized with moderate effort. Requirements that are too broad leave too much room for errors and misunderstandings.

Testable — Requirements need to be testable, so that you can determine whether they have been implemented or delivered.

Table B.1 provides a sample scope matrix. The order of the columns varies with the needs of your project. In any case, the column headings mean the following:

- *Item #*: Maintain a unique numbering scheme for all project requirements. It can be helpful to freeze this column once the scope is defined and officially closed.

---

[1] Extreme programming actually does not speak of functional requirements but "user stories" (Wake, 2001). "A user story describes desired functionality from the customer or user perspective. A good user story describes who wants it, and how and why the functionality will be used" (Gadodia, 2010). For a good introduction to user stories, see Cohn (2004).

Table B.1 Scope Matrix

Item #	Project Requirements	Customer Value	Technical Complexity	Effort Estimate	Phase	Owner	Description	Supporting Documentation or Bounding Assumptions	Required By	Contact Person	Source	Status
1	**Deliverables Group 1**											
1.1	\<List deliverables and committed activities related to Deliverables Group 1\>											
1.1.1	…											
1.1.1.1	…											
1.1.1.1.1	…											
1.1.1.1.1.1	…											
2	**Deliverables Group 2**											
2.1	\<List deliverables and committed activities related to Deliverables Group 2\>											

2.1.1	...						
2.1.2	...						
#	**Deliverables Group #**						
#.1	\<List deliverables and committed activities related to Deliverables Group #\>						
#	...						
#.1	...						
#	**Non-functional requirements**						
#.1	...						

- *Project requirements*: Capture a concise description of the requirement.
- *Customer value*: Indicate the customer value of this item. For example, you can use the parameters "high," "medium," and "low." Define the meanings of the various parameters with your project team to secure consistency and coherence of the requirements evaluation. An alternative approach is to follow the MoSCoW rule proposed by the Dynamic Systems Development Method (DSDM) (VersionOne, 2010). The M stands for "must have requirements," the S for "should have if at all possible," the C for "could have but not critical," and the W for "won't have this time but would like in the future"
- *Technical complexity*: Indicate the technical complexity to realize this item. Possible parameters may be "high," "medium," and "low." Define the meanings of the various parameters with your project team to secure consistency and coherence of the requirements evaluation.
- *Effort estimate*: Use this column to enter any effort estimates you and your team have come up with for the respective item.
- *Phase*: Identify the phase in which this item will be delivered. The phase could be part of the running project or may refer to a future project.
- *Owner*: Identify the high-level entity responsible for the respective requirement.
- *Description*: Enter a more detailed description of this item (as needed).
- *Supporting documentation or bounding assumptions*: Capture a reference to the detailed specifications for this item. Include specific document name and chapter or section reference.
- *Required by*: Create dependencies between line items, so that you can identify potential problems when you want to delete or scope out an item. Enter in this column the IDs of all items that depend on this. Do this later in the process so that line numbers will be moderately stable.
- *Contact person*: Optional column to track the person driving the definition of this item.
- *Source:* Optional column to indicate the source of this scope item in the event that discussions arise.
- *Status:* Optional column to use for any "working status" regarding this item.

Note that the scope document also includes nonfunctional requirements. Although they are often technical in nature, it is crucial to capture them early in the process. Examples of nonfunctional requirements include performance, availability, capacity, security, fault tolerance, scalability, maintainability, modularity, reliability, reusability, usability, etc. Nonfunctional requirements constrain the functional requirements and thus must not be neglected.

B.2 Auxiliary Tables

Table B.1 is the heart of the scope matrix. However, it is not complete. In addition to the list of project requirements, the following tables are part of the scope matrix file:

1. Project overview
2. General assumptions
3. Change log

Let's look at each one individually.

B.2.1 The Project Overview

The project overview table (Table B.2) provides an overview of the key parameters of the project. The project overview is a snapshot of the project. Complete this sheet to allow readers to have a basic context about the project before reading the scope matrix. This sheet can also facilitate mining this information once the project has been completed. Make sure every member of the project team is familiar with the content of this table.

Table B.2   Project Overview

Project [Name] Overview	
Department/Project Name	...
Project ID	...
Project stage	...
Other related documents	...
Timeframe	...
Project / Program Manager	...
Vision *[taken from Project Vision Document]*	
Project Motivation Statement	...
Project Vision Statement	...
Product or Solution Position Statement	...
SMART Project Objectives	...
Key Features & Benefits	...
Future Enhancements	...
Last Modified Date	[Date]
Scope Owner	NN

Table B.3   General Assumptions

General Assumptions, Prerequisites, Decisions
Last updated on [enter date]

ID	Area	Prerequisites, Assumptions, and Decisions	Initiator	Mitigation/ Action Item	Owner	Decision Date	Status	Supporting Documentation
1							open	\<Reference any documentation that supports this assumption\>
2							in progress	
3							approved/ accepted	
...								

Table B.4   Change Log

[Project Name] | Scope Change Log
Use this table to make changes to the scope of the Scope Matrix

Date	Scope Line Item	Change Request ID (if a scope change)	Who Made This Change	Nature of Change	Original Description	New Description	Status/ Comments

B.2.2 General Assumptions, Prerequisites, Decisions

Use Table B.3 to list all general assumptions, prerequisites, decisions, and known constraints that are not specific to a project requirement or deliverable listed in the actual scope matrix.

B.3 Change Log

You may want to know all project requirements at the beginning of the project. Alas, in most cases this is unrealistic. By the same token, it is rather unlikely that all requirements will be stable over time. Thus, it is important that you keep track of any changes to your requirements. The sample change log presented in Table B.4 can help you do so. The columns have the following meanings:

- *Date*: Enter the date the change is made.
- *Scope line item*: Refer to the line item number of the project requirement that is undergoing a change.
- *Change request ID*: Capture the exact ID of the change request. If the entry log is simply a clarification, leave this cell blank.
- *Who made this change*: Enter the name of the person making this change.
- *Nature of change*: Explain the nature of the change. Possible entries include "added," "updated," or "deleted."
- *Original description*: Capture the original description or other cell changed, or enter "N/A" if not relevant.
- *New description*: Enter the new description, or "N/A" if irrelevant.
- *Status/comment*: Enter additional information about the status of the change (e.g., "open," "under discussion," "approved," "implemented," etc.) or any other comment about the change.

References

Cohn, M. (2004). *User Stories Applied: For Agile Software Development*. Amsterdam: Addison-Wesley Longman.

Gadodia, V. (2010). *Six Features of a Good User Story — INVEST Model*. Retrieved from http://agilesoftwaredevelopment.com/blog/vaibhav/good-user-story-invest.

VersionOne. (2010). *Dynamic Systems Development Method (DSDM)*. Retrieved from http://www.versionone.com/Resources/AgileMethodologies.asp#DSDM.

Wake, W. C. (2001). *Extreme Programming Explored*. Indianapolis, IN: Addison-Wesley Professional.

Appendix C: Sample Scope Phase 2-Week Plan

Scoping can be time consuming. If done right, however, it helps save you and your team a lot of time. This is one reason it is so crucial to do it correctly at the beginning of the project. Scoping is not limited to the initiation phase of a project. The longer a project runs, the more likely the scope will change over time. This does not mean that the scoping phase lasts forever. You and a performing team can conduct a scoping phase within 1 to 4 weeks. This may be ambitious for some projects, but possible.

Let's look at the following 2-week plan of a project I managed. The objective of the project was to integrate a new software application for the call center of an online bank. The project was moderate in size. It lasted 15½ weeks, with a core project team of eight full-time plus two part-time external consultants and one full-time and four part-time individuals on the client side. We started the project with a 2-week scope phase. Tables C.1 and C.2 list the most important sessions conducted. The colors of the cells indicate the participants of the various sessions.

We started the first day with a core project-internal team norming. At that time, the high-level scope of these 2 weeks was already known. The team norming focused less on the business and technical requirements of the client. Those were analyzed in subsequent sessions with the client. The team norming covered the roles and responsibilities, team and individual expectations and motivations, as well as communication rules for the 2 weeks. In the afternoon kickoff session with the client we introduced the schedule and methodology we would follow during the next days.

Starting with the second day, the core project team conducted daily stand-up meetings of 15 minutes each. We covered our accomplishments of the previous day, the daily plan, as well as any impediments. The morning of the second day was filled with a vision-building workshop with the complete project team. It laid the foundation for all subsequent sessions in which we evaluated

Table C.1 Week 1 of Sample Scope Schedule

	Day 1	Day 2	Day 3	Day 4	Day 5
8:30		Daily Team Stand-Up*	Daily Team Stand-Up*	Daily Team* Stand-Up	Daily Team Stand-Up*
8:45					
9:00					
9:15					Finetuning of data model requirements***
9:30					
9:45			Team sync & documentation of interim results*		
10:00					Further evaluation of functional and non-functional requirements. Consolidation with Scope Matrix*
10:15					
10:30					
10:45		Vision Building Workshop*		Creation of initial Scope Matrix*	
11:00			Evaluation of existing and target business processes III**		
11:15	Team Norming* (Core Project Team)				
11:30					
11:45					
12:00					
12:15					
12:30	Lunch	Lunch	Lunch	Lunch	Lunch
12:45					
13:00					
13:15					

Time			
13:30	Evaluation of existing and target business processes I**	Analysis of existing IT architecture, data models, interfaces***	Evaluation of existing and target business processes I**
13:45			
14:00			
14:15			Evaluation of target IT architecture, data models, interfaces II**
14:30			
14:45			
15:00			
15:15	Evaluation of existing and target business processes II*	Evaluation of target IT architecture, data models, interfaces I***	
15:30			Team sync & documentation of interim results (core project team)*
15:45			
16:00	Scope Kickoff:* - Introduction of project team - Overview of weekly plan - Critical success factors - Risks - Ground rules	Team sync & documentation of interim results (core project team)*	
16:15			
16:30			
16:45			
17:00			
17:15			
17:30			
17:45			
18:00	Team Dinner		

Presentation and discussion of initial scope matrix*

Interview with project sponsor about initial results and next steps

Evaluation of data model requirements***

Team sync & documentation of interim results (core project team)*

Update of scope matrix*

Team sync & weekly wrap-up (core project team)*

Evaluation of technical options*

Legend: *Sessions of and by Core Project Team; **Sessions of and by Business Team; ***Sessions of and by IT Team; *Sessions of and by Complete Team

Table C.2 Week 2 of Sample Scope Schedule

	Day 6	Day 7	Day 8	Day 9	Day 10
8:30					
8:45					
9:00	Daily Team Stand-Up*	Daily Team Stand-Up*	Daily Team Stand-Up*	Daily Team Stand-Up*	Daily Team Stand-Up*
9:15					
9:30		Assessment of Scope Matrix. Prioritization of Scope Matrix (business value)*	Final prioritization of Scope Matrix*	Consolidation of all results*	
9:45					
10:00					
10:15	Update of Scope Matrix. Weekly plan. Documentation of interim results*				Final presentation of project phase results. Delivery of Scope Document*
10:30					
10:45					
11:00					
11:15		Prioritization of Scope Matrix (organizational readiness)*	Guidelines for software development and technical documentation requirements***		
11:30					
11:45					
12:00					
12:15					

Time					
12:30	Lunch	Lunch	Lunch	Lunch	Lunch
12:45					
13:00					
13:15					
13:30	Further evaluation of functional and nonfunctional requirements. Consolidation with scope matrix(*)	Prioritization of scope matrix cont'd. Planning of scope of project phases/sprints(*)	Review of documentation Clarification of any open issues Assumptions for next project phase/sprint*	Preparation of final presentation of project phase results Final documentation Planning of next project phase/sprint Team sync*	Next steps (meeting with project sponsor)(*)
13:45					
14:00					
14:15					
14:30					
14:45					
15:00	Technical evaluation of scope matrix. Final assessment of target IT architecture and data requirements***				
15:15					
15:30					
15:45					
16:00					
16:15					

(continued)

Table C.2 Week 2 of Sample Scope Schedule (Continued)

	Day 6	Day 7	Day 8	Day 9	Day 10
16:30					
16:45					
17:00	Team sync & documentation of interim results. Technical estimation*	Team sync & documentation of interim results*	Team sync & documentation of interim results*		
17:15					
17:30					
17:45					
18:00					

Legend: *Sessions of and by Core Project Team; **Sessions of and by Business Team; ***Sessions of and by IT Team; (*)Sessions of and by Complete Team business and technical requirements and designed a solution. Whenever possible, we built focus groups. This allowed us to work in parallel work groups and gather the material for the solution design faster. At the end of each day we documented our interim findings and results. At the end of the second day the complete project team went out for dinner together. This social event helped foster team unity.

On the fourth day we started consolidating the project requirements in a scope matrix. From then on it was updated on a daily basis. It formed the foundation for estimating the specification and implementation effort in the second week. The scope matrix was prioritized with the client on days 7 and 8. Those requirements that had to be implemented in the first release of the new call center application were included in the final estimation and planning exercises, which resulted in a project plan for the design and specification project phase that followed the first 2 weeks.

The key ingredients for a successful scope phase of only 2 weeks were the functioning project team (both core and extended teams), a common understanding of the project vision, parallel focus groups, and consolidating and discussing interim results on a daily basis. The presented schedule is only a sample, but it may give you a good idea how to structure an initial scoping phase for your project.

Appendix D: The Scope Document

The purpose of a scope document is to describe the agreed scope of a project. It is based on the project vision document and it documents all requirements of the project. A sample outline of a scope document for a software development project is provided here.

D.1 Executive Summary

The purpose of the first project phase was to examine the overall business requirements, discuss potential new functionality, and develop an implementation plan. During this engagement the project team discussed the need to ... *[insert initial project objectives statement; for example, to improve the systems that support the business process]*:

- Briefly highlight the major business challenges/drivers.
- Briefly highlight the major business benefits.
- Briefly highlight the next steps or recommendations.

D.2 Business Context

This chapter contains the latest version of the official project vision document. As such, it lists the project motivation, vision, and objectives statements. In addition, it describes the critical success factors of the project and the project's organizational environment. Optional subchapters: company background, business vision, and strategy.

D.3 Future Process Flows

The project requirements must be put into context; i.e., they need to be referenced to the future process flow from an end-user perspective. For example, you need to describe how a call center agent will use the new call center application. You can describe the process flow verbally or with the help of diagrams. Describing the future process flow is important because it helps identify dependencies with other processes, functional and nonfunctional requirements, as well as systems. It also serves as a foundation for the creation of test cases.

D.4 Prioritized Scope

This chapter includes or refers to the scope matrix, which structures functional and nonfunctional requirements and models the solution requirements to an appropriate level of detail.

D.5 Target Infrastructure of the Solution

The infrastructure of the solution is what needs to be in the background for your solution to work. For example, when you build a house you need to secure access to water and electricity, garbage collection, etc. To operate a preschool you need to have the necessary permits and warrants. When you build new software, you need to know something about the target technical architecture, the data model, etc.

D.6 Business Case

Unless it was already covered in the project vision document, this chapter shows the value of the described requirements to the customer of the project. The benefits of the finished project results are identified in this section. An analysis and evaluation of the customer benefits permit prioritization of the project requirements and confirm the justification for proceeding with the recommended next steps.

D.7 Next Steps

This chapter includes a timeline along with effort estimates for the next phase(s) of the project. The level of detail depends on the needs of the respective project.

D.8 Issues and Assumptions

List all open issues and impediments that require further consideration. Also, list all assumptions that guided decisions during the first phase of the project and assumptions you made preparing the scope document. Why? There is no way that you know every possible detail about your requirements at the beginning of your project. If you are missing information about a certain requirement and you know that the requirement is essential for the project, you may have to make an assumption about it. For example, you assume that a certain building material for your new house is readily available in the local hardware store. At other times, you may not be sure about a requirement. For example, who will pay for an additional technical expert to develop software?

D.9 Optional Chapters

- Project chronology
- Project organizational set-up, including information about the project team, other project participants, roles and responsibilities, rules of engagement, etc.
- Project approach: which methodology you are applying in your project (e.g., an Agile or traditional "waterfall" approach to software development)
- Project glossary

Appendix E: Virtual Team Room

One of the key factors for successful collaboration is the open and free flow of information. The ideal scenario is when you and your team can work in the same location and share a project room. In cases when this is not possible, you can create a virtual team room in the form of a Website or a file you share over the Internet. It should include the same information you would find in a project room. I recommend the following structure for a virtual team room:

- Project overview
- Roles and responsibilities and team rules
- Regular meetings
- Weekly goals and deliverables
- Issues and impediments tracker
- Prerequisites, assumptions, and decisions
- Lessons learned
- Team morale board
- Project glossary

Let's look at each of these elements.

E.1 Project Overview

Table E.1 provides an overview of the key parameters of the project. It is a snapshot of the project. As such it is crucial that every single team member is familiar with the content of this table.

Table E.1   Project Overview

Department/Project Name	...
Project ID	...
Project stage	...
Other related documents	...
Timeframe	...
Project/Program Manager	...
Vision [taken from Project Vision Document]	
Project Motivation Statement	...
Project Vision Statement	...
Product or Solution Position Statement	...
SMART Project Objectives	...
Key Features & Benefits	...
Future Enhancements	...

E.2 Roles and Responsibilities and Team Rules

In Table E.2, for each team member, enter the role, responsibilities, key deliverables, expectations of and by this role, and key persons with whom this team member interacts. In addition, list the rules of engagement the team defines, agrees on, and commits to during the team norming workshop.

E.3 Regular Meetings

In Table E.3, list the regular team meetings, including information about the purpose, objectives and expected outcomes, time and location, the owner (i.e., the person accountable for the meeting), as well as mandatory and optional participants.

Next to this information, agree on and publish guidelines for effective meetings. For example:

Table E.2 Roles and Responsibilities and Team Rules

Roles and Responsibilities
[Date]

Team Member	Role	Responsibility	Key Deliverables	Expectation(s) in Role	Expectation(s) by Role	Key Contacts	...
NN							
NN							
NN							
NN							
NN							

Team Rules of

1
2
3
4
5
6
7
8
9
10

Table E.3 Regular Meetings

Project [Name] | Regular Meetings

Objectives/ Milestones	Frequency	Duration	Time	Focus	Agenda	Room	Owner	Mandatory Audience	Optional Audience
Daily stand-up meeting/team sync	Daily	15 min	hh:hh	Delivery	(1) Accomplishments since the day before (2) Planned activities of the day (3) Impediments	Project Room			
Weekly team sync	Weekly	45 min	hh:hh	Delivery	(1) Project plan/achieved & upcoming milestones (2) Weekly and daily team objectives & deliverables (3) Weekly and daily individual objectives & deliverables (4) Team issues and open action items (5) Feedback and lessons learned	Project Room			
Track lead meeting	Weekly	30 min	hh:hh	Delivery	(1) Project status (2) Individual status (3) Issues (4) Risks and mitigation plan	tbd			

Project review/ audit	Monthly	60 min	tbd	Delivery	(1) Project progress (2) Review of known project level risks and mitigation plan (3) Identification of new project level risks.	tbd			
...	...	...	...	...	...	...	...	...	...

Guidelines for effective meetings:

1. Every meeting request should include the following information:
   (1) Purpose of the meeting (why do we need this meeting?)
   (2) Objectives of the meeting (agenda)
   (3) Deliverables/expected results of the meeting

   If the meeting request did not include this information, start the meeting with agreeing on the POD statement. Meetings without a POD statement are often times ineffective and time killers.

2. Start and finish on time.

3. Assign minute taker prior to the meeting.

4. Capture results/decisions on white board, flip chart or file in real time.

5. Communicate results to all relevant people.

6. Update the issue tracker after a meeting, if necessary.

1. Every meeting request must include the following POD information:
   - Purpose of the meeting (why do we need this meeting?)
   - Objectives of the meeting (agenda)
   - Deliverables/expected results of the meeting
     If the meeting request did not include this information, start the meeting by agreeing on a POD statement. Meetings without a POD statement often are ineffective and time killers.
2. Start and finish on time.
3. Assign a minute-taker prior to the meeting.
4. Capture results/decisions on a whiteboard, flip chart, or file in real time.
5. Communicate results to all relevant people.
6. Update the issue tracker after the meeting, if necessary.

E.4 Weekly Goals and Deliverables

In Table E.4, you will list the weekly goals and deliverables of the complete team and each individual. Use and update this overview in your daily stand-up meetings. This means every team member first reviews the accomplishments of the previous day and explains how they relate to the weekly goals of the complete team and the respective individuals. Second, each team member provides an outlook for the present day. At the end of each week or the beginning of a new week, the outlook is expanded to the complete week.

Planned deliverables are prefixed by a "_" and accomplished deliverables by an "x." Deliverables overdue are highlighted in red.

E.5 Issues & Impediments Tracker

In Table E.5, capture any open and unresolved questions or impediments that need clarification. Typically, there is one assigned person who administers this list on a daily basis. However, it is best when every team member visits and updates the tracker at least once a week.

E.6 Prerequisites, Assumptions, and Decisions

In Table E.6, capture any prerequisites, assumptions, or important decisions that affect the project. Typically, there is one assigned person who administers this list on a daily basis. However, it is best when every team member visits and updates the tracker at least once a week.

E.7 Lessons Learned

In Table E.7, capture, categorize, and prioritize lessons learned within and by your team.

Table E.4 Weekly Goals and Deliverables

	Weekly Goal(s)	Place	Mo 13.11.06	Place	Tu 14.11.06	Place	Wed 15.11.06	Place	Thu 16.11.06	Place	Fri 17.11.06
Project Goals/Milestones											
Team Member's Name	x deliverable x _ deliverable y _ deliverable z		x deliverable x		_ deliverable y						_ deliverable z
NN											
NN											
NN											
NN											

	Weekly Goal(s)	Place	Mo 20.11.06	Place	Tu 21.11.06	Place	Wed 22.11.06	Place	Thu 23.11.06	Place	Fri 24.11.06
Project Goals/Milestones											
Name											
Name											
Name											
Name											
Name											

Table E.5 Issues and Impediments Tracker

				Last update: [date]						
Issues & Impediments Tracker										
No.	Prio	Topic	Issue/Impediment	Impact	Next Steps / Resolution	Status	Owner	People Involved	Due Date	Updates	Date Closed
1	1					open					
2	2					in progress					
3	3					postponed					
4	1					closed					
5											
6											
7											
8											
...											

Table E.6 Prerequisites, Assumptions, and Decisions

Prerequisites, Assumptions, Decisions
Last Updated on [enter date]

ID	Area	Prerequisites, Assumptions and Decisions	Initiator	Mitigation / Action Item	Owner	Decision Date	Status	Supporting Documentation
1							open	<Reference any documentation that supports this assumption>
2							in progress	
3							approved/ accepted	
4								
5								
6								
..								

Table E.7 Lessons Learned

Lessons Learned
Last updated on [date]

Prio	Category	Background	Feedback		Lesson(s) Learned	Next Steps	Submitted by	Decision Date	Status	Additional Comments
			Positive	Delta						
	Vision								open	
	Collaboration								in progress	
	Performance								approved/ accepted	
	Learning									
	Results/Delivery									
	…									

Table E.8 Team Morale Board

Team Members	Enter the morale of individual team members at the end of a reporting period (min. 1 week).	1 = miserable, 2 = poor, 3 = ok, 4 = good 5 = excellent +++ please enter a brief comment if your morale score is less than 3 +++				
		CW 39		*CW 40*		*...*
		Score	Comment	Score	Comment	Score	Comment
NN		5 ☺		3 ☺	logistical and access issues	4 ☺	
NN		4 ☺		4 ☺		2 ☹	
NN		3 ☺	logistical and access issues	2 ☹		3 ☺	contractual issues
NN		2 ☹	sick	3 ☺	still sick	4 ☺	
NN		1 ☹	no training	2 ☹	no training	3 ☺	contractual issues
...							
...							
...							
Team's Overall Morale Score		3.0 ☺		2.8 ☹		3.2 ☺	

Table E.9   Project Glossary

Project [Name] | Glossary		
Term	*Explanation*	*Source*

E.8 Team Morale Board

In Table E.8, enter the morale of individual team members at the end of a reporting period.

E.9 Project Glossary

In Table E.9, capture project-related terms and store them in a central location where every team member can access and update it.

Appendix F: Status Report

This sample template of a status report is a one-page summary of a project. It fulfills the minimum requirements of a status report, as described in Chapter 11. (See Table F.1.) The status report is outlined as follows.

F.1 Executive Summary

In one or two sentences, describe where the project stands. What is relevant is how the project progresses with respect to achieving the project vision and objectives.

The traffic lights in the top left corner signal the overall status of the project with respect to its plan and project risk. For the traffic light of the column "Plan," a green light signals that the project is on track, a yellow light signals that it is behind schedule at the moment but that the ultimate delivery date is not threatened, and a red light means that the project is behind schedule and the final delivery date is threatened. With respect to the traffic light in the "Risk" category, a green light means that no significant risks exist at the time of the report, a yellow light means that risks may endanger project delivery, and a red light is an alert for serious risks. Whenever there is a red light, it has to be explained either in the executive summary or in the listing of top three issues or top three risks.

The arrows next to the traffic lights indicate whether the status has improved (arrow pointing upward), deteriorated (arrow pointing downward), or remained stable (horizontal arrow) since the last reporting period.

F.2 High-Level Plan

This high-level plan illustrates the project schedule. Each cell represents a reporting period. In the sample in Table F.1 the reporting period is 1 week. The color of the cell indicates whether the respective work package has been completed, is on track, is behind schedule, or is facing issues. The red dashed line indicates the reporting date.

F.3 Accomplishments

List the top three accomplishments of the past reporting period. Focus on actual, tangible results that add value to the project organization and show that you and your team are moving in the right direction.

If you have missed an originally planned date, state so and enter the actual delivery date in the column "Date (actual)."

F.4 Upcoming Milestones

List the top three expected milestones of the next reporting period. Similar to the past accomplishments, state these as expected results rather than ongoing activities. Note that when you are reporting upcoming milestones you give a commitment to deliver them in the mentioned time period. Make sure prior to the report that you and your team can deliver them. If you cannot commit to a delivery date, state so. Raising the wrong expectations will eventually haunt you. If you and your team face impediments, explain them.

F.5 Top Three Issues or Impediments

Spell out the top three issues or impediments you and your team are dealing with at present *and* explain how you plan to solve or at least mitigate them. Do not describe a problem without pointing out its source and suggesting a resolution. If you need help from the outside, state this and suggest a resolution. A green status signifies that an issue or impediment is fully under control. A yellow status means that an issue is significant and requires additional attention. A red status means that an issue is critical and may need to be escalated to the next management level.

F.6 Top Three Risks

Spell out the top three risks you and your team have identified *and* explain how you plan to mitigate them. Do not describe a risk without pointing out its source and suggesting a resolution. If you need help from the outside, state this and suggest a resolution. The meaning of the status colors is similar to the colors of the top three issues or impediments.

F.7 Resolved Top Issues or Risks Since Last Report

List the top three issues and top three risks you and your team have resolved since the last reporting period.

Table F.1 Sample Status Report

| Project Manager: NN | | | Reporting Period | [date] till: [date] | [date] | Status as of: | [date] |

Executive Summary

Overall	Plan	Risk
	Green ➚	Green ➚
Sub-Project 1	G ➚	G ➚
Sub-Project 2	Y ↑	Y ↑
Sub-Project 3	R ↗	R ↗

...

High Level Plan

Dates	Nov	Dec				Jan				Feb				Mar				Apr				May				Jun				Jul				Aug	
CW	47	48	49	50	51	52	1	2	3	4	5	6	7	8	9	10	11	12	13	14	15	16	17	18	19	20	21	22	23	24	25	26	27	28	29	30	31	32	33

Overall Progress	Inprogress
Work Package 1	Critical
Work Package 2	Not started
Work Package 3	Complete
...	Not started
	Not started

Today

Legend:					
Activity and status:	on-track	some issues	Not started	Completed	Delayed	Delayed and Critical
	critical				
Milestones:	✓ Achieved Milestone	⊗ Missed Milestone			

Key accomplishments since last reporting period

Description	Date (plan)	Date (actual)	Status	Owner
...			Green	NN
...			Yellow	NN
...			Red	NN

Planned accomplishments for next reporting period

Description	Date (plan)	Date (actual)	Status	Owner
...			Green	NN
...			Yellow	NN
...			Red	NN

(continued)

Table F.1 Sample Status Report (Continued)

Top Issues & Impediments

| | | | | | 1 Critical 2 Significant 3 Moderate | | |
Track	Priority	Description	Impact	Next Steps	Date	Status	Owner
Overall	1	...	...		...	open	NN
Track 1	2	...	...		...	in progress	NN
Track x	3	...	...		...	overdue	NN

Top Risks

| | | | | | 1 Critical 2 Significant 3 Moderate | | |
Track	Priority	Description	Impact	Next Steps	Date	Status	Owner
Overall	1	...	...		...	open	NN
Track 1	2	...	...		...	in progress	NN
Track x	3	...	...		...	overdue	NN

Resolved Top Issues & Impediments Since Last Report

| | | | | | 1 Critical 2 Significant 3 Moderate | | |
Track	Priority	Description	Impact	Next Steps	Date	Status	Owner
Overall	1	...	...		...	closed	NN
Track 1	2	...	...		...	closed	NN
Track 1	3	...	...		...	closed	NN

Resolved Top Risks Since Last Report

| | | | | | 1 Critical 2 Significant 3 Moderate | | |
Track	Priority	Description	Impact	Next Steps	Date	Status	Owner
Overall	1	...	...		...	closed	NN
Track 1	2	...	...		...	closed	NN
Track 1	3	...	...		...	closed	NN

BIBLIOGRAPHY V

Bibliography

Aiyer, J., Havelka, D., & Rajkumar, T. M. (2005). A staged framework for the recovery and rehabilitation of troubled IS development projects. *Project Management Journal, 36*(4), 32–43.

Andersen, E. S., Grude, K. V., & Haug, T. (1987). *Goal Directed Project Management: Effective Techniques and Strategies.* London: Kogan Page.

Atkinson, R. (1999). Project Management: Cost, Time and Quality, Two Best Guesses and a Phenomenon, It's Time to Accept Other Success Criteria. *International Journal of Project Management, 17*, 337–342.

Baccarini, D. (1999). The Logical Framework Method for Determining Critical Success/Failure Factors in Projects. *International Journal of Project Management, 14*, 141–151.

Baghai, M., White, D., & Coley, S. (1999). *The Alchemy of Growth: Kickstarting and Sustaining Growth in Your Company.* New York: Texere.

Bailey, II, R. W. (2000). Six steps to project recovery. *PM Network, 14*(5), 33–38.

Baker, B. N., Murphy, D. C., & Fisher, D. (1988). Factors Affecting Project Success. In D. I. Cleland & W. R. King, *Project Management Handbook* (2 ed., pp. 669–685). New York: Van Nostrand Reinhold Company.

Bass, B. M. (1985). *Leadership and Performance Beyond Expectations.* New York: The Free Press.

Bass, B. M. (1990). *Bass and Stodghill Handbook of Leadership: Theory, Research, and Applications.* New York: The Free Press.

Beedle, M., Bennekum, A. V., Cockburn, A., Cunningham, W., Fowler, M., Highsmith, J., et al. (2001). *Manifesto for Agile Software Development.* Retrieved from http://agilemanifesto.org/.

Bennis, W. (1989). *On Becoming a Leader.* London: Hutchinson.

Blanchard, K. H., Bowles, S., Carew, D., & Parisi-Carew, E. (2001). *High Five! The Magic of Working Together.* New York: HarperCollins.

Blanchard, K. H., Carlos, J. P., & Randolph, A. (1998). *Empowerment Takes More Than a Minute.* San Francisco: Berret-Koehler Publishers.

Block, T. R. (1998). Project recovery: Short- and long-term solutions. In *Proceedings of the 29th Annual Project Management Institute 1998 Seminars & Symposium.* Long Beach, CA: Project Management Institute.

Cockerrell, L. (2008). *Creating Magic: 10 Common Sense Leadership Strategies from a Life at Disney.* London: Vermilion.

Cohen, J., & Stewart, I. (1994). *The Collapse of Chaos: Discovering Simplicity in a Complex World.* New York: Viking Penguin.

Cohn, M. (2004). *User Stories Applied: For Agile Software Development*. Amsterdam: Addison-Wesley Longman.

Collins, J., & Porras, J. I. (1994). *Built to Last: Successful Habits of Visionary Companies*. New York: HarperCollins.

Cooke-Davies, T. (2001). The Real Project Success Factors. *International Journal of Project Management, 20*(3), 185–190.

Covey, S. R. (1989). *The 7 Habits of Highly Effective People: Powerful Lessons in Personal Change*. New York: Free Press.

Covey, S. R. (1991). *Principle Centered Leadership*. New York: Fireside.

Covey, S. R. (2004). *The 8th Habit: From Effectiveness to Greatness*. New York: Free Press.

Crowe, A. (2006). *Alpha Project Managers: What the Top 2% Know That Everyone Else Does Not*. Kennesaw, GA: Velociteach.

Davis, K. (1999). Project recovery: Short- and long-term solutions. In *Proceedings of the 30th Annual Project Management Institute 1999 Seminars & Symposium*. Philadelphia, PA: Project Management Institute.

DeMarco, T. (1997). *The Deadline: A Novel about Project Management*. New York: Dorset House Publishing Company.

DeMarco, T., & Lister, T. (1999). *Peopleware: Productive Projects and Teams*. New York: Dorset House Publishing Company.

Denning, S. (2005). *The Leader's Guide to Storytelling: Mastering the Art and Discipline of Business Narrative*. San Francisco: Jossey-Bass.

Denning, S. (2010). *The Leader's Guide to Radical Management: Re-Inventing the Workplace for the 21st Century* (to be published: 10/24/10). San Francisco: Jossey-Bass. p. 217

Drucker, P. F. (1974). *Management*. New York: Harper & Row.

Drucker, P. F. (2006). *The Effective Executive: The Definitive Guide to Getting the Right Things Done* (rev. ed.). New York: Harper Paperbacks.

Drucker, P. F. (2008). *The Essential Drucker: The Best of Sixty Years of Peter Drucker's Essential Writings on Management*. New York: Collins Business Essentials.

Egolf, D. B. (2001). *Forming Storming Norming Performing: Successful Communication in Groups and Teams*. Lincoln, NE: Writers Club Press.

Einstein, A. (1934). On the method of theoretical physics. *Philosophy of Science, 1*(2), 163–169.

Emerson, R. W. (2000). *The Essential Writings of Ralph Waldo Emerson* (B. Atkinson, Ed.). New York: Modern Library.

France, A. (1896). *Discours de réception, Séance De L'académie Française*. Retrieved from http://en.wikiquote.org/wiki/Anatole_France.

Gadodia, V. (2010). *Six Features of a Good User Story — INVEST Model*. Retrieved from http://agilesoftwaredevelopment.com/blog/vaibhav/good-user-story-invest.

Geoghegan, L., & Dulewicz, V. (2008). Do Project Managers' Leadership Competencies Contribute to Project Success? *Project Management Journal, 39*(4), 58–67.

Gladwell, M. (2007). *The Tipping Point: How Little Things Can Make a Big Difference*. New York: Black Bay Books/Little, Brown and Company.

Goffee, R., & Jones, G. (2000). Why Should Anyone be Led by You? *Harvard Business Review, 78*(5), 63–70.

Goleman, D., Boyatzis, R. E., & McKee, A. (2002). *The New Leaders: Transforming the Art of Leadership*. Boston, MA: Harvard Business School Press.

Greenleaf, R. K., Covey, S. R., & Senge, P. M. (2007). *Servant Leadership: A Journey into the Nature of Ultimate Power & Greatness*. Mahwah, NJ: Paulist Press.

Hass, K. (2007). Living on the edge: Project complexity management. In *PMI Global Congress 2007*. Atlanta, GA: Project Management Institute.

Hass, K. (2009). *Managing Complex Projects: A New Model*. Vienna, VA: Management Concepts.

Haugan, G. T. (2006). *Project Management Fundamentals: Key Concepts and Methodology*. Vienna, VA: Management Concepts.

Higgs, M. (2003). Developments in Leadership Thinking. *Organisational Development and Leadership Journal, 24*, 273–284.

Hutchens, D. (2007). *Emerging Principles of Complexity Theory*. Retrieved from http://www.davidhutchens.com/Biz Writing/articles/emergingprincipl.html.

Hutchens, D., & Webber, P. G. (2007). *Leadership Beyond the Baseline: New Thinking about Leadership for a New World of Business*. Retrieved from http://www.davidhutchens.com/Biz Writing/articles/leadershipinthen.html.

Iacocca, L. (2007). *Where Have All The Leaders Gone?* New York: Simon and Schuster.

Jenewein, W., & Morhart, F. (2006). Sieben Manöver zum Teamerfolg. *Harvard Business Manager, July*, 2–12.

Johns, T. (2008). The art of Project Management® and complexity. In *2008 PMI Global Congress Proceedings*. Denver, CO: Project Management Institute.

Juli, T. (1997). The Logic of Social Interactions in Foreign Policy: The 1994-1996 US-Chinese Negotiations on Intellectual Property Rights. Dissertation, University of Miami. Retrieved from http://www.thomasjuli.com/Logic of Social Interactions in Foreign Policy - December 1997 - by Thomas Juli - all rights reserved.pdf.

Juli, T. (2002). Closer to the customer: The successful CRM strategy of HVB Direkt. *Banken & Sparkassen, 3*, 40–42.

Juli, T. (2003). Work smart, not hard! An approach to time-sensitive project management. In *2003 PMI Global Congress Proceedings*. The Hague, Netherlands: Project Management Institute. Retrieved from http://www.thomasjuli.com/work_smart_not_hard.pdf.

Juli, T. (2008). Realigning project objectives and stakeholders' expectations in a project behind schedule. In *2008 PMI Global Congress Proceedings*. Denver, CO: Project Management Institute. Retrieved from http://www.thomasjuli.com/Realigning_Project_Objectives_by_Thomas_Juli,Ph.D._v1.0.pdf.

Juli, T. (2009). *It Takes a Team to Realign a Project: Lessons from Rescue Missions*. Orlando, FL: Project Management Institute. Retrieved from http://www.thomasjuli.com/It takes a team to realign a project_ Article_by Thomas Juli, Ph.D..pdf.

Juli, T. (2009). *Online Survey: Team Involvement in Re-Aligning a Project*. Edingen, Germany. Retrieved from http://www.thomasjuli.com/Team Involvement and Project Re-Alignment - Results of Online Survey - Spring 2009.pdf.

Juli, T., & Wutz, A. (2001). Implementing a CRM help desk solution within 15 weeks: The OptiFrend Project at HVB Direkt, Oct 2000–Feb 2001. In *Proceedings of the Helpdesk World 2001*. Cologne, Germany: Euroforum.

Katzenbach, J. R. (1997). *Teams at the Top: Unleashing the Potential of Both Teams and Individual Leaders*. Boston, MA: Harvard Business School Press.

Keith, C., & Cohn, M. (2008). How to Fail with Agile: Twenty Tips to Help You Avoid Success. *Better Software, July/Aug*, 24–28. Retrieved from http://www.mountaingoat-software.com/system/article/file/40/HowToFailWithAgile.pdf?1267552459.

Kelley, T. (2000). *The Art of Innovation*. New York: Doubleday.

Kerzner, H. (1998). *In Search of Excellence in Project Management*. New York: Van Nostrand Reinhold Company.

Kerzner, H. (2006). *Project Management: A Systems Approach to Planning, Scheduling, and Controlling*. Hoboken, NJ: John Wiley & Sons.

Kets De Vries, M. F., & Florent-Tracy, E. (2002). Global Leadership from A to Z: Creating High Commitment Organizations. *Organization Dynamics, 30*, 295–309.

Kliem, R., & Anderson, H. (1996). Teambuilding Styles and their Impact on Project Management Results. *Project Management Journal, 27*(1), 41–50.

Kotter, J. (1990). What Leaders Really Do. *Harvard Business Review, 68*(3), 103–111.

Ludwig, E. (2008). Your project is spiraling out of control. Now what? The road to recovery. *PM Network, 22*(11), 46–53.

Lundin, S. C., Paul, H., & Christensen, J. (2000). *Fish! A Remarkable Way to Boost Morale and Improve Results*. New York: Hyperion.

Mendeley. (2009). *Getting Started with Mendeley*. *Mendeley Desktop*. London: Mendeley Ltd. Retrieved from http://www.mendeley.com.

Miller, G. A. (1956). The magical number seven, plus or minus two. *The Psychological Review, 63*, 81–97. Retrieved from http://www.musanim.com/miller1956/.

Morgan, G. (2006). *Images of Organizations*. London: Sage Publications.

O'Brochta, M. (2005). Getting executives to act for project success. In *Proceedings of the PMI Global Congress 2005*. Toronto, Canada: Project Management Institute.

O'Brochta, M. (2006). How executives can act for project success. In *Proceedings of the PMI Global Congress 2006*. Seattle, WA: Project Management Institute.

O'Brochta, M. (2008). How to Get Executives to Act for Project Success. In *Proceedings of the PMI Global Congress 2008*. Denver, CO: Project Management Institute.

O'Brochta, M. (2009). Great Project Managers. In *Proceedings of the PMI Global Congress 2009*. Amsterdam, Netherlands: Project Management Institute.

Patton, G. S., & Atkinson, R. (1995). *War as I Knew It*. New York: Mariner Books. Retrieved from http://en.wikiquote.org/wiki/George_Patton.

Peters, T. J. (1987). *Thriving on Chaos*. New York: Alfred A. Knopf.

Peters, T. J. (2007). The Wow Project. *FastCompany*. Retrieved from http://www.fastcompany.com/magazine/24/wowproj.html.

Piante, J. D. (2008). The remarkably ordinary leader. In *2008 PMI Global Congress Proceedings*. Denver, CO: Project Management Institute.

Pinto, J. K., & Slevin, D. P. (1988). Critical Success Factors in Effective Project Implementation. In D. I. Cleland & W. R. King, *Project Management Handbook* (2 ed., pp. 479–512). New York: Van Nostrand Reinhold Company.

Pinto, J. K., & Slevin, D. P. (1988). Project Success: Definition and Measurement Techniques. *Project Management Journal, 19*, 67–71.

Porthouse, M., & Dulewicz, V. (2007). *Agile Project Managers' Leadership Competencies*. Henley Working Paper Series.

Pinto, J. K., & Trailer, J. W. (1998). *Leadership Skills for Project Managers*. Newtown Square, PA: Project Management Institute.

Project Management Institute. (2008). *A Guide to the Project Management Body of Knowledge* (4th ed.). Newtown Square, PA: Project Management Institute.

Rasiel, E. M., & Friga, P. N. (2001). *The McKinsey Mind: Understanding and Implementing the Problem-Solving Tools and Management Techniques of the World's Top Strategic Consulting Firm*. New York: McGraw-Hill.

Rees, D., Turner, R., & Tampoe, M. (1996). On Being a Manager and Leader. In J. R. Turner, K. V. Grude, & L. Thurloway, *The Project Manager as Change Agent* (pp. 99–115). Maidenhead, UK: McGraw-Hill.

Rossy, G., & Archibald, R. (1992). Building Commitment in Project Teams. *Project Management Journal, 23*(2), 5–14.

Senge, P. M. (1990). *The Fifth Discipline: The Art and Practice of the Learning Organization.* New York: Currency Doubleday.

Simmons, A. (2006). *The Story Factor: Inspiration, Influence, and Persuasion Through the Art of Storytelling.* New York: Perseus Books Group.

Sliger, M. (2008). Little scrum pigs and the big, bad wolf. *Stickyminds.com Weekly Column.* Retrieved from http://www.stickyminds.com/sitewide.asp?ObjectId=14404&Functio n=DETAILBROWSE&ObjectType=COL&sqry=*Z(SM)*J(MIXED)*R(relevance)* K(simplesite)*F(sliger)*&sidx=6&sopp=10&sitewide.asp?sid=1&sqry=*Z(SM)*J(MI XED)*R(relevance)*K(simplesite)*F(sliger)*&sidx=6&sopp=10.

Steinfort, P., & Walker, D. H. (2008). *A Critique of the PMI-Disaster Rebuild Methodology.* Newtown Square, PA: Project Management Institute.

Sutherland, J., Schoonheim, G., Rustenburg, E., & Rijk, M. (2008). Fully distributed scrum: The secret sauce for hyperproductive offshored development teams. Paper presented at the Agile Conference 2008. Retrieved from http://www.stevedenning.com/ Documents/XebiaAgile08.pdf.

Takeuchi, H., & Nonaka, I. (1986). The new new product development game. *Harvard Business Review, 1986*(January–February), Reprint 86116: 2–11.

Taylor, W. C., & Labarre, P. G. (2006). *Mavericks at Work: Why the Most Original Minds in Business Win.* New York: HarperCollins.

The Standish Group. (2009). *CHAOS Summary 2009.* West Yarmouth, MA.

The Standish Group. (2009). *News Release on the New 2009 Chaos Report.* April 23, 2009. Retrieved from http://www1.standishgroup.com/newsroom/chaos_2009.php.

Thomas, M., Jacques, P. H., Adams, J. R., & Kihneman-Wooten, J. (2008). Developing an Effective Project: Planning and Team Building Combined. *Project Management Handbook, 39*(4), 105–113.

Todryk, L. (1990). The Project Manager as Team Builder: Creating an Effective Team. *Project Management Journal, 21*(2), 17–22.

Turner, J. R., & Müller, R. (2005). The Project Manager's Leadership Style as a Success Factor on Projects. *Project Management Journal, 36*(2), 49–61.

Ulrich, D., Zenger, J., & Smallwood, N. (1999). *Results-Based Leadership.* Boston, MA: Harvard Business School Press.

VersionOne. (2010). *Dynamic Systems Development Method (DSDM).* Retrieved from http:// www.versionone.com/Resources/AgileMethodologies.asp#DSDM.

Verzuh, E. (2008). *The Fast Forward MBA in Project Management.* Hoboken, NJ: John Wiley & Sons.

Waitley, D. E. (1980). *The Winner's Edge: The Critical Attitude of Success.* New York: Berkley.

Waitley, D. E. (1985). *The Psychology of Winning: Ten Qualities of a Total Winner.* New York: Berkley.

Wake, W. C. (2001). *Extreme Programming Explored.* Indianapolis, IN: Addison Wesley Professional.

Ward, J. L. (2007). Five critical first steps in recovering troubled projects. In *2007 PMI Global Congress Proceedings.* Hong Kong: Project Management Institute.

Weinberg, G. M. (1985). *The Secrets of Consulting: A Guide to Giving and Getting Advice Successfully.* New York: Dorset House Publishing.

Whitten, N. (2005). *Neal Whitten's No-Nonsense Advice for Successful Projects.* Vienna, VA: Management Concepts.

Yourdon, E. (1999). *Death March: The Complete Software Developer's Guide to Surviving "Mission Impossible" Projects*. Upper Saddle River, NJ: Prentice Hall.

Zaccaro, S. J., Rittman, A. L., & Marks, M. A. (2001). Team Leadership. *Leadership Quarterly, 12*, 451–483.

Zenger, J. H., & Folkman, J. (2002). *The Extraordinary Leader. Turning Good Managers into Great Leaders*. New York: McGraw-Hill.

Zenger, J. H., & Folkman, J. (2004). *The Handbook for Leaders: 24 Lessons for Extraordinary Leaders*. New York: McGraw-Hill.

INDEX

Index